[RG] 1982

A History of British Industrial Relations
1875–1914

The Working Class in the Victorian Age: (joint editor with Max Goldstrom) (4 vols., Gregg, 1973)

David Lloyd George and the British Labour Movement (Harvester, 1976)

A.J.P. Taylor: A Complete Annotated Bibliography and Guide to his Historical and Other Writings (Harvester, 1980)

A History of British Industrial Relations 1875–1914

Edited by

Chris Wrigley
Senior Lecturer in Economic History,
Loughborough University

THE HARVESTER PRESS

First published in Great Britain in 1982 by
THE HARVESTER PRESS LIMITED
Publisher: John Spiers
16 Ship Street, Brighton, Sussex

British Library Cataloguing in Publication Data

A History of British industrial relations
1875–1914.
1. Industrial relations – Great Britain –
History
I. Wrigley, Chris
331'. 0941   HD8390

ISBN 0-7108-0316-8

Typeset in 10 on 12 Sabon by Inforum Ltd, Portsmouth
Printed in Great Britain by
Mansell Limited, Witham, Essex

Contents

List of Contributors

DR. GREGORY ANDERSON is Lecturer in Economic History at the University of Salford.

DR. PHILLIP BAGWELL is Professor Emeritus of Economic History at the Polytechnic of Central London.

DR. JOHN BENSON is Senior Lecturer in History at The Polytechnic, Wolverhampton.

DR. KENNETH BROWN is Reader in Economic History at Queen's University, Belfast.

DR. JAMES CRONIN is Associate Professor of History at the University of Wisconsin, Milwaukee.

DR. ROGER DAVIDSON is Lecturer in Economic History at the University Edinburgh.

DR. W.R. GARSIDE is Senior Lecturer in Economic History at the University of Birmingham.

MR. VAN GORE is Senior Lecturer in History at the Sheffield City Polytechnic.

DR. HOWARD GOSPEL is Lecturer in Industrial Relations at the University of Kent, and Research Fellow of the Business History Unit at the London School of Economics.

DR. JAMES HINTON is Lecturer in History at the University of Warwick.

DR. JEFFREY PORTER is Lecturer in Economic History at the University of Exeter.

DR. JOSEPH WHITE is Associate Professor of History at the University of Pittsburgh.

DR. CHRIS WRIGLEY is Senior Lecturer in Economic History at Loughborough University.

List of Tables and Graphs

Preface

Interest in the history of British industrial relations has grown markedly since the time of the Donovan Commission (1965–8). In the past decade historians have carried out much research — and even more is underway — on industrial relations in a broader context than purely institutional studies of, say, specific trade unions. This book is the first of several which are intended to provide an up-to-date broad survey of British industrial relations since the Industrial Revolution.

There are potential strengths and inevitable weaknesses in approaching a survey of a forty-year period by twelve essays by different authors. In planning the book I have attempted to identify eight themes which collectively cover most of the more important areas, yet do not overlap unduly. In addition, in view of the way industrial relations varied markedly from industry to industry and from region to region as well as over time, I have ended the book with four case studies dealing with important sectors of the late nineteenth-century British economy. In inviting authors to contribute the essays and in editing the resulting contributions I have tried to minimize repetition; but some repetition is inevitable if topics are dealt with in a sensible and balanced manner. Another problem with such a set of essays by different contributors is the variety of outlook which is likely to occur. However, after consideration of possible contributors, I felt the best criterion to use in inviting contributions was that the author was likely to provide a stimulating, sound and original essay rather than restrict invitations to persons who all hold a common outlook on the subject.

I hope that the book will prove to be a useful basic survey for people from many disciplines who are interested in the history of industrial relations as well as providing a starting base for future researchers.

CHRIS WRIGLEY

Introduction

To generalize about nineteenth-century industrial relations is most hazardous. For one thing there was a wide diversity of experience with considerable variations between industries and within industries, from one region or area to another, as well as patterns changing over time (often with features recurring rather than 'evolving'). Strikes or lock-outs could result in famous victories for masters or men and set the pattern of industrial relations for many years in an area, yet leave the practice of industrial relations elsewhere in Britain unchanged. For another, until recently historians have tended to work the most accessible material: institutional sources (such as trade union records) or information relating to sensational events (such as major disputes or court cases).

Nevertheless in this book an attempt is made to survey the period 1875–1914. Drawing divisions in time in nineteenth-century industrial relations is necessarily arbitrary. 1875 as a starting date has some merits, and not solely for trade union history. By 1875 the unions had gained strength from the upsurge in membership of 1872–4, although this was to be eroded later in the decade. Collective bargaining, with its necessary concomitants, was established at law in the legislation of 1871 and 1875. The change in attitude to trade unionism, reflected in such legislation, was also reflected in the way trade unions and trade unionists were granted further recognition in the political system. As the Webbs commented, 'In 1875 the officials of the great societies found themselves elected to the local School Boards, and even to the House of Commons, pressed by the Government to accept seats on Royal Commissions, and respectfully listened to in the lobby'.[1]

The harsher international climate for British manufactures in the quarter century from the early 1870s pressurized employers to make further savings in labour costs. This took various forms including speeding up machinery, attacking other established workplace prac-

tices, and cutting back on sub-contracting. Employers' organizations, usually hitherto shadowy or transient affairs, became firmly
established during this gloomier economic period and, alongside the
growing unionization of major sectors of the economy, were prime
elements in the widening spread of collective bargaining.

Some employers found a regular system of formal negotiation
with representatives of their workers more attractive than the danger
of irregular disruption of work. For them such negotiations could
not only forestall strikes but could amend workshop practices and
help them to discipline their labour force. In some industries, collective bargaining spread from workplace to workplace in an area; and
eventually bargaining between unions and employers expanded,
with first local and then national agreements.[2]

One feature of the late 1860s was the widespread adoption of
conciliation and arbitration agreements in many areas. 'By 1875',
Vic Allen has written, 'there was barely a trade where trade unions
existed which did not have either a standing joint committee of
employers and workmen to settle disputes, with provision for arbitration, or the experience of settling disputes through arbitration on
an *ad hoc* basis'.[3] For a period these and sliding-scale wage agreements were attractive to some trade unions. Even in 1892 Tom
Mann and others could speak favourably of conciliation and arbitration agreements when questioned by the Royal Commission on
Labour. Generally, however, such arrangements tended to lessen
labour's advantages in good times and not protect them in such
periods of falling prices as the last quarter of the century.[4] In 1911
and later, when faced with serious industrial unrest, governments
turned to joint committees of employers and trade unionists to help
defuse the situation.

To the annoyance of government, employers and some trade
union leaders the clash of interests at work continued to lead to
periodic violence in industrial relations. George Howell, in a book
published in 1891, expresses well the attitude of 'progress' in industrial relations held by some of the trade union leadership of the
period.[5]

> Some of the leaders have openly proclaimed their mission is to preach the
> gospel of discontent. Of course there is discontent and discontent. In so
> far as discontent leads to emulation, to vigorous effort to better the
> conditions of the workers, it is healthful; it stirs the stagnant pool. But
> there is discontent of another kind, which aims at lawlessness and license;

we have seen examples of it during the last few years in strikes without
reason; in the exercise of brute force, without compunction; and in
capitulation without honour. Violent methods are, or rather, they should
be, things of the past. They belonged to an age when freedom of association was denied; when persecution drove men to something like frenzy;
when long hours, low wages, dear provisions, scarcity of work, and
demoralising conditions, had degraded the working classes almost to the
level of brutes.

To those holding such views the norm was to be the avoidance of
conflict by bringing together all those who, in the words of Charles
Macara at the time of the 1911 National Industrial Council, shared
the ideal of 'the substitution in the industrial sphere of co-operation
for antagonism in relations between employers and employed'.
Those who did not share this ideal, the leaders of the New Unionism
of the 1880s, were beyond the pale. Howell's alarm at the ways of the
New Unionist leaders in leading the poor, frequently unemployed,
unskilled workers in their struggle to win for themselves better
conditions, was echoed twenty years later in Cabinet Papers prepared by the Board of Trade during the upsurge of unrest of
1910–1912.[6]

The interconnection between industrial struggles and political
struggles, always implicit in the economic system, was made explicit
in the 1880s by the committed socialist leaders of the New Unionism.
In their activities on behalf of both the unskilled and the unemployed, Tom Mann, John Burns and the others revived British socialism, which had been relatively dormant for some decades; though
the Owenite and Chartist traditions, in terms of ideas and old
Chartists, was stronger at the local level of trade unionism in some
areas than historians have usually recognized. Again in the 1910–14
period the struggles of the poorer-paid workers were encouraged by
socialist ideas and in turn helped to foster socialist ideas. Even
religious sectarianism was eclipsed temporarily in the class conflicts
of 1910–1912 (and indeed, of 1910–26). Thus Fred Bower, the
syndicalist stonemason, recalled of the 1911 Merseyside transport
strike:

From Orange Garston, Everton and Toxteth Park, from Roman Catholic
Bootle and the Scotland Road area, they came. Forgotten were their
religous feuds . . . The Garston band had walked five miles and their
drum-major proudly whirled his sceptre twined with orange and green
ribbons as he led his contingent band, half out of the Roman Catholic, half
out of the local Orange band.[7]

Within the economy and within the Labour Movement in the period 1875–1914 there was a rise in importance of the transport and mining sectors. This was accompanied by a greater proneness of these workers to strike in the period before the First World War. Mining and transport disputes had considerable potential for disrupting the national economy. Hence it is not surprising that direct government interventions to settle disputes should begin in these areas — and that in 1911–12 the government had to take special measures and not rely on its civil servants and conciliation machinery.

Before the First World War only a minority of the British labour force was in trade unions; though the number of trade unionists had risen from just over two million in 1900 to over four million in 1913. Many aspects of trade unionism in the 1875–1914 period are as diverse as the industrial relations of the period.

Within trade unionism there were wide divisions between craft and craft, sometimes as much as between skilled and unskilled. Within the skilled there were a variety of ways of achieving recognition of a skill; and during the period 1875–1914 there appears to have been a growth of non-apprenticed skilled work.[8] Even in a trade such as engineering, in the 1890s, Amalgamated Society of Engineers' average wage rates could vary between 23 shillings and 40s 6d. per week.[9] Similarly there was a wide variety of structure to trade union organizations — and accompanying that a range of attitudes amongst the rank and file to their full-time officials.[10]

The First World War brought a greater unity to British industrial relations and, eventually, to the British Labour Movement. Whilst many of the changes of 1914–20 were eroded in the subsequent recession and afterwards, British industrial relations did not return to the extreme diversities of the pre-1914 pattern of industrial relations.

References

1   Sidney and Beatrice Webb, *The History of Trade Unionism*, Revised Edition, (1920), pp. 325–6.

2   For an important interpretation of nineteenth-century industrial relations in one industry, building, see R. Price, *Masters, Unions and Men*, (1980).

3   'The origins of industrial conciliation and arbitration',

reprinted in his *The Sociology of Industrial Relations* (1971), p. 68.

4 See H. A. Clegg, A. Fox & A. F. Thompson, *A History of British Trade Unions Since 1889*, Vol. 1, (1964), especially chapters 3 and 4.

5 In his *Trade Unionism New and Old*; cited in *Workers and Employers*, ed. J. T. Ward & W. H. Fraser, (1980), pp. 119–20.

6 On Howell at this time see F. M. Leventhal, *Respectable Radical*, (1971), pp. 208–10. For similar complaints twenty years later see 'The Present Unrest in the Labour World', June 1911; CAB 37/107.

7 Cited in Bob Holton's *British Syndicalism 1900—1914* (1976), p. 99; a book which makes the case for taking British syndicalism as seriously as that in Europe and the USA.

8 On this see C. More, *Skill and the English Working Class 1870–1914*, (1980). For a survey of the aristocracy of labour issue, see R. Q. Gray, *The Aristocracy of Labour in Nineteenth Century Britain, c.1850–1914*, (1981).

9 K. Burgess, *The Origin of British Industrial Relations*, (1975), p. 27.

10 Sidney and Beatrice Webb's *Industrial Democracy* (1897), remains a valuable starting point on this subject. For an invaluable guide to work published on British industrial relations between 1880 and 1970 see G. S. Bain & G. B. Woolven *A Bibliography of British Industrial Relations*, (1979).

1
Some Aspects of the Labour Market in Britain c.1870–1914

Gregory Anderson

The purpose of this essay is to explore some interesting and important areas of the British labour market in the period 1870–1914. It is not intended, partly through the physical constraint of space, to provide a more general picture of how the market worked. In any event the macro-aspects of the labour market, whether movements in real/money wages, the share of wages in national income, the squeeze on regional wage variations, the changing elasticity of labour supply, participation rates or unemployment, have been covered, to a greater or lesser extent, elsewhere[1]. It was felt that within the scope of this essay a more intensive treatment of a number of issues in the labour market would be more feasible. The three areas chosen — variations between skilled and unskilled labour markets, the growth of service occupations and the role of trade unions — are significant either as topics of debate between historians (as in the role of the skilled workers and trade unions) or reflect important long-term changes occurring in the labour market in this period (sectoral change and the expansion of service occupations).

Skilled and Unskilled Workers

At the top end of the manual labour market was a category of skilled workers separated traditionally from the unskilled labourers below them by a higher degree of manual dexterity/knowledge, greater control over the finished product, higher wages and more secure employment. Historically, straightforward skill differentials alone have not separated the skilled workers from the unskilled below them. In any assessment of the position of the skilled worker two lines of inquiry have to be distinquished, one which examines relative movements in measurable criteria such as earnings, and a second which is concerned with changes in status and class position. Historians committed to the concept of the 'labour aristocracy' believe that the two approaches are inseparable and argue that the superior position of the skilled worker rested on conditions of cultural and class advantage (they were more respectable, moderate and had closer links with employers) as well as a lead in economic terms. Moreover these class/cultural and skill differentials changed over time, with any 'deskilling' leading to an increasing class consciousness. This is not the place to test the validity of the 'class approach' to the skilled worker but suffice it to say that the labour aristocracy has been elevated (initially by Eric Hobsbawm and more recently by R. Gray and G. Crossick) to a key position in any appreciation of longer-term changes from 1850 both in the social structure and the class system[2]. Its importance, both as a key occupational category and in terms of its links with new and ultimately more important groups (such as white-collar workers) as well as its changing relationship with the wider working class and later the labour movement, are not in dispute. However, the most recent synthesis on British labour history has challenged both its distinctiveness-/homogeneity and its central role in the inhibition and/or development of class consciousness.[3]

It is difficult to know exactly what the size of the skilled sector was at any time, partly because of difficulties over definition (only in a minority of occupations was the dividing line between skilled and unskilled clear) and partly through the changing composition of the skilled workforce over time. Hobsbawm thought that at any particular point in the period 1890–1914 the labour aristocracy included not more than 15 per cent of the working class, although he deliberately excluded skilled non-manual white-collar workers, and qualified the inclusion of manual workers who though skilled in a technical sense, were in trades with a long unskilled 'tail', i.e. a large amount of low-paid unskilled labour.[4] Significant changes occurred within the composition of the skilled workforce in this period. In the middle of the century the labour aristocracy was concentrated in handicrafts, such as cabinetmaking and watchmaking, the top end of cotton textiles, engine-driving and shipwrighting. From the 1880s its centre of gravity had shifted towards the metal industries, in line with structural changes in Britain's economy away from handicrafts and older staples (textiles) towards metals and engineering. Moreover, in line with this shift the majority of skilled workers increasingly found their employment not in customer work in small workshops but in large-scale, highly-capitalized factories with less control over the whole of the finished product. Charles More has recently shown that the number of employers and own-account artisan workers in England in the traditional skilled trades was declining in the period 1891–1911.[5]

Labour market differences between skilled and unskilled workers rested on the wage gap. This earnings differential is not in doubt. Most observers indicate a 30–40 per cent differential between craftsmen's and labourers' wages in the same trade, although there were large variations across industries. Sidney Pollard has recently argued that 'the position of the labour aristocracy was being strengthened very substantially in a number of major industries [in the second half of the nineteenth century] while in several of the same industries the contrast with unskilled labour increased'.[6] This view is reinforced by Jeffrey Williamson's recently revised estimate of intra-occupational earnings distribution which suggests that earnings inequality, in line with skill differences, among manual workers engaged in commodity production rose in the period 1881–1901.[7] Traditionally, Eric Hobsbawm argued that this wage differential rested on restrictionist devices (e.g. the power of craft unions to restrict entry through apprenticeship) combined with the size of the 'unskilled army of under/unemployed' which kept unskilled wages low. More recently, some scholars have adopted a human capital approach to the skilled worker. Williamson, therefore, argues that the widening gap between skilled and unskilled manual workers (thus confirming Hobsbawm's early contention) was in contrast to the general economy-wide levelling of intra-occupational earnings distribution (which Hobsbawm denied) but that both movements can be explained by the convergence of pay by skill. More has argued that the existence of skilled workers 'cannot be satisfactorily explained as a result of union control over apprenticeship'.[8] According to this thesis skill was genuine and was acquired via apprenticeship which for most of its length gave real instruction and was not merely a restrictionist device'.[9] According to this approach, the main development occurring within the labour aristocracy was changing patterns of training and skill acquisition within the workplace. In many industries, such as engineering, apprenticeship by regular service was still the main form of training. In some new or technically-innovated trades (papermaking, clothing, machine-made boots and shoes, bicycles or electrical engineering) the acquisition of skill was by migration (movement from shop-to-shop or machine-to-machine) or following up (attachment to a gang or skilled worker while carrying out a full-time job) rather than by the conventional 4–7-year trade apprenticeship. The main impact of these changes, apart from the loss of position of some who were previously labour aristocrats, was the growth of a new semi-skilled sector in which there was no defined period of training (apprenticeship) but nevertheless some skill requirement usually acquired through 'picking up', i.e. by long acquaintance with the work.[10]

The growth of the semi-skilled sector at the end of the century was indeed one element, according to the proponents of the concept of the labour aristocracy, in the narrowing of the gap (in status, *not* earnings) between skilled workers and the rest of the working class (as reflected both in the growth of non-apprenticed skilled labour, outside the control of the craft unions, and in the corresponding emergence of all-grades trades unions as opposed to exclusive craft unions) and a cause of skilled workers' integration into the mainstream of the labour movement.[11] Whatever the force of this 'class' argument it is clear that in labour market terms the growth of a semi-skilled sector was a most important development. In the traditional skilled trades, recruitment from the external labour market had been restricted. The largest single source of recruits was the use of family networks in the same firm or occupation. In many of the older crafts (cutlery, basketmaking and coach-building) the apprenticeship was used as a privilege enabling fathers to bring their sons into the trade. The recent work of Crossick and More reinforces this process of self-recruitment.[12] By and large, it was the sons of skilled fathers who received apprenticeships. There were several sound reasons for this. First, employers, by favouring the sons of their workers, could hope to maintain harmony within the firm; secondly the sons of skilled fathers might be more likely to make good skilled workers through 'inheritance of talent or the greater scope they had for emulation'; and thirdly, in the craft shops a strong empathy existed between master and men. Even within the skilled trades 50–60 per cent of recruits were made by contacts with the external labour market. A few boys initially recruited into 'blind-alley' jobs (e.g. errand boys) might later be taken on as probationers (a period of aptitude testing) before entering apprenticeships. Probationers drawn from the external market did not have to possess any high level of intelligence or proven manual dexterity, neither, given the decline of indentured 'premium' apprenticeships, were they required to pay an entry fee.[13] Local residence and elementary education were the most obvious criteria for entry. In addition the pecuniary sacrifices incurred *during* apprenticeships may have been exaggerated. In any event, young workers were willing to discount present in the expectation of future earnings.[14]

If even within the skilled trades there were likely to be half as many recruits from outside the trades as within them, the growth of semi-skilled or intermediate occupations further widened the job opportunities available to those in the external labour market. Here workers did not enter an apprenticeship at all, thus eliminating the closed entry qualifiction, but acquired their skill by a longer period of training, often extending well into adult life. Some might even expect to make the transition in a few industries from semi-skilled to skilled status.[15] The growth of the semi-skilled element reinforces Williamson's idea that employment was shifting out to more skilled occupations and that the decisive factor in all of this was supply side changes associated with the post-1870 spread of basic literacy and numeracy.[16] Entry requirements into the skilled and especially semi-skilled sectors were fairly rudimentary and were loosening but for those without such basic advantages, the chance of mobility between markets was limited.

Beneath the skilled/semi-skilled sectors of the workforce was a variety of unskilled labour, much of it characterized by casual unemployment. This, of course, was Karl Marx's classic 'disposable industrial reserve army' but the size of the sector is, in fact, impossible to determine precisely. Stedman Jones, using Charles Booth's survey of London labour in the 1880s, calculated that casualized workers and their families comprised 10 per cent of the capital's population. It seems likely that most of the 10 per cent living in primary poverty in 1911 (according to Seebohm Rowntree in his study of York) were concentrated at the unskilled, casual end of the labour market.[17] Although it seems certain that basic conditions were moving in favour of the unskilled labour force in the period 1870–1914, (whether through the decline of rural/urban and Irish migration, the mechanization of domestic 'sweatshop' trades, the impact of elementary education (after 1870) on the juvenile labour market or the gains from real wage movements which affected labour as a whole) there was still a large casual element in the labour force. Indeed it was this section of labour which was re-discovered, effectively for the first time for half a century, from the 1880s onwards.[18] The problem of unemployment among the casual labourers concentrated the minds and activities of a generation of professional middle-class investigators in the decades before the First World War. The investigations of H. L. Smith, Charles Booth, William Beveridge and Sidney and Beatrice Webb led to the first real classification of unemployment, emphasizing initially (with the Fabians) differences between seasonal, cyclical and casual employment and moving by the time of Beveridge in 1907 to a more modern kind of 'frictional' approach to the labour market which highlighted information costs and sought a remedy in the form of labour exchanges.[19]

In a sense the late Victorian and Edwardian inquiries anticipated the more recent formulations by labour economists of dual labour markets, in which workers are characterized by either primary or secondary labour market characteristics.[20] Those workers in the primary labour market are, therefore, typified by higher incidence of skill, better pay, job security and upward mobility — indeed, all the qualities of the nineteenth-century skilled worker. In contrast the workers with low wages, little job security and high turnover are in the secondary labour market. Fluidity and casualness are the hallmarks of the secondary labour market. On the face of it, there is an undeniable attraction in the very simplicity of a dual labour market for late Victorian Britain and there is no doubt that the concept focuses on the very important reality of labour market segmentation. In the most obvious terms many unskilled workers certainly exhibited secondary labour market characteristics.

Low pay was a feature of unskilled work, but there were large variations across industries and between workers. Although low wages characterized many occupations which were associated with no skill and ease of entry (e.g. for females, charwomen/washerwomen, waitresses and many 'sweatshop' trades; and for males, 'blind-alley' employment such as carmen, messengers, general labourers and porters) it would be a mistake to equate casual work solely with poverty and destitution. In the building industry, for example, James Treble has suggested that despite the checks and gains to unskilled labourers' wages through the operation of a distinctive building cycle in the post-1850 decades, the long-term 'secular gains are unmistakable', and that in times of full employment unskilled building workers and their families could live without any supplementary income above the primary poverty line.[21] Moreover, in the docks (the classic casual employment 'discovered' by the late

Victorian investigators) there existed an entire 'skilled' sector of the casual workforce (stevedores and lightermen) which possessed specialist knowledge/experience which was highly valued by port employers. Such men, given the high daily wage rates, could earn reasonable wages in a relatively short period of time. These workers were rarely forced on to Poor Relief (an indication of slippage below the primary poverty line) and were in terms of living standards and work habits more akin to semi-skilled workers rather than the mass of unskilled dockworkers.[22]

Irregular employment (casualness) was the distinguishing hallmark of unskilled work in the nineteenth century. This disrupted the regular flow of earnings and affected most seriously those workers already in receipt of low wages, probably driving them below Rowntree's primary poverty line. Like all workers, unskilled labour was subject to unemployment associated with fluctuations in the business cycle and such downturns were probably the biggest single cause of distress for labour as a whole. In addition, unskilled workers were particularly vulnerable to seasonal variations in demand which impinged continuously on any longer business cycles — agricultural labour was traditionally affected by this problem but in the urban labour markets it was commonplace in the building and dock industries. Irrespective of business or seasonal cycles, the casual labourer had by definition no security of employment, he was hired on a day-to-day or even an hour-to-hour basis. Although the unskilled labour market was overstocked (by men attracted in period of high demand, or by others who evinced a preference for casual against regular work) the main problem was often a 'frictional' one of matching up labour supply and demand at any particular time. The realization of these information costs was common to the middle-class investigators of the time, from the Fabians through to Beveridge, and in turn led to their conviction that government intervention was necessary in order to rationalize the labour market, a view shared by modern dual labour market theorists who argue strongly that one of the implications of segmentation is that measures need to be taken (usually by government) in order to improve information and reduce barriers between markets.[23]

Some historians taking a structural approach have pointed strongly to the rigidities and arbitrariness of the casual labour market suggesting that (i) employers 'rigged' the market (using a kind of 'divide and conquer' strategy) by encouraging a labour surplus in order to keep wages low in recessions, and ensure rapid expansion in boom times; (ii) workers were caught in a vicious or self-perpetuating circle because of the nature of casual employment which demanded not only their geographical proximity to work in order to be known by recruiting agents, but also that of their wives, whose employment was in similar warehouses and workshops, and whose income was sometimes essential to keep families above the poverty line. Such market characteristics help explain the geographical immobility of the casual workforce despite the chronic underemployment.[24]

There is much of substance in this approach, but it could be that the imperfections are only part of the picture. The existence of marked wage differentials within casual labour markets indicates that pay was determined by conventional market forces, with wages linked to variations in skill and experience. Moreover, within the confines of these geographically and organizationally distinct casual labour markets the informal networks based on neighbourhood/kinship/friendship ties were very important and probably quite successful in matching up labour supply and demand. Intervention in these labour markets was hardly successful. José Harris has criticized the role of the labour exchanges (from 1909 onwards) in reducing frictional unemployment and suggests that any vacancies filled by them might just as adequately have been filled through the market.[25] Official attempts at decasualization in the docks before 1914 mostly failed and partly because of 'the unwillingness of casual hands to move from their own narrowly-defined areas'.[26] Dockers quite simply refused to conform to such schemes, and they were only tolerated because they did not work.[27] The main problem would appear to have been the absence of inter-occupational mobility *between* manual labour markets. While recognizing that the structure of the casual labour market rendered workers geographically immobile, it seems plausible, given Williamson's suggestion that 'labour supply by skill was highly wage elastic'[28] in this period, that most casual labourers were restricted less by discrimination/exploitation, rigidities and vicious circles, than by their own pre-labour market disadvantages, especially in the areas of education and skill. Such a human capital approach reinforces the upsurge in interest in technical training and the acquisition of industrial skills shown by late Victorian social scientists and reformers themselves. It would certainly confirm Rowntree's findings that 'failure to reach the seventh standard of elementary education was twice as common among unemployed juveniles as in the whole juvenile workforce'.[29]

Sectoral Change and the Labour Market: The growth of Service Occupations

Another development which directly affected the labour market was the process of structural change. As various sectors of the economy contracted and/or expanded under the impact of economic growth this had a spin-off in terms of changing employment opportunities between sectors. Nowhere was this felt more than in the absolute and relative decline of agricultural employment in the half-century after 1850. Down to 1851, despite the employment effect of the growth of manufacturing/mining, agriculture remained the largest single employment sector for men, and still occupied nearly 22 per cent of the total British labour force. By 1911 only 8.3. per cent of occupied Britons were in agriculture. Although this sectoral shift of the occupied population was in part a result of the long-run agricultural price fall in the last third of the century, it was well under way in the period 1850–70 and had as much to do with structural changes in the economy as a whole. Part of the rural exodus was taken up by the manufacturing/mining sector, especially in coal mining and building, but this sector was not growing as fast as it had been in the first half of the century. Most of the contraction of agriculture's share of employment can be explained by the expansion of the service/tertiary sector. This is not to say that agricultural workers were simply transferring directly into service occupations. With the large exception of domestic service they did not possess the skills/background to do so. Rather, they were entering industrial semi-skilled and unskilled occupations, thus releasing both other urban workers and future increments to the labour force for service employment. Between 1851 and 1911 the percentage distribution of the labour force in the tertiary sector as a whole increased from 35.5–45.3 per cent. By the First World War, virtually as many people were engaged in tertiary occupations as in manufacturing/mining. Of course within the tertiary sector there were variations between the employment effects of major subgroups. Much of the increase in employment was actually in the transport sector (21.5 per cent of the labour force by 1911) which some observers would prefer to group separately rather than link either with the 'service' or 'industrial' categories.[30] Certainly, the rise of transport activity had a major employment effect with advanced sectors like the railways, apart from their own permanent staffs, helping to generate an enormous increase in labour-intensive urban road services. Even if transport is regarded separately, the more traditional white-collar service occupations were growing rapidly, concentrated mainly in the areas of finance and commerce, local/central government and the professions. Neither would it be true to say, as J. Gershuny has suggested, that the growth of services was little more than a domestic service revolution.[31] Admittedly domestic service continued to be the largest service occupation, as well as one of the largest of all employment categories, but it had peaked in 1890 and the English servant population declined slightly both in absolute terms and as a proportion of the labour force in the period down to the First World War.[32]

In fact the new representative service worker of the late nineteenth century was the clerk. Clerks fulfilled supportive functions not merely in the service sector itself (commerce and finance) but also in manufacturing, and part of the explanation for the shift towards services lies in the extent to which white-collar personnel were increasing in purely manufacturing establishments. However, the bulk of the increase came in those firms (banks, insurance companies, shippers and merchants) not directly concerned with the manufacture of tangible goods but linked more to the lowering of transaction costs in the distribution of goods. Between 1861 and 1911 the number of men in commercial occupations rose from 130,000 to 739,000 and it is difficult to identify any other male occupational category which increased as rapidly.

When considering the main characteristics of the clerical labour market it is important to distinguish between changes occurring within it and the impact of its growth upon the wider labour market. One of the main developments was the changing sexual composition of the clerical labour force. In mid-century virtually no female commercial clerks were recorded, but by 1911 there were 157,000 in commercial occupations (mainly as clerks). Moreover, female penetration of the white-collar sector in government was just as impressive with 17,000 employed in public administration in 1891 and 50,000 in 1911. The implications of these developments for the general female labour market are important. Traditionally women, either by custom/prejudice or human capital deficiencies, were both excluded from the apprenticed trades and every other occupation which led to the acquisition of skill, and were paid less than men even when they did the same work. The overwhelming majority of women were employed in three sectors: domestic service (much the most important), textile/dressmaking, and agriculture (up to 1851). In the period 1870–1914 these sectors were either fairly static/growing slowly or, as in the case of agriculture, in rapid decline. The decline in these traditional outlets was partly compensated by the emergence of white-collar opportunities. The new office technology of the period 1880–1914 (mainly typewriters and telephones) attracted lower-middle-class and upper-working-class women rather than traditional male clerks because (i) the technical skills were easily and cheaply acquired, (ii) the technology was labour-intensive and only replaced highly-specialized labour such as copy and/or corresponding clerks, (iii) it did not attract men because it was not associated with any long-term promotion prospects. The increased participation of women in white-collar employment illustrates the widening of female employment opportunities after 1870 and especially the shift of qualified women to more skilled occupations, which in turn goes part of the way towards explaining the narrowing of wage differentials between men and women in this period.[33]

In contrast to female white-collar employment the male clerical sector was characterized by its heterogeneous structure. There were wide variations based on social background and status, skills, wages and type of employer. The best placed clerks in the leading merchant or banking houses were on a par with the professionals and small businessmen. Many others earned no more than skilled or even some semi-skilled manual workers but they generally had greater regularity of wages and security of employment. Not all were so fortunate, and a section of the male clerical workforce experienced unemployment, as evidenced by the growth of voluntary associations providing unemployment benefits and 'job search' information.[34]

There were strong connections between the increased demand for white-collar labour after 1870 and the rise in occupational/social mobility. This worked in a number of ways. At one level some manual workers simply made the transition to white-collar work within their own firms. More importantly there was an increase in inter-generational mobility as the sons of working-class fathers entered the clerical labour market. Within the clerical sector itself there were both gains and losses in terms of social mobility. Down to 1870 many white-collar workers were upwardly mobile into the employer class (as merchants and brokers) and this pattern has some striking similarities with the experience of skilled manual workers (entry into the small master class).[35] For both groups after 1870 such mobility was probably less frequent but it was matched, at least in the case of the white-collar workers, by mobility within firms. The rise in the scale of business organization in the last third of the century probably registered a greater impact upon white-collar than manual employment. Among the largest employing institutions and firms many, such as banks, insurance companies and government itself, were either exclusively or mainly employers of white-collar workers. In other industries, such as the railways, while there was a hierarchy of unskilled to highly-skilled manual jobs, there was an additional white-collar/managerial component. At one level the growth of large-scale, country-wide, multi-branch employers had an effect on the narrowing of regional wage differentials and at another they established avenues for upward mobility.[36]

Some of these white-collar firms/industries operated as virtually-closed labour markets, characterized by a growing division of labour and specialization *within* firms or industries and with little contact with the external labour market. The banks are a good example. From their mid-century expansion the joint-stock banks mainly recruited at low-level 'ports of entry', usually taking on young men who served an apprenticeship before being singled out for special training and promotion. These forms of internal promotion are an important, if little known, aspect of late Victorian and Edwardian mobility. Certainly this form of social mobility qualifies any simple conclusion to be drawn from 'snapshots' of the labour market. At any particular point in time many white-collar workers were en route to some other occupations. Despite the opportunities accruing to workers inside the internal labour markets their operation has been criticized as inhibiting the access of workers from the market outside and in the sense that there were fewer entry points, this is true. However, the fact that these large white-collar bureaucracies were expanding in this period meant that the opportunities for entry at the base level were increasing. This reinforces Williamson's contention that, in the wake of the spread of literacy after 1870, employment was shifting out to more skilled sectors generally and particularly to urban service activities.

Trade Unions

There is no question that trade unions exerted a more powerful influence upon the labour market in the period 1870–1914 than they had in earlier decades. This influence operated at several levels. First, the trade unions were expanding in size and influence not only in the traditional 'staple' occupations, but also in previously non-unionized occupations and in new sectors of the economy; moreover this expansion was matched by a shift in attitudes from mid-Victorian 'quietism' to late Victorian and Edwardian 'militancy'. Secondly, the trade unions exerted a more discreet influence upon the course of wages, labour's share of national income and working conditions.

The increase in trade union membership (from 750,000 in 1888 to 4.1 million by 1914) did not accelerate along a continuously upward-moving curve. Rather membership was closely linked to cyclical fluctuations moving forward strongly in upturns (1888–92, 1896–1900, 1910–14) and contracting/stablizing in periods of economic uncertainty (1893–6 and 1901–09). The rise in membership meant that, in numerical terms at least, the trade unions were, effectively for the first time, the most representative working-class institution. This had not always been so. In the early and middle decades of the century far more workers were members of friendly and co-operative societies than trade unions. In terms of the changing composition of the trade unions many historians have traditionally emphasized the so-called switch in the 1880s from old-style craft unions committed to the interests of a privileged minority of labour aristocrats to politicized new unions among the semi-skilled and unskilled workers, especially in the transport sector. In fact much of the increase in union membership occurred in the staple industries (metal/engineering, textiles and mining) or traditional sectors like building which had already been heavily unionized from mid-century but in which, as we have already seen, the distinctions between skilled and semi-skilled were becoming blurred in this period. Among the most significant developments occurring within the composition of trade union membership was the penetration by trade unions of the service sector of the economy. This affected both manual and white-collar service workers in two distinct areas: government and transport. The white-collar unions were concentrated almost exclusively in the public sector among civil servants, teachers and post office workers, and their expansion has been strongly linked with the increase in bureaucratization associated with government employment.[37] The bureaucratic principle underpinned the growth of railway unionism as well, as country-wide collective bargaining became the norm between a small, distant and anti-union group of employers and a more unified 'all-grades' workforce, increasingly conscious of its industrial power.

For some historians the class or political role of trade unions in this period has been regarded as far more significant than their impact upon the labour market in any narrower sense. In some respects the years c. 1880–1914 witnessed the revival of class conflict (and in a sense the first real emergence of a wider working-class consciousness) which had been largely dormant since the heyday of Chartist activity in the 1830s and 1840s.[38] In the later period, trade unions played a more fundamental, if sometimes ambivalent, role whereas in the 1830s and 1840s they had been much less important. Moreover, against this background a section of the trade union leadership was comitted to socialist and/or syndicalist views which at various times impinged upon industrial relations as in the socialist stand of the new unions in the 1880s, and in the syndicalist element in the Triple Alliance period before the First World War. These radical leaders were very critical both of the reformist position of Lib-Labism and of the 'conservatism' of the rest of the trade union leadership and its structures. Such leaders were in a minority and attempts at syndicalist control of the trade unions before the First World War were unsuccessful. Neither was a large element of the membership imbued by notions of 'class war', although historians adopting the 'revolt of labour' approach argue that trade unions acted as vehicles for a rank-and-file revolt which represented part of a long-term struggle for workers' control in which conservative union leadership and bureaucratic/concilatory systems of collective bargaining as well as capitalism itself were the objects of attack.[39] Such an approach is concerned to place trade unions (especially the more radical leaders and members) in the wider context of workers' control and working-class solidarity and sometimes explicitly rejects attempts to view trade unions primarily as 'maximizing agents' operating in such areas as wages, hours, conditions and membership.[40]

In these 'narrower' areas of the labour market the trade unions were certainly exerting more influence in this period. Both Hunt and

Pollard have recently drawn attention to the role of trade unions as one agent (the other being government) in the reduction of working hours.[41] These reductions occurred in brief periods of strong union bargaining power when money wages were high, with the engineers in the vanguard in the years 1871–4 and the miners and building workers forcing the pace from the 1890s. The connections between trade unions and movements in wages is part of a larger development: labour's changing share of national income. It is now generally accepted that before 1850 a greater than proportionate share of Britain's rising national income went to the upper and middle classes as opposed to the working classes, but that from the middle decades of the century, and especially after 1870, labour's share of the national income rose. It is worth noting, as Phelps-Brown initially and more recently S. Pollard have pointed out, that in the long term (i.e. the century or so since 1850) the share of wages in the growth of national income has been remarkably constant.[42] The reasons for the change in the distribution of national income in the second half of the nineteenth century cannot be attributed to any single factor. During the period 1873–96 the fall in prices, falling rate of profit and decline of agricultural rents constrained non-wage incomes while money wages were rising, despite falling prices. Moreover the nature of changes in the terms of trade, which led to the price fall down to the mid-1890s, benefited workers, who spent a higher proportion of their incomes upon basic foodstuffs, more than other groups. Whether trade unions played an independent influence in this period, lifting wages in proportion to the rise in national income, is much less certain. A. G. Hines was among the first to argue that they did, independent of the state of demand for labour, although his model has been heavily criticized on theoretical grounds and Pollard has recently suggested that if, before 1914, higher wages coincided with a higher rate of union density it is unclear which was cause and which effect.[43] It seems certain that in the period 1873–96 trade unions were one important influence which held up money wages even though unemployment was higher than in the pre-1873 or post-1896 years, prices/profits were falling and employers were seeking wage reductions. This is in line with the well known pattern identified by A. W. Philips, i.e. 'that workers are reluctant to offer their services at less than the prevailing rates when the demand for labour is low'.[44] Pollard, in line with Hines, has suggested that 'it is difficult not to associate that reluctance with the attitude and power of the trade unions'.[45] However, it seems likely that most of the gains to labour in this period, apart from the favourable price movements already mentioned, came through long-term gains in productivity with output outstripping population growth between 1850 and the 1880s, and with economies of scale and technical advances improving labour productivity. Associated with improvements in labour productivity was a high rate of occupational/sectoral change with employment rising fastest where pay/skill levels were relatively high-.[46] Against this background of sectoral/occupational/technical changes the trade unions were probably of secondary importance in the period down to 1896. Between 1896 and 1914 the position changed in a number of ways. First, in these years, the terms of trade switched against British workers and brought distinct checks to real wages, which were probably fairly static for labour as a whole. This led to more awareness of the cost of living on the part of organized labour and was an important element in the unrest of the Edwardian years, especially when employers sought to impose wage reductions at low points in the trade cycle as in 1908. Secondly the trade unions, reinforced by the legislative gains following the 1906 General Election (particularly the Trade Disputes Act of 1906 which gave trade unions immunity from civil liabilities) increasingly adopted a more independent and even opportunistic role in industrial relations, notably in the militant and widespread labour unrest associated with the years 1910–14. Some observers have argued that increasing trade union interference in the labour market was an important cause of the decline in labour productivity between 1890 and 1914. W. A. Lewis, drawing in part upon Phelps-Brown's earlier work, has depicted trade unions, committed to job preservation and resistant to new technology, as one element in the productivity trap from which Britain suffered in the 'climacteric' years before 1914.[47] Interestingly, Hunt has concluded that trade union 'impediments to efficiency' were gradually beginning to erode/outweigh many of the more substantial advantages, in terms of wages and conditions, which they had brought workers in earlier decades.[48]

References

1   Recent important surveys of the labour market in Britain during the nineteenth century which have formed the basis for much of the discussion in this paper include E. H. Hunt, *British Labour History 1815–1914* (1981) and S. Pollard, 'Labour in Great Britain,' (in *Cam-*

bridge Economic History of Europe (ed.) P. Mathias & M. M. Postan VII, Part 1 (1978)). See also E. H. Hunt, *Regional Wage Variations in Britain 1850–1914* (1973) and E. J. Hobsbawm, *Labouring Men* (1968).

2 Eric Hobsbawm opened the debate on the labour aristocracy in the 1950s with a 'classic' essay reprinted in his *Labouring Men* ch. 15. The debate continues, and in the 1970s there were major contributions by G. Crossick, *An Artisan Élite in Victorian Society* (1978) and R. Gray, *The Lab our Aristocracy in Victorian Edinburgh* (1976).

3 See E. H. Hunt, *British Labour History* pp. 277–8.

4 E. J. Hobsbawm, *op.cit.*, p. 285.

5 C. More, *Skill and the Working Class in England 1870–1914* (1981) p. 46.

6 S. Pollard, *op.cit.*, p. 172.

7 J. Williamson, 'Earnings Inequality in Britain,' *Journal of Economic History*, Volume XL, September 1980, No. 3.

8 C. More, *op.cit.*, p. 228.

9 *Ibid.*

10 *Ibid.*, p. 231.

11 See E. Hobsbawm, *op.cit.*, pp. 295–6.

12 G. Crossick, *op.cit.*, p. 117, and C. More, *op.cit.*, p. 228.

13 C. More, *op.cit.*, p. 69.

14 *Ibid.*

15 *Ibid.*, p. 231.

16 J. Williamson, *op.cit.*, p. 473.

17 See J. H. Treble, *Urban Poverty in England* (1979) pp. 186–7, for an analysis of Rowntree's notions of 'primary' and 'secondary' poverty.

18 The first major inquiry was Henry Mayhew's investigation of *London Labour and the London Poor* published in the 1850s.

19 For a good account of the various approaches to unemployment from the 1880s to the First World War see J. Harris, *Unemployment and Politics, A Study in English Social Policy, 1886–1914*, (1972) ch. 1.

20 Any basic primer in labour economics is likely to contain information on dual labour market theory. See, for example, F. R. Marshall, A. M. Carter & A. G. King, *Labour Economics*, (1976) pp. 268–70.

21 J. H. Treble, *op.cit.*, ch. 1.

22 N. Whiteside, 'Welfare Insurance and Casual Labour 1906–1926,' *Economic History Review*, (1979).

23 William Beveridge represented the 'highwater mark' of the pre-1914 school of investigators who were critical of the workings of the 'free' labour market. For Beveridge, deficiencies in the labour market could only be remedied by government agencies such as labour exchanges. See J. Harris, *op.cit.* p. 24. In similar fashion, contemporary dual labour market economists argue for government-sponsored 'social action' programmes in order to reduce discrimination and exploitation. See, for example, G. C. Cain, 'Dual Labour Market Theories: A Neoclassical Assessment,' in J. E. King (ed.) *Readings in Labour Economics* (1980).

24   A good example of this approach is Gareth Steadman Jones, *Outcast London* (1971). For Steadman Jones there was no equilibrium between supply and demand in the unskilled labour market, as reflected in the chronic over-supply (p. 97). Moreover workers in the unskilled labour market suffered in an arbitrary fashion from both 'the sentence of destitution' and 'the equally arbitrary cascade of charity' (p. 344). In combination, these factors inhibited the development of class consciousness among the unskilled workers which, in turn, restricted the general growth of a radical metropolitan labour movement before 1914.

25   J. Harris, *op.cit.*, p. 355.

26   J. H. Treble, *op.cit.*, p. 60.

27   N. Whiteside, *op.cit.*, p. 518.

28   J. Williamson, *op.cit.*

29   Quoted by J. Harris, *op.cit.*, fn. p. 32.

30   S. Lebergott in *Manpower in Economic Growth* (1964) p. 113, argues that employment in transportation in the American economy should be included in a new functional grouping distinct from services and manufacturing.

31   S. Lebergott, *Ibid.*, suggests that the much vaunted rise of service employment is a myth because in the USA, in the twentieth century, the growth of general service employment was matched by the decline of domestic service. Conversely, J. Gershuny, in *After Industrial Society* (1978) p. 62., argues that the growth of services in Victorian Britain was primarily a function of the growth of domestic service.

32   T. McBride, *The Domestic Revolution*, (1976) p. 34.

33   Much of the information on female employment is derived from E. H. Hunt, *op.cit.*

34   See G. Anderson, *Victorian Clerks* (1976) for evidence of clerical unemployment.

35   For E. Hobsbawm, and other historians of the labour aristocracy, this pattern of upward mobility into the small master class is one of the distinguishing characteristics of aristocratic status.

36   See E. H. Hunt, *Regional Wage Variations*, for the effect of trade unions, firms and government on narrowing regional wage differentials.

37   For the bureaucratization theory, see G. S. Bain, *The Growth of White-Collar Unionism*, (1970), ch 6.

38   For a critical appraisal of the revival of class conflict and extent of working-class consciousness by 1914 see E. H. Hunt, *British Labour History*, pp. 329–34.

39   In sharp contrast to E. H. Hunt, see R. Price, *Masters, Unions and Men, Work Control in Building and the Rise of Labour 1830–1914*, (1980) in which a revolt of rank-and-file labour is fused to a crisis of authority in the years before 1914.

40   R. Price, *op.cit.*, p. 240 argues that rank-and-file militancy 'can't be patronizingly dismissed as just another stage of simple union militancy, . . . its significance can't be gauged by the measurement of statistical

indices of any sort'.
41 See E. H. Hunt, *British Labour History*, pp. 78–9 and S. Pollard, *Cambridge Economic History of Europe*, p. 172.
42 S. Pollard, *op.cit.*, p. 168.
43 *Ibid.*, p. 176.
44 *Ibid.*
45 *Ibid.*
46 On changes in labour productivity, see E. H. Hunt, *British Labour History*, pp. 109–16.
47 W. A. Lewis, *Growth and Fluctuations*, (1978) p. 127.
48 E. H. Hunt, *British Labour History*, p. 340.

2

The Rise of a Mass Labour Movement: Growth and Limits

James Hinton

Between the 1870s and the First World War a mass labour movement was formed in Britain. Trade union membership grew from about half a million in the mid–1870s to over four million by 1914. Most of this growth took place in the two great strike explosions of 1889–90 and 1910–14, though there were also two lesser spurts in the late 1880s and the mid-1900s. By 1914 nearly a quarter of the occupied population belonged to trade unions, compared with a mere 4 per cent in 1880. This was only one facet, if the major one, of the growing power of working-class organization within British society.

Membership of the co-operative movement grew, in line with the unions, from about 600,000 in 1880 to over three millions by 1914. Trades councils, previously confined mainly to the larger industrial towns, spread rapidly over the whole country, reflecting a growing identification among working-class activists with a national movement, broader and more political than mere sectional trade unionism. The formation of the Labour Party in 1900 gave further expression to this sense of a working-class movement. By 1912 more than half the total trade union memebership was affiliated to the Labour Party, though the co-operative movement as a whole remained aloof from independent labour politics. Labour won forty-two seats in the General Election of December 1910, and, despite setbacks in the last years before the war, it continued to advance strongly in municipal elections.[1]

The growth was impressive, but it should not be exaggerated. At one moment, in 1889–90, it had seemed possible that an alliance between socialist politics and the poorer sections of the workers who were exploding into trade union organization, could remake the whole working-class movement. In fact, the promise of New Unionism was not fulfilled. The formation of the Labour Party at the turn of the century represented not a victory of the socialists, but the effective containment of the socialist impulse within older traditions of trade union politics and class collaboration. Within the unions sectional division and conflict remained endemic, and organized labour, for all its growth, remained a minority of the working class. Paradoxically, its very expansion involved the consolidation of certain patterns of organization and of ideology – in the approach to women, for example, or the poor – which tended to confine the movement within its minority position.

Historians of trade unionism have tended to reflect, more or less unconsciously, the assumptions of the trade union activists about whom they are writing. Some, identifying with socialists, exaggerate the coherence and ambition of the movement – or indulge in a rather superior pessimism about the capacity of ordinary workers to measure up to the demands that 'History' makes upon them. Others, more sympathetic to the pragmatic behaviour characteristic of trade union officials (including most socialist ones), see only sectionalism and a readiness to settle for modest gains. Both standpoints are too narrow. Over-rehearsed arguments about the relative influence of socialism and of trade union pragmatism in the movement obscure more important questions. We need to stand outside the assumptions of the activists, to view the labour movement from without. The growth of organized labour, and its limitations, can only be understood in relation to broader economic, social and political changes in the society of which it formed a part. The purpose of this essay is to review trade union growth between the 1880s and 1914 within this broader context.

During the last quarter of the nineteenth century Britain lost its supremacy as the workshop of the world. While the rate of growth of British manufacturing industry slowed down, rapid industrialization in other parts of the world reduced the British share of world industrial production from over 30 per cent in 1870 to under 15 per cent by 1913.[2] British capitalism responded to the challenge of the new industrial economies largely along traditional lines, storing up problems for the future. Manufacturers, facing stiffer foreign competition in the more industrialized areas of the world, turned increasingly towards the Empire and developing countries to sell the textiles, iron and steel, railway rolling stock and basic machinery which German and American capitalism no longer needed to import from Britain. At the same time the relative weakness of Britain's export performance was compensated by a huge expansion of the income from overseas investment. Between 1870 and 1914 capital export was the fastest growing sector of the British economy. Increasingly funds went, not to Europe and the United States, but to the Empire and other developing countries. This contributed to the expansion of markets on which British exporters relied, while at the same time it yielded an influx of dividend and interest payments to sustain the British balance of payments.

By thus retreating from the most dynamic sectors of the world economy, British capitalism was able to remain viable with a manufacturing base geared to producing the textiles and heavy capital goods characteristic of the first industrial revolution, and to evade the necessity to modernize industry in line with the more advanced technology emerging in Germany and the United States. Before 1914 the relative backwardness of British industry, although becoming increasingly apparent, had not yet reached crisis proportions.[3]

Underpinning the emergence of a mass labour movement in the last quarter of the nineteenth century was the growing predominance of regular industrial wage-earners, concentrated in substantial work units, within the working-class population. The proportion of the occupied population involved in agriculture was halved, falling from 15 per cent in 1871 to 7.5 per cent in 1901. The mass of rural immigrants went, not into manufacturing industry, but into the most rapidly expanding sectors of the domestic economy, transport and mining. Together these two industries accounted for over 15 per cent of the occupied population by 1911. This involved a major shift from worse to better paid jobs, from less to more regular employment. By 1911 there were nearly 1¼ million miners, providing a powerful and relatively prosperous bedrock for the labour movement. In transport, casual labour persisted on the waterfront and in road transport, but it was the steady work on the railways that expanded fastest.

Manufacturing industry remained constant at about 40 per cent of the occupied population, the relative decline of textiles and clothing being balanced by a rapid growth of metal working and food processing industries.[4] It was during this period that the factory became the predominant form of organization in almost all industries, at the expense of outwork and petty workshop production. There were seven or eight clothing factories in Leeds in 1881, fifty-four ten years later, the larger of which employed up to 1250 people. During the 1890s the factory very largely superseded outwork in provincial shoemaking. A similar shift occurred in tailoring, hosiery, furniture and the light metal trades of Birmingham, London, Glasgow and Sheffield. Many of the independent and anarchic file- and toolmakers of Sheffield found themselves working in one of the five factories employing over 1000 workers each by 1890. By 1911 women were less likely to go into domestic service, or to take in work at home, and more likely to find employment in the new food processing, metalworking and chemical factories.* The number of washerwomen declined in face of the factory laundry. Overall, by 1913 4.5 million people were employed in factories (average size 40–50), slightly more than half a million in workshops (average size 4–5). In 1907 less than 3 per cent of the manufacturing workforce were outworkers.[5]

The growth of the mines, railways and factories swelled the intermediate stratum of the working class, the semi-skilled, the 45 per cent or so who, by the 1890s, were earning between 22 shillings and £2 a week. This stratum was the chief beneficiary of the great price fall between 1873 and 1896. Falling prices, which worried manufacturers, contributed to a general rise in working-class living standards by 30–50 per cent . For the first time some of the material gains of industrialization were being reaped by more than a small aristocratic élite of the working class. The huge expansion of the co-operative movement, and of food, clothing and footwear chain stores is an indication of the trend. Better fed, better clothed, better shod, even, after the building boom of the 1890s, a little better housed, the prospect of a richer and more varied life outside of work itself opened up to large numbers of workers and their families. Other changes pushed in the same direction. The gains made in shorter hours in the 1870s were extended further. Some of this gain was consumed by increasing time spent travelling to work as towns grew in size, but some remained to be devoted to domestic life and recreation.[6]

With more leisure and more money to spend, working people could construct more stable and satisfying cultural patterns. For the higher paid pianos, gramophones and bicycles became the means to

---

*There was, however, no overall increase in the proportion of women workers, except in white-collar work, because the relative decline of textiles, which employed the largest percentage of women, masked their advance in other manufacturing industries, and because they were virtually excluded from the most rapidly expanding sectors, mining and transport.

a richer family life, as well as symbols of status within the neighbourhood. As new populations settled down after the upheavals of industrialization kinship and neighbourhood networks could be consolidated, sheltering working-class people against the harshness of the urban environment. For most working-class people the possibilities of recreation broadened. Music Hall peaked after 1890, and the cinema was well established in working-class areas before 1914. Every conceivable working-class institution had its own brass band. Football spread as a participant and spectator sport, aided by the emergence of the Saturday half-holiday which enabled sportsmen to circumvent the killjoy prohibitions of sabbatarian local authorities. Meanwhile, cheap railway excursions opened up the seaside to the working class and made it easier to spend Sunday in the country or visiting relatives.[7]

It was in the last decades of the nineteenth century that the main features were created of a working-class culture that, by the 1950s, had come to be seen as 'traditional'. This culture embodied real gains for a large section of the working class. Rising living standards, and a more established, settled, less hand-to-mouth existence, contributed to the strengthening of the labour movement. Larger workplaces and steadier employment made it easier to maintain trade union organization. Higher real wages released cash to finance union activity. For a small, but significant section increased leisure time could be devoted to adult education, trade union and political activism.

It would however be easy to exaggerate the degree to which a socially and culturally homogenous working class had emerged by 1914. Profound divisions persisted within the working class, and these continued to set limits to the expansion of the labour movement until after the First World War. The growth of the intermediate stratum of the working class did not mean the disappearance of the labour aristocratic élite. The superior status of the labour aristocracy was eroded by the rapid growth of white-collar employment, particularly where salaried clerical, technical and managerial staff interposed themselves between skilled workers and the bosses. Similarly, rising standards of living among the mass of respectable workers immediately below the aristocrats in the social hierarchy tended to diminish the starkness of their privilege by closing the gap beneath them. Wage differentials between skilled and unskilled workers, however, seem to have changed little between 1870 and 1910, and in big cities suburbanization may have led to an increasing residential segregation of better-off from less fortunate workers.[8]

In some expanding occupations, food manufacture and transport for example, status divisions among the workforce were less extreme than in the craft sectors – although on the railways engine drivers retained separate organization and a position of exceptional privilege. The spread of mechanization and the factory undermined the position of handicraft artisans. Nevertheless, craftsmen in the shipyards, in engineering and foundry work, in printing and building, spinners in cotton mills, rollers and puddlers in iron and steel, hewers in pits all continued to lord it over their less skilled helpers. Craftsmen resisted the encroachments of the less skilled, often, as in engineering, maintaining their monopoly of work whose real skill content had been reduced by technological change.[9] Unless forced to do so by irresistible technological change, skilled workers resisted accepting the less skilled as equals. One result of the relative technological and managerial backwardness of British capitalism before 1914 was to prolong the viability of craft unionism, enabling skilled workers to resist novel doctrines of all-grades, industrial unionism.[10] Many of the new unionists of the 1880s or the syndicalists of 1910–14 were themselves craftsmen, but most labour aristocrats before 1914 viewed the organization of the less skilled within their own workplaces with suspicion or downright hostility. 'New Unionism' often appeared as a direct challenge to aristocratic privilege. The early 1890s saw a rash of bitter conflicts between skilled and less skilled trade unionists – spinners and their piecers, platers and their holders-up, hewers in the North East and their putters.[11] Robert Knight expressed a common attitutde to signs of independence on the part of the less skilled when he declared in 1893: 'The helper ought to be subservient, and do as the mechanic tells him.'[12] Twenty years later skilled engineers took a dim view of the (highly successful) drive of the Workers' Union to organize the less skilled: 'When the membership of a semi-skilled union rises from 5000 to 65,000 in less than four years, and nearly trebles in less than twelve months, we get dictatorship.'[13]

While the exclusiveness of the aristocracy remained an important factor in the working-class movement, it was the hopelessness of the poor which presented the movement with its most critical problems. Despite the general rise in living standards, in 1900 'the poor' constituted up to 40 per cent of the working class – families living on an income of 21 shillings a week or less. Poverty was endemic among the unemployed, casual and seasonal workers, or simply low-paid regular wage earners. In the absence of any system of social security, apart from the Poor Law, ill-health or accident could deny even a subsistence income to a respectable worker and his family, unless trade union benefits could tide him over. The largest concentrations of poverty were to be found in London and the other great port towns where casual labour prevailed. Other black sports included the sweated workshop and outwork trades of London, the West Midlands, Leeds and Manchester, the Yorkshire woollen and Scottish jute industries, the building trades and the food processing factories generally. The old suffered worst, and women and children. While a casual labourer might get sufficient food to maintain physical efficiency, his wife and children would go without.[14] Although infant mortality fell substantially, as late as 1913 one in every four funerals was the funeral of a child under five years. The effects of undernourishment on those who lived were revealed in 1917 when little more than a third of the young men medically examined for military service were without 'marked' or 'partial' disabilities.[15]

The problem posed by poverty for the labour movement was an intractable one. The urban poor were intensly parochial. Dependent on kin and friends for help in times of crisis, needing to be known locally in order to get credit from shopkeepers and jobs from employers, unable to pay the transport costs involved in living at a distance from the workplace, their lives were narrowly circumscribed by the immediate locality.[16] Denied status or power in the wider society, and ignorant of the world outside the slum, the poor could retain their self-respect only by limiting their horizons to those in the same situation as themselves. Hence the indignation – so well recorded by Robert Tressell in *The Ragged Trousered Philanthropists* – against those idealists who threatened to bring them up against the larger parameters of their deprivation. Since experience taught that nothing could be achieved by collective action, the missionaries of the labour movement tended to be seen as either naîve or self-seeking.

This was not invariably the case. In the mid-1880s, when unemployment peaked, the nascent socialist movement had some success among the London poor, leading protest marches and demonstrations. For a moment in February 1886 middle-class London, terrified by the riotous behaviour of an East End crowd led by socialists, was ready to believe that insurrection was imminent. But the fear was exaggerated and the poor were as likely to support zenophobic imperialists as to march behind the red flag.[17] More important was the trade union explosion of 1889–90 which pulled in sections of the casual poor who had previously appeared to be beyond the reach of organized labour. The New Unionism organized among dockers, seamen, gasworkers, building labourers and the less skilled and low paid throughout industry. After the success of the London Dock Strike in August 1889 it seemed to many that trade unionism, no longer the property of a privileged élite within the working class, held the key to the self-emancipation of the poor.

In reality there was little basis for this optimism. The success of New Unionism during 1889–90 rested on full employment, on the readiness of the police to tolerate vigorous picketing, and on the absence of concerted opposition from employers. None of these conditions lasted long, and the counter-attack devastated the new organizations. In 1890, at their peak, the seven largest New Unions claimed 320,000 members, though this was probably an inflated figure. On more reliable figures this total had fallen to 130,000 in 1892 and 80,000 in 1896, a mere 5 per cent of the total number of trade unionists in the latter year. The more lasting expansion of trade unionism occurred among the relatively secure and well-paid, semi-skilled workers in cotton, coal, iron and steel and the railways, and in the old-established unions of the craft industries.[18] Even in the New Unions the sectional logic of trade unionism was quick to assert itself against the notion of an all-embracing class unionism. After the first flush of success, for example, the gasworkers unscrambled their 'general' branches reorganizing on the basis of trade and place of employment. In face of the employers' counter-attack and the return of unemployment, those sections which could not win union recognition dropped out, leaving the general unions as federations of sectional bargaining units rather than organs of a united industrial offensive against capitalism.[19] Even before the counter-attack the New Unionism was clearly something less than a coherent revolt of the poor as a whole. Thus the fight to establish trade unionism in the London docks was also a fight to make dockwork 'respectable' – at the expense of the weakest competitors for jobs. In 1890 the Dockers' Union decided to close its books, and Tom Mann explained that 'the other men at the Dock gates must clear off; with us there is no room for them'.[20] Trade union action by itself might expand the size of the respectable working class. But despite occasional spasms of revolt, the great mass of the urban poor remained impermeable to working-class organization.

The inability of the labour movement to come to grips with the problem of poverty was matched by its failure to recruit among the female half of the working class. In 1901, women made up over 30 per cent of the labour force, but only 7.5 per cent of the total number of trade unionists. About one in six working men were organized in unions. The equivalent figure for wage-earning women was less than one in thirty.[21] The main reason for this difference was not that women were intrinsically less clubbable, but that they were concentrated in those occupations most difficult to organize whatever the sex of the workforce. Despite some valiant efforts, trade unionism could make little headway in such a personalized employment situation as domestic service – and in 1911 39 per cent of all employed women were domestic servants. The large numbers of women employed in outwork or in small workshops in dressmaking, millinery, tailoring, shoemaking or the light metal trades, women who often worked on a part-time or seasonal basis, were almost equally difficult to organize. Where employment was secure, regular and concentrated in large workplaces women did organize, most notably in the Lancashire cotton mills which in 1914 accounted for nearly half the total number of women trade unionists. Outside cotton much of the growth of women's trade unionism occurred in the expanding semi-skilled factory trades – food processing, box-making, engineering – and among white-collar workers in shops, telephonists, postal sorters and, a major growth area, elementary school teachers.[22]

Trade union attitudes to the organization of women were complicated by the widespread hostility of working-class men to women working at all. Since women's wages were generally much lower than men's, they were seen as a potential threat to the maintenance of the male wage. Most skilled unions excluded women, and bitterly resisted employer attempts to introduce them into the workforce. The fact that such exclusiveness was one reason for women being low paid in the first place did nothing to allay the men's fears. Feminists and craft unionists could agree, in the 1880s, on a TUC resolution in favour of equal pay, but for the men the point of insisting on equal pay was to make it uneconomic for employers to take on women workers. Over the issue of 'protective' legislation designed to exclude women from certain occupations – women in the chain and nail trades of the Black Country and the pit brow lasses became *cause célèbres* in the 1880s – advocates of women's rights fought extended battles against the TUC. As late as 1911, cotton spinners in Wigan were demanding an amendment of the Factory Acts to ban women from the mule room, though the TUC took a more enlightened attitude when the brassworkers proposed a similar measure in 1908.[23]

Fear of cheap labour was only one aspect of the problem. Central to the emergence of a more settled and respectable working-class way of life, which underpinned the growth of trade unionism in the period, was the construction of the home as an arena of physical comfort and emotional support. Given large numbers of children and the labour-intensive character of housework the fulfilment of the domestic ideal required the full-time labour of housewives.[24] Better-off workers in most parts of the country preferred their wives to stay at home. The notion of the 'family wage' – that a man's earnings should be sufficient to keep his wife and young children out of the labour markct – was an important element in late nineteenth century working-class respectability, and it militated against any serious consideration of the case for equal work opportunities for women. In 1911 less than 10 per cent of married women were in paid employment.[25] While the resulting predominance of young, single women in the female labour force did nothing to discourage militancy, it may have had some influence on the capacity of women workers to sustain stable trade union organization.

Where women workers did oragnize successfully, male concern to protect job monopolies kept them in a subordinate position. Although most cotton trade unionists were women, there were very few women officials, and the men took care to keep women out of the most specialized and highly paid jobs. On the few occasions when Lancashire women set up independent organizations they met with determined opposition from the male leaders of the established unions.[26] Efforts to organize women were further bedevilled by conflict between the middle-class women who took the lead in the Women's Trade Union League (founded in 1874 as the Women's Provident and Protection Society), and male class consciousness. The WTUL operated as an entrepreneur of organization, helping to set up women's unions and persuading existing unions to recruit women. At the same time it worked as a parliamentary lobby, at first opposing protective legislation, later playing a leading role in the agitation for Trade Boards to establish a minimum rate in sweated industries. The finance for these activities was provided by wealthy philanthropists. In the 1880s the hostility of these women to strikes and militancy and their attempts to organize low-paid women along craft union lines, limited their effectiveness. While their approach improved from the 1890s, the WTUL and its offshoot the National Federation of Women Workers (1906) continued to be disparaged as organs of middle-class charity rather than proper trade unions.[27] The rapid growth of women's organization from the mid-1900s made some impact on male attitudes, but in 1914 the predominant view was still that stated by Will Thorne, the socialist leader of the gasworkers: 'Women do not make good trade unionists and for this reason we believe that our energies are better used towards the organization of male workers.'[28]

One further qualification to the emergence of a more homogeneous working class should be noted. There was little diminution during this period in regional variations in the standard of living, and the growth of trade union organization probably did more to intensify than to reduce the relative advantage of the more prosperous areas.[29] The shape and pace of economic and social change differed markedly from one part of the country to another, and many of the cross-currents of working-class politics can only be understood in terms of variations in local conditions. There is little space in this essay to discuss the peculiarities of class relations in the metropolis, the special features of the coalfields where Lib-Labism found its most enduring base, or the contrasting pattern of development in the factory towns of the North which led in the development of independent labour politics. The great diversity of local experience which lie behind the generalizations inevitable in an essay of this kind should be remembered.

If the labour movement remained a minority within the working class, socialism remained a minority position within the movement. Socialist penetration reflected the growing frustration of working class activists with the collaborationist stance of the established Lib-Lab leadership. During the later 1880s that leadership was challenged over a wide front – ideologically on its Gladstonian hostility to social legislation, politically on its failure to promote labour representation in parliament, industrially on its pacifism and its narrow aristocratic exclusiveness. Socialists were at the forefront of this challenge in all its aspects, but they were neither cause nor masters of the revival of working-class militancy which underpinned it. Scornful of the squabbles and sectarianism of the early socialist movement, Engels had looked forward to an explosion of mass unrest that would engulf these tiny organizations and create the basis for a mass socialist party. In the event nothing so simple occurred. For one thing, the explosion when it came proved less elemental in its force, less class conscious in the attitudes it embodied, and more short-lived than Engels imagined it would be.[30] Moreover, socialism was too weakly established, too inadequately articulated in Britain, to master the movement: rather, the socialists themselves were mastered by the limitations of the mass movement.

While the pioneer socialist party, the Social Democratic Federation (SDF), took a dim view of the opportunities provided by the trade union explosion,[31] a growing number of independent socialists made their mark both as organizers and by their capacity to translate the ideological challenge to Lib-Labism into immediate agitational demands. Above all it was the campaign for the statutory eight-hour-day, launched by Tom Mann in 1886 and seen as a panacea for unemployment as well as an end in itself, which enabled socialists to capture the imagination of trade unionists in new and old unions alike.[32] From the outset this campaign was closely linked with attempts to establish labour representation in parliament on an independent basis. Urged on by Engels, who valued practical activity over socialist purity in the political as well as in the industrial field, dissident members of the socialist parties were attempting from the late 1880s to launch an independent labour party. The breakthrough came in the North with the foundation of the Independent Labour Party (ILP) as a federation of local labour clubs and parties at a conference in Bradford in 1893.[33]

The establishment of the ILP was very largely a result of the activity of socialists in the trade union explosion. The subsequent development of the new socialist party, however, owed as much to the limitations and failures of New Unionism as to its successes.

It is significant that the ILP emerged out of a defeated strike in Bradford, and that the West Riding of Yorkshire, where trade unionism was particularly weak, remained for many years its strongest area of support.[34] The growth of socialist politics in the 1890s represents less a political generalization of industrial militancy, than a reaction to defeat in the industrial struggle, a search for political solutions where industrial ones had failed. Behind this lay the incompleteness and weakness of trade union organization. During the explosion of 1889–90, socialist leaders of New Unionism had been anxious to repudiate the allegation made by Gladstonian trade union leaders that their policy would lead workers into craven dependence on the state. 'The keynote,' wrote Mann and Tillett, 'is to *organize* first, and take action in the most effective way . . . instead of looking specially to the government.'[35] Nevertheless, their emphasis on the demand for the statutory eight-hour-day and on labour representation in parliament reflected an awareness that the groups of workers they were organizing were too weak to win their trade union battles without positive support from the state. The decline of New Unionism in the early 1890s confirmed socialists in their conviction that it was to legislative intervention, rather than to the direct action of the poor themselves, that they must look for the solution to the problem of poverty.

It was not only the new unions that came under attack during the 1890s. Major conflicts occurred in cotton and coal. In the lockout of 1897–8 the engineering employers made the most determined assault on trade union power. Meanwhile, a series of adverse court decisions culminated in the Taff Vale judgment of 1901 which undermined the legal status enjoyed by the unions since the 1870s. But employers stopped short of an all-out attempt to destroy trade unionism. The early years of the twentieth century saw a period of exceptional industrial peace. This was a result not so much of trade union defeat as of the stalemate reached in many industries during the 1890s. Most of the major confrontations had ended not in outright defeat for the unions, but in the establishment of procedures for collective bargaining. More and more employers were willing to accept trade unionism as a fact of life, and were prepared to rely on 'responsible' trade union leaderships rather than the weapon of the lockout to hold rank-and-file rebelliousness in check.[36]

One effect of the employers' counter-attack was to open the way for the conversion of the trade unions to independent labour politics. Socialist attempts to persuade the TUC to promote working-class candidates independent of the Liberals in the early 1890s were defeated. The agreement of the TUC in 1899 to convene a conference of co-operative, socialist and trade union organizations to 'devise ways and means for securing the return of an increased number of labour members to the next Parliament', reflected a widespread belief that British employers, like their American counterparts, were poised for an all-out attack on trade unionism.[37] (That these fears were exaggerated goes some way to explain why the outcome of the 1899 decision was not as radical as some of its socialist advocates had hoped it would be.) At the ensuing conference the ILP steered a careful course between Lib-Lab attempts to restrict the new organization to the pursuit of limited trade union demands, and the SDF's call for the adoption of a clear socialist objective. The delegates accepted Hardie's compromise resolution, voting to establish 'a distinct labour group in Parliament, who shall have their own whips, and agree upon their policy'. By 1905 most major unions except the miners – whose numerical dominance in a number of constituencies enabled them to gain representation in parliament through the Liberal Party – had affiliated. The foundation of the Labour Representation Committee was a triumph for the socialists, but it did not overnight transform the character of working-class politics.[38] What the unions sought from the LRC, however, was not any long-term alternative to Liberalism, but a sufficiently strong bargaining position to force the next Liberal government to repeal the effects of the Taff Vale judgment. Ramsay MacDonald and the leadership of the LRC concurred. What they had in mind was bargaining strength *vis à vis* the Liberals, rather than strict independence from both established parties. In 1903 MacDonald negotiated an electoral pact with the Liberal Whip, Herbert Gladstone. In the Liberal landslide of 1906, twenty-nine Labour candidates were elected, twenty-four of them without Liberal opposition. The new Labour Party – formally constituted as such after the election – had arrived on the political scene not as the gravedigger of Liberalism, but as an integral part of a great Liberal revival.

The Labour Party, as it emerged in 1906, rested on two sets of alliances. In the first place it involved what Keir Hardie called the 'Labour Alliance' – the co-operation of socialists and trade unions to promote Labour members of parliament. Trade union numbers and money dominated the new party and ensured that within it the pursuit of socialism was firmly subordinated to the immediate legislative needs of organized labour. The unions' concern with parliamentary effectiveness dictated a second alliance – the accommodation with the Liberals which alone enabled the Labour Party to secure a significant parliamentary presence. This further weakened the impact of socialism, since in order to sustain Liberal willingness to allow Labour candidates a free run against the Tory, it was important that these candidates conciliate local Liberal opinion by playing down any socialist convictions they may have held. As a result little could be done to build up the independent socialist electorate without which Labour would inevitably remain little more than an interest group within the Liberal coalition. Within the Labour Party, then, socialism was doubly subordinated – to trade union pragmatism and to the need to maintain an electoral accommodation with the Liberals.

In 1906 there was no significant current of socialist politics, apart from that represented by the rather sectarian Social Democratic Federation, outside the Labour Party. This reflected the impasse in which the socialist movment had found itself since the heady days of the early 1890s. At the core of the impasse was the ambiguous and problematic relationship of socialism to the central problem confronting the Labour movement prior to the First World War, the problem of poverty. Any effective socialist party must be rooted in a powerful trade union movement. But, as the experience of New Unionism demonstrated, the building of such a movement required, as a precondition, the amelioration of that great morass of poverty which undermined effective union organization. As one historian has written, summarizing Keir Hardie's views:

> Before the real agitation for socialism could begin, the unemployed and underemployed must be materially elevated so that they would become morally fit for the responsibilities of the labour movement. Before its agitation for socialism could become effective, the Labour Party must first agitate effectively for the improvement of the poor.[39]

Since the poor could not help themselves, socialists were forced to look to the legislative intervention of the state. Perhaps, had the political establishment proved totally resistant to demands for social reform, the socialists would have been driven to pursue revolutionary alternatives. In fact the socialists' concern with the problem of poverty met with an answering response in the Liberal Party.

During the 1890s, inspired by Charles Booth's great survey of *London Life and Labour*, a programme of welfare legislation designed to ameliorate the worst evils of capitalism began to take shape among middle-class intellectuals in and around the Liberal Party. Aware that the Gladstonian remedy of individualism and self-help held no solution, these New Liberals were equally opposed to any root-and-branch attack on the capitalist organization of the economy. Booth was a characteristic advocate, describing his programme as one of 'limited socialism', and calling on the organized workers to turn aside from revolutionary ideas in favour of a 'socialism which shall leave untouched the forces of individualism and the sources of wealth'.[40] It was with advocates of such views that the socialists had to make an alliance if they were to have any chance of securing the legislative attack on poverty which appeared to be the precondition of any class offensive against capitalism as such.

The alliance was all too easily formed. The social composition of the ILP – young skilled workers and their wives, shop assistants, teachers, clerks – made it, at best, a movement *on behalf of* the poor, rather than a movement *of* the poor. Among the leaders of the ILP the problem of poverty was perceived less as a problem for the poor themselves, more as a problem created by the poor for the organized and respectable working class. Many of their favoured remedies – notably the resettlement of the urban unemployed in rural farm colonies – owed less to any understanding of the economic forces producing poverty, than to a straightforward desire to remove the poor from competition with organized labour in the market place.[41] The SDF took a more robust view and frequently took the lead in building up agitation among the unemployed themselves.[42] But its leaders' hostility to the unions restricted its ability to sustain a viable socialist alternative to the compromising politics of the ILP. Within the emerging politics of New Liberal social reform there was a clear convergence between a labour aristocratic distain for the moral incompetants in the slums, and a middle-class view of the poor as something less than responsible citizens, appropriate objects of pity and of social engineering.

Given this background it is not surprising that socialists were unable to sustain an effective alternative to the reform programme of the Liberal government after 1906. School meals for children, medical inspection in schools and non-contributory pensions were introduced. The Trades Boards Act made it possible to fix legal minimum wages in sweated trades, putting a floor under the competitive driving down of wages. Labour exchanges, not very successful in their prime purpose of ending the anarchy of the labour market, did provide a test, more acceptable than the workhouse test, of the willingness of the unemployed to work – a test used by Lloyd George in establishing unemployment insurance. The 1911 National Insurance Act also established sickness and accident insurance schemes.[43] None of these reforms made much impact on poverty. Their importance for working-class politics lay, rather, in the promise they appeared to hold of a gradual expansion of state action against poverty. To the Labour Party leaders support for this legislation seemed the only way forward. In face of the stated anti-socialist intentions of their prime movers, leading socialists, rather quixotically, presented the reforms as stepping-stones on the road to socialism.[44] But hidden within the politics of welfare reformism was a quite contrary process. Whatever its ameliorative effects early twentieth-century social reform embodied a counter-attack on democratic and working class institutions at least as formidable as the employers' attack on trade unions in the 1890s. Already in 1902 the directly-elected School Boards which facilitated popular control of the education system had been abolished in favour of the more remote authority of the LEAs. Similarly the National Insurance Act of 1911 was constructed in such a way as to subordinate the participatory democracy of the most successful of all nineteenth-century working-class institutions – the Friendly Societies – to the bureaucratic procedures of the commercial insurance industry. What was at issue was whether the growth of state provision for social welfare would represent an extension of democracy and working-class power, or whether it would tend to supress existing democratic forms in favour of the construction of a bureaucratic welfare machine concerned more with discipline and control than with opening up new opportunities for popular self-government. By the end of the first decade of the century a growing number of socialists were pointing anxiously to the clauses in reform legislation, from old age pensions to unemployment insurance, intended to reinforce labour discipline and establish new ways of rewarding the 'deserving' and punishing the 'undeserving' poor. In recent years historians of the welfare state, increasingly conscious of the repressive aspects of the New Liberal reforms, have tended to endorse their views.[45]

The limitations of the labour movement as it emerged before 1914 are perhaps most clearly revealed in its attitude towards the parliamentary franchise. The Reform Acts of 1867 and 1884 had made it possible to contemplate building a Labour Party. But the franchise, hedged around with a complex system of registration, residence qualifications and the exclusion of paupers, remained very restricted. Only about two-thirds of the adult male population qualified for the vote, and all women were excluded. It has been calculated that before 1918 no more than ninety-five of the 670 Members

95

of Parliament were elected from constituencies predominantly working-class in character, despite the overwhelming preponderance of the working class in the population as a whole.[46]

What is revealing, in view of these figures, is that after 1884 the extension of the franchise never again became a central issue in working-class politics. Indeed Labour and socialist leaders often spoke as though parliamentary democracy was already an accomplished fact. Certainly, among unenfranchised males there was little demand for the vote. They tended to be among the poorer, less organized sections of the working class, and few were excluded permanently. Depending on his particular circumstances, a man might fall in and out of the suffrage from one election to the next.[47] This was not, however, the case with women. In the early twentieth century the campaign for women's suffrage became a major political issue, and it struck deep roots in the labour movement – especially in the ILP and among the female operatives of Lancashire. But relations between the Labour Party and the women's movement were never easy.

On the surface, the problem was over tactics. The suffragettes demanded the immediate granting of votes to women on the same terms as men. The Labour Party rejected this, arguing that the enfranchisement of women under the existing electoral law – 'Votes for Ladies' – would tend to increase the anti-working-class bias of the electorate. The question of women's suffrage, they asserted, should be tied to a general extension of the franchise – to the demand for adult suffrage. Labour fears that the women's movement might develop in a reactionary direction were born out by the behaviour of the suffragettes under their élitist leader Christabel Pankhurst. But bitter experience of the sexism rampant in the labour movement could not be assuaged by a token gesture towards adult suffrage. Those suffragists who worked for unity with the labour movement would have achieved more had the Labour Party been prepared to place the demand for adult suffrage at the centre of its programme. In reality the Party did little to promote the demand.[48]

The mental and institutional world of labour, as it had emerged by 1910, socially restricted and politically unambitious, constituted a challenge to capitalist power only in the most qualified and limited sense. A Labour Party struggling for political muscle which nevertheless failed to promote an agitation against the exclusion from the franchise of more than two-thirds of the working class, male and female, was clearly something less than the all-embracing political movement of the class. The exclusive attitudes of organized labour towards women and the poor might derive, in part, from the difficulty of organizing those sections of the population. But such attitudes in turn, powerfully reinforced the inability of the movement to break out of its minority position. Even the more radical activists – the socialists – often premised their politics on the assumption that the working class, for the time being at least, was too weak to embark on the independent pursuit of its own emancipation.

During the five years before the First World War the whole pattern began to shift. A new trade union explosion laid the basis for a widening of the movement's social base and of its political horizons. These developments called sharply into question the adequacy of the established institutions of the labour movement.

Between 1910 and 1914 trade union membership grew by more than 50 per cent and strike activity ran at more than four times the level of the previous decade.[49] Behind this lay a low level of unemployment, the failure of wages to keep up with the rising prices, and an accumulation of unsolved grievances over conditions, hours and the pace of work which had been building up beneath the façade of industrial truce. In one industry after another strike action, often unofficial, brought previously unorganized workers flocking into the unions.[50] The general unions catering for less skilled workers grew much faster than the movement as a whole.[51] Few industries were untouched by the labour unrest, but its focus was in the two most rapidly expanding sectors of the economy: coal mining and transport.

A dispute at the Cambrian Combine pits in South Wales lasted for nearly a year in 1910–11, and was marked by violence and rank-and-file revolt against the established conciliatory leadership. Though defeated, the Cambrian strike helped to precipitate the first national coal strike in March 1912, a strike involving nearly a million miners, which threatened to close down much of British industry and forced the government to intervene.[52] Meanwhile the transport industry had exploded during the hot summer of 1911. This was no ordinary strike movement. The spontaneity and breadth of the strikes posed unprecedented problems both for union leaders, whose ability to gain permanent recognition and bargaining rights for their unions depended on their ability to control the strikers, and for the forces of the state. Sparked off by a successful strike of seamen in June, the strikes radiated outwards among dockers, carters, tramwaymen, railway workers, and the miscellaneous factory operatives around the waterfront areas. The poorest workers were drawn into the movement. In London, many women in the sweated workshops of Bermondsey came out, closely followed by cleaners working for the London County Council. Union leaders, taken by surprise, rushed to formulate demands and to recruit unorganized bodies of strikers. George Askwith, the ubiquitous Board of Trade conciliator, toured the affected areas, grinding out settlements. In Manchester alone he spent five days in the Town Hall co-ordinating the simultaneous negotiations of eighteen different unions representing a bewildering variety of workers all pledged not to go back until the other seventeen were satisfied. And the longer settlements were delayed the more the strikers took on the character of a general social war. In Liverpool, with a gunboat standing by on the Mersey, two strikers were shot dead by the Army following three days of guerrilla warfare in the streets around the city centre. In response to the national railway strike, 58,000 troops were moblized, and martial law declared over large areas of the country. Revolvers sold like hot cakes to the alarmed inhabitants of London's West End. In Llanelly, troops protecting a blackleg train fired on the strikers, killing two men; five more were killed when a goods shed, raided by strikers, caught fire detonating a van-load of gunpowder.[53]

The transport strikes of 1911, and the miners' strike of 1912, were the most dramatic engagements of the pre-war labour unrest. But militancy continued right up to the outbreak of war. Outside the coalfields, which were quiescent following the national dispute of 1912, the figures show a continuing strike movement drawing in workers from a wide variety of industries.[54] Among the more notable was the 'prairie fire' strike which swept through the largely unorganized metal industries of the Midlands, accompanied by the familiar clashes between strikers and the police, and the novel tactic of fund-raising hunger marches dispatched throughout the country. Women workers played a major role in this strike movement. Using the economic power of the new classes of semi-skilled workers to jack up minimum labourers' rates, the general unions registered a spectacular growth in membership, and established a permanent foothold in the factories.[55]

The trade union explosion of 1910–14 represented a fundamental challenge to the restricted horizons, both sociological and ideological, within which the development of the labour movement had been confined since the 1870s, and, indeed, since the defeat of Chartism. The penetration of trade union organization into the poorer strata of the working class, deeper than in 1889–90, made it possible to believe that the labour movement could solve its own 'problem of poverty' by methods of direct industrial action, rather than by an exclusive concentration on achieving social reform through parliament. At the same time, the realization that the most powerfully organized groups (notably the miners) were now capable of national strike action that could bring the whole economy to a halt, reinforced the appeal of direct action as a weapon in the socialist arsenal. The growth of revolutionary syndicalism reflected this novel sense of trade union power most clearly. But it was by no means confined to those who rejected parliamentary action altogether. In practice, syndicalism shaded over into a militant parliamentarianism which stressed, not the superiority of industrial over parliamentary action, but the necessity of co-ordinating the two tactics.[56] After the war direct action was to achieve broad support in the labour movement, understood not as the revolutionary general strike, but as the use of concentrated industrial force to wrest reforms from the capitalist state.[57]

Increased strength and militancy in the industrial field was reflected in a growing impatience with the hesitant performance of the Labour Party. In the two general elections of 1910 the Labour Party, fearful of provoking Liberal retaliation, made little effort to expand its parliamentary representation beyond the foothold achieved in 1906.[58] By 1914 the contrast between the strength and self-confidence at the grass roots and the timidity of the parliamentary leadership was creating intense pressure within the Party for a break with the Liberals and a re-orientation of working-class politics along more genuinely independent lines. Despite the force of the pre-war upheaval, the immediate prospects for the labour movement were not bright. There was no easy resolution in sight for the growing tensions within the Labour Party. By 1914 there was little sign that the Liberals were in imminent danger from Labour. Any electoral confrontation between the two would have hurt the Liberals by letting in Conservative candidates, but it would have decimated Labour's representation in the House of Commons. Negotiations for an electoral pact would probably have broken down in the run up to the general election due in 1915 (but postponed as a result of the war).[59] It is difficult to see how the Labour Party itself could have survived. A large minority of trade unionists continued to oppose the Labour Party.[60] Many of those who supported the Labour Party did so because they saw it as the working-class element of a broader progressive alliance rather than as the nucleus of an independent, socialist party. If the Labour Party had been forced by its own activists into pursuing real independence, it is doubtful whether the majority of trade unionists would have still been prepared to finance electoral campaigns which let the Conservatives in.

The growing strength and ambition of some sections of the working class threatened to burst the institutional form in which working-class politics had taken shape since the turn of the century. Perhaps a more authentically socialist party would have been the result. In any event it took the enormous social and political changes wrought by the First World War to enable the labour movement to consolidate its gains of the pre-war period and make the break from Liberalism without destroying what, in 1914, was still a fragile alliance between socialists and the major trade unions.

Between the First World War and the early 1920s the labour movement presented a potentially revolutionary challenge to the state. I cannot discuss that here. What should be said however is that when the crisis was finally resolved many of the limitations of labour's mobilization identified in this essay were once again apparent. Much of the pre-war trade union growth had been concentrated in industries – coal, cotton, shipbuilding, heavy engineering – which were to be decimated in the structural transformation of the economy between the wars. Despite the efforts of the Communists there was little effective organization of the unemployed victims of that transformation. Trade union organization remained weak in the new expanding industries of the 1930s. Especially after the general strike of 1926 the narrowly electoral politics of the Labour Party grew at the expense of extra-parliamentary forms. Whole areas of potential mobilization – the street, the housing estate, the workplace – were systematically fenced off by the nervous and conciliatory leadership of an increasingly bureaucratized movement. While their control was never absolute, it was certainly debilitating. The inability of the movement to develop trade union strategies and political demands appropriate to the needs of the female half of the working class continued to limit is potential base. In some ways the syndicalist

Table 1:1   Trade Union Statistics

Year	1 Trade union membership (1000s)	2 Trade union density %	3 Strikes: No. working days lost (1000s)	4 Unemployment %
1892	1576	–	17,382	6.3
1893	1559	–	30,468	7.5
1894	1530	–	9529	6.9
1895	1504	–	5725	5.8
1896	1608	–	3746	3.3
1897	1731	–	10,346	3.3
1898	1752	–	15,289	2.8
1899	1911	–	2516	2.0
1900	2022	12.7	3153	2.5
1901	2025	12.6	4142	3.3
1902	2013	12.4	3479	4.0
1903	1994	12.1	2339	4.7
1904	1967	11.9	1484	6.0
1905	1997	11.9	2470	5.0
1906	2210	13.1	3029	3.6
1907	2513	14.7	2162	3.7
1908	2485	14.4	10,834	7.8
1909	2477	14.2	2774	7.7
1910	2565	14.6	9895	4.7
1911	3134	17.7	10,320	3.0
1912	3416	19.1	40,915	3.2
1913	4135	23.1	11,631	2.1
1914	4145	23.0	9878	3.3

Sources:
Column 1: B. Mitchell and P. Deane, *Abstract of British Historical Statistics*, 1962, p.68.
Column 2: A.H. Halsey (ed.), *Trends in British Society Since 1900*, 1972, p. 123.
Column 3: B. Mitchell and P. Deane, *op cit.*, p. 72.
Column 4: *Ibid*, pp. 64–5.

current, with its stress on the primacy of class struggle at the point of production, tended to reinforce the traditional male-centredness of the movement. After the First World War, as before, the labour movement turned an excluding face towards sections of the working class which it had failed to organize. It resisted forms of activism which appeared to threaten the authority of its leaders and the viability of their various accommodations with capitalism. Consequently, it remained an accomplice in its own continuing impotence.

Table 1:2   *Trade Union Densities*

	1888 %	1901 %	1910 %
Mining and quarrying	19	56	60
Metals, engineering and shipbuilding	15	21	18
Shipbuilding alone	36	60	46
Cotton textiles	16	35	44
Railways	9	24	31
Building	10	19	13
Printing	21	34	36
Clothing	3	5	5

Source:
H.A. Clegg, A. Fox and A.F. Thompson, *A History of British Trade Unions Since 1889*, Vol. 1, (1964), p. 468).

References

1   E. Hunt, *Regional Wage Variations in Britain, 1850–1914*, (1973), ch. 9; A. Clinton, *The Trade Union Rank and File. Trades Councils in Britain, 1900–1940*, (1977), pp. 189–198; D. Butler & J. Freeman, *British Political Facts 1900–1968*, (1969), pp. 107, 141; M. G. Sheppard & J. L. Halstead, 'Labour's Municipal Election Performance in Provincial England and Wales, 1901–1913,' *Bulletin of the Society for the Study of Labour History*, 39, (1979), pp. 39–62; G. D. H. Cole, *A Century of Co-operation*, (1945), p. 371. See also Appendix.

2   D. H. Aldcroft & H. W. Richardson, *The British Economy 1870–1939*, (1969), p. 65.

3   E. J. Hobsbawm, *Industry and Empire*, (1968), Chs. 7 & 9.

4   B. Mitchell & P. Deane, *Abstract of British Historical Statistics*, (1962), p. 60.

5   J. H. Clapham, *An Economic History of Modern Britain*, Vol. 3, (1938), pp. 181–5, 194–5; S. Pollard, *A History of Labour in Sheffield*, (1959), p. 132; P. Stearns, *Lives of Labour. Work in a Maturing Industrial Society*, (1975), p. 33; B. Mitchell & P. Deane, *op.cit.*, p. 60.

6   E. J. Hobsbawm, *op.cit.*, pp. 135–7; P. Stearns, *op.cit.*, chs. 7 & 8; J. Burnett, *A Social History of Housing*, (1978), ch. 6; S. Pollard & D. W. Crosseley, *The Wealth of Britain*, (1968), pp. 232–7; E. J. Hobsbawm, *Labouring Men*, (1968), p. 285.

7   G. S. Jones, 'Working-class Culture and Working-class Politics in London, 1870–1900. Notes on the Remaking of a Working Class,' *Journal of Social History*, (1974); S. Meacham, *A Life Apart. The English Working Class, 1890—1914* (1977), chs. 1 & 2; M. J. Daunton, *Coal Metropolis: Cardiff 1870–1914*, 1977, ch. 11; K. S. Inglis, *Churches and the Working Class in Victorian England*, (1963), pp. 75ff.

8   E. J. Hobsbawm, *op.cit.*, ch. 15. Hobsbawm's essay on the labour aristocracy has been much debated. For a recent survey see R. Gray,

The Labour Aristocracy in Nineteenth Century Britain, (1981).

9   For a recent review of the position of skilled workers in this period, see C. More, *Skill and the English Working Class, 1870—1914*, (1980).

10   The strength of craft unionism may also have been one factor in causing the British technological lag. W. A. Lewis, *Growth and Fluctuations, 1870–1913*, (1978), ch. 5; E. Phelps Brown & M. H. Browne, *A Century of Pay*, (1968), pp. 174–98.

11   H. A. Clegg, A. Fox & A. F. Thompson, *A History of British Trade Unions since 1889*, Vol. 1, (1964), pp. 104–05, 112, 132; H. A. Turner, *Trade Union Growth Structure and Policy*, (1962), p. 149; A. Reid, 'Division of Labour in the British Shipbuilding Industry, 1880–1920,' Cambridge Ph.D., (1980), p. 116f.

12   Quoted in E. J. Hobsbawm, *Labour's Turning Point*, (1948), p. 4.

13   Quoted in J. Zeitlin, *Craft Regulation and the Division of Labour*, Ph.D. Warwick, (1981), p. 415.

14   E. J. Hobsbawm, *Labouring Men*, pp. 310–15; S. Pollard & D. W. Crosseley, *op.cit.*, pp. 238–46.

15   B. Mitchell & P. Deane, *op.cit.*, pp. 39, 41 & 12; E. J. Hobsbawm, *Industry and Empire*, p. 137.

16   G. S. Jones, *Outcast London*, (1971), pp. 81–8; J. Burnett, *op.cit.*, pp. 149–51.

17   G. S. Jones, *op.cit.*, pp. 290 & 343.

18   H. A. Clegg et al., *op.cit.*, pp. 83, 97 and *passim*.

19   E. J. Hobsbawm, *Labouring Men*, ch. 10.

20   Quoted in P. Thompson, *Socialists, Liberals and Labour. The Struggle for London, 1885–1914*, (1967), p. 51; J. Lovell, *Stevedores and Dockers*, (1969), p. 134f.; G. S. Jones, *op.cit.*, ch. 17.

21   A. H. Halsey (ed.), *Trends in British Society since 1900*, (1972), p. 123.

22   S. Lewenhak, 'The lesser trade union organization of women then men,' *Bulletin of the Society for the Study of Labour History*, 26, (1973); S. Lewenhak, *Women and Trade Unions*, (1977); N. Solden, *Women in British Trade Unions, 1874–1976*, (1978). Except where otherwise noted the following three paragraphs are based on these works. See also ch. 1 of this book.

23   J. White, *The Limits of Trade Union Militancy*, (1978), p. 39; T. Olcott, 'Dead Centre: the Women's Trade Union Movement in London, 1874–1914,' *London Journal*, 2, (1976).

24   S. Meacham, *op.cit.*, ch. 4.

25   P. Stearns, 'Working-class Women in Britain, 1890–1914,' in *Suffer and be Still*, (ed.) M. Vicinus (1972); E. H. Hunt, *op.cit.*, 1973, pp. 118–24; T. Olcott, *op.cit.*

26   J. White, *op.cit.*, pp. 53–5; J. Liddington & J. Norris, *One Hand Tied Behind Us*, (1978), p. 87f.

27   T. Olcott, op.cit.

28   *Ibid*, p. 43.

29   E. Hunt, *op.cit.*

30   K. Marx & F. Engels, *On Britain*, (1962), pp. 566–9.

31   Henry Collins, 'The Marxism of the Social Democratic Federation,' in *Essays in Labour History*, Vol. 2, (ed.) A. Briggs & J. Saville (1971).

32 A. E. P. Duffy, 'The Eight-Hour Day Movement in Britain, 1886–1893,' *Manchester School*, (1968).
33 H. Pelling, *The Origins of the Labour Party*, (1954); S. Pierson, *Marxism and the Origins of British Socialism*, (1973).
34 E. P. Thompson, 'Homage to Tom Maguire,' in *Essays in Labour History*, Vol. 1, (ed.) A. Briggs & J. Saville (1960); C. Pearce, *The Manningham Mills Strike*, 1975.
35 Tom Mann & Ben Tillett, *The New Trades Unionism*, (1890).
36 J. Saville, 'Trade Unions and Free Labour. The Background to the Taff Vale Decision,' in *Essays in Labour History*, Vol. 1, 1960; H. A. Clegg et al., *op.cit.*, pp. 326–8, 361–3.
37 H. Pelling, *America and the British Left*, (1956), pp. 66–88.
38 This and the following two paragraphs are based on accounts to be found in H. Pelling, *The Origins of the Labour Party* (1965); F. Bealey & H. Pelling, *Labour and Politics 1900–1906*, (1958); H. A. Clegg et al., *op.cit.*, ch. 10; P. Poirier, *The Advent of the Labour Party*, (1958); P. Clarke, *Lancashire and the New Liberalism*, (1971); K. O. Morgan, *Keir Hardie: Radical and Socialist*, (1975); D. Marquand, *Ramsay MacDonald*, (1977).
39 F. Reid, *Keir Hardie*, (1978), p. 148.
40 C. Booth, *Life and Labour of the People of London*, Vol. 1, (1902), p. 177. On the development of New Liberal social thinking in general, see J. Harris, *Unemployment and Politics, A Study in English Social Policy, 1886–1914*, (1972); H. V. Emy, *Liberals, Radicals and Social Politics, 1892–1914*, (1973); B. B. Gilbert, *The Evolution of National Insurance in Great Britain*, (1966). There is a valuable review of the literature on New Liberalism in R. Hay, *Origins of the Liberal Welfare Reforms, 1906–1914*, (1975).
41 D. Hopkins, 'The Membership of the ILP 1904–1910. A Spatial and Occupational Analysis', *International Review of Social History*, 20, (1975); S. Pierson, *op.cit.*, pp. 209–10; F. Reid, *op.cit.*, chs. 6, 7 & 8.
42 K. D. Brown, *Labour and Unemployment, 1900—1914*, (1971).
43 See, *inter alia*, the sources listed in note 40 above.
44 R. Barker, 'Socialism and Progressivism in the Political Thought of Ramsay MacDonald,' in (ed.) A. J. Morris, *Edwardian Radicalism 1900–1914*, (1974).
45 E.g., the essays by J. Brown and J. R. Hay in (ed.) P. Thane *The Origins of British Social Policy*, (1978); B. Holton, *British Syndicalism 1900–1914: Myths and Realities*, (1976), pp. 137–8, 182–3; S. Yeo, 'Class Struggle and Associational Form,' unpublished paper.
46 N. Blewitt, 'The Franchise in the United Kingdom, 1885–1918,' *Past and Present 32*, (1965); H. Pelling, *The Social Geography of British Elections*, (1967), pp. 419–20.
47 M. Pugh, *Electoral Reform in War and Peace, 1906–1918*, (1978), ch. 1.
48 A. Rosen, *Rise Up Women!*, (1974); J. Liddington & J. Norris, *op.cit.*; D. Morgan, *Suffragists and Liberals. The Politics of Women's Suffrage in Britain*, (1975).
49 A. Halsey, *op.cit.*, pp. 123 & 127.

50 The following account is largely based on G. Dangerfield, *The Strange Death of Liberal England*, (1935); E. Phelps Brown, *The Growth of British Industrial Relations*, (1959); H. Pelling, 'The Labour Unrest,' in *Popular Politics and Society in Late Victorian Britain*, (1968); R. J. Holton, *op.cit.*; J. E. Cronin, *Industrial Conflict in Modern Britain*, (1979).

51 G. D. H. Cole, *Trade Unionism and Munitions*, (1923), p. 24.

52 R. P. Arnot, *South Wales Miners*, Vol. 1, (1967); R. P. Arnot, *The Miners*, (1953).

53 P. Bagwell, *The Railwaymen*, (1963), ch. 12; G. Askwith, *Industrial Problems and Disputes*, (1920), p. 152; H. Hikins, 'The Liverpool General Transport Strike of 1911,' in *Transactions of the Historical Society of Lancashire and Cheshire*, 113, (1961).

54 B. Mitchell & P. Deane, *op.cit.*, pp. 71–2.

55 R. Hyman, *op.cit.*, pp. 59–61.

56 R. Holton, *op.cit.*, pp. 176–86; E. Phelps Brown, *op.cit.*, pp. 342–3. Militant workers looked to the new Triple Alliance of Miners, Railwaymen and Transport Workers to lead a general strike. Most of the union leaders involved, however, were more concerned to moderate than to maximize militancy. G. A. Phillips, 'The Triple Alliance in 1914,' *Economic History Review*, 24, (1971).

57 A. Gleason, *What the Workers Want*, (1920), *passim*.

58 N. Blewitt, *The Peers, the Parties and the People*, (1972), ch. 12.

59 R. McKibbin, 'J. R. MacDonald and the problem of the Independence of the Labour Party,' *Journal of Modern History*, 42 (1970).

60 R. McKibbin, *The Evolution of the Labour Party, 1910–1924*, (1974), p. 81

3
Rank-and-File Dissent

Van Gore

Although the term 'rank and file' now carries certain fashionably populist and militant connotations, analytically it still lacks precision. As its origins in a military metaphor for the common soldiery may suggest, the phrase acquires meaning only in the context of power, organization and hierarchy. Rather than a descriptive category it designates a dialectical relationship between leaders and led; it focuses attention on the ambiguities and problems of popular participation and control. Its relevance to the study of industrial relations, therefore, presupposes not simply the emergence of trade union organization, but also a dynamic process of social differentiation whereby power is concentrated in a distinctive stratum elevated above and, in an important sense, opposed to the mass of workers. Defined thus, rank-and-file dissent was not a major phenomenon before 1875; it only became so as the multiform institutionalization of labour within capitalist society gathered pace in the late Victorian and Edwardian eras.

The differentiation of leaders from the rank and file was a complex process and never the simple or inevitable product of organizational growth, whether this is conceived in terms of the supposed imperatives of 'administrative efficiency', the 'iron law of oligarchy', or 'goal displacement'. These formulations often pay insufficient attention to contradiction and contingency in history and neglect the 'external' forces and relationships shaping working-class struggle; capital, state and sociocultural experience beyond the workplace.

In their well-known study of trade union government the Webbs identified an early and formative tradition which they styled, somewhat pejoratively, 'primitive democracy'. *Industrial Democracy* recorded with analytical scholarship, but evident impatience, the profound reluctance of workers to abandon such ideals during the nineteenth century and their futile resistance against successive innovations involving the centralization of union power in a representative executive employing a professional staff. The latter features were, of course, precisely those which the Webbs, not without some justification, regarded as essential for administrative efficiency and whose arrival by the 1890s they correctly understood to have constituted a 'silent revolution' in trade union government.[1]

The conditions of primitive democracy, exemplified for the Webbs in the eighteenth-century trade club, render the term 'rank and file' anachronistic. For these essentially local bodies possessed a small, homogeneous and active membership which governed itself directly through frequent general meetings. Considering it appropriate only to an era of highly localized organization, minimal administration and simple finances, the Webbs concluded that 'the early trade club was thus a democracy of the most rudimentary type, free alike from differentiated officials, executive council, or representative assembly'.[2]

Gradually modified and finally superseded, the tradition of primitive democracy was a persistent and powerful influence upon trade union development, formal and informal. As the scale and complexity of union business increased with federation and centralized funds, so certain tasks were delegated to a full-time, salaried official. But this move was accompanied by, indeed occasioned, the adoption of written constitutions containing democratic safeguards such as rotation of office, annual election, the popular initiative and referendum. The same purpose underlay the practice whereby the newly emergent executive committees were drawn from the local lay members and moved from branch to branch.

Not until the consolidation of continuous national unions in the third quarter of the nineteenth century does the concept of the rank and file acquire real significance. For in the evolution and practice of the 'new models' may be seen the beginnings of the bureaucratic and centralizing tendencies which were to separate union from men and stimulate growing rank-and-file resistance.

Distinguished by greater size, stability and longevity, the amalgamated craft societies such as the Engineers (1851) and Carpenters (1860) combined a professional general secretary with a centralized system of finance and strike control. Strict actuarial criteria and high contributions made for exclusiveness in recruitment and purpose. Confined to the skilled minority, more friendly society than trade society, the craft unions were self-consciously 'respectable', tending to discourage strikes or other activities likely to jeopardize their funds or status. Viewed from below, such caution constituted complacency. The north-east nine-hours' agitation, 1870–1, initiated independently of the ASE, evinces the emergence of a 'recurrent rank-and-file militancy'.[3] Earlier, in 1867, the ASE Council had been denounced for its 'backwardness' and senior officials, Allan and Danter, blamed for a narrow-mindedness induced 'by the routine of years of service within certain limits'.[4]

This argument, that the transformation of the labour leader from unpaid agitator to salaried administrator engenders a profound conservatism, was repeated in subsequent analyses. Thus, although flawed by a mechanistic pessimism, the famous Michels' thesis of an 'iron law of oligarchy' affecting all organizations predicted as one consequence an inexorable drift to conservatism.[5] This insight was rendered more powerful by his recognition of social pressures working in the same direction and summed up in the term 'embourgeoisement'. Modern organization theory offers a similar explanation in 'goal displacement', a process whereby formal objectives are overriden by institutional needs. The need for security and stability, financial solvency, unity and cohesion, and administrative efficiency have been cited as major determinants of trade union practice, both prompting and legitimating the concentration of power in the hands of a professionalized leadership.[6]

Tracing the impact of one organizational imperative, administrative efficiency, the Webbs identified two resultant authoritarian trends after 1870, either dictatorship by the general secretary or the domination of a 'closely combined and practically irresistable bureaucracy'.[7] Prior to 1895, when the rank and file finally imposed constitutional reform upon recalcitrant officials, the Boilermakers' Society exhibited both these features, the general secretary, Robert Knight, having become an autocrat backed by an 'informal cabinet of permanent officials which is unknown to the printed constitution'.[8] The classic devices of primitive democracy had proved ineffectual, subject to evasion or manipulation.

This is useful, but a purely organizational focus risks narrowness and reification. The history of the new model unions demonstrates that the enhanced authority of the leader over the rank and file and the resultant tensions were primarily the exogenous outcome of progressive entanglement in compromising relations with employers and the state. The role of politics and ideology was especially important in the formation of an élite exercising a moderating influence within the unions and the wider working class.[9] The process was admittedly highly contradictory. The legal and parliamentary reform activities of the Junta, for example, achieved substantial gains – suffrage extension in 1867, and improvements in trade union legal status in 1871 and 1875. The struggle for legal recognition was prompted by a crisis of essentially external origins; a threatening combination of adverse judicial verdicts, a co-ordinated employer offensive, and the use of the 'Sheffield Outrages' to create a hostile climate of public opinion.[10] However, opportunistic liaisons with middle-class intellectuals and politicians possessed a less favourable side. Exposure to such contacts and the seductive social milieu of the metropolis nurtured an ideological dependence damaging to workers' interests. Thus the 'growing adhesion of the Junta to the economic views of their middle-class friends was marked by the silent abandonment by Allan, Applegarth and Guile of all leadership in trade matters'.[11] A further and related source of differentiation was the opening up of new and prestigious opportunities for personal advancement through public service, local and national. By 1875, 'The officials of the great societies found themselves elected to School Boards and even to the House of Commons, pressed by the Government to accept seats on Royal Commissions, and respectfully listened to in the lobby'.[12]

The third quarter of the nineteenth century is important then in so far as it marks the beginning of those state-sponsored processes of incorporation which were to find much fuller expression in the hybrid strategies of Edwardian social imperialism. In the 1870s and 1880s the ideological subservience and occasional material corruption of the leaders were the first signs that institutions created by and for workers in one period had the disturbing potential to become a means of control over and against workers in another.

The politics of class collaboration inaugurated by franchise reform and favourable labour legislation was consolidated in the subsequent Lib-Labism of the Trade Union Congress Parliamentary Committee and paralleled at the industrial level by the widespread introduction of arbitration and conciliation procedures. In 1875 there were five industries where joint boards or their sliding-scale equivalents were in operation; hosiery, boot and shoe manufacture, cotton spinning, iron foundry and coal mining. A number of employers in new or expanding industries undergoing a period of relative prosperity but faced with competition and an organized workforce came to realize the advantages of permanent negotiating machinery in which official representatives of the workers participated. The explicit intention was that their involvement would induce greater 'realism' through a practical education in conventional economics, whilst joint endorsement of decisions promised a less hostile response from the rank and file. A mixture of rational calculation and varying degrees of ideological conviction ensured a welcome for such schemes from union leaders who were quick to recognize the benefits of employer recognition and strike avoidance, both for their own authority and the stability and strength of the union. Trade union enthusiasm is shown by the role of the TUC as the virtual author of the 1872 Arbitration Act.[13]

In retrospect, it seems that conciliation boards were more cause than effect of union officials losing contact with the grassroots. Shopfloor suspicion turned to hostility after 1873, when the onset of the 'Great Depression' signalled the start of a downward spiral of wage cuts in many trades. Between 1873 and 1896, we are told, in only nine out of sixty-one decisions did the boards of the five industries award a wage improvement.[14] Detailed evaluation of the workings of arbitration and conciliation procedures up to 1914 has shown that in times of prosperity wage increases were smaller and in times of depression wage cuts greater than might have been expected had alternative methods of direct bargaining been in force.[15] The bias in favour of capital has been attributed to the restricted criteria informing the boards' deliberations. The most important was the assumption that wage levels were solely determined by the selling price of the finished product. Consideration of productivity or profits was deliberately excluded, so too the concept of a minimum wage.[16]

Rank-and-file discontent was particularly acute where the use of the sliding-scale effectively meant an *automatic* adjustment of wages to prices. Acceptance of arbitration on this basis may have been, as in coal mining after 1874, necessary for union survival during adverse conditions.[17] Experience varied, but in South Wales the cost of survival was high: the emasculation of an already weak organization and its reduction to a form of company unionism.[18] Union membership declined since frequent and marked fluctuations in the selling price of coal and hence wages made the regular payment of union dues difficult. To this may be added the discouragement of the compulsory levy imposed by the owners on all miners to defray the administrative costs of the boards.[19]

The union officials, such as William Abraham (Mabon), acted as the virtual agents of the colliery companies and blocked all attempts from below to secure a minimum wage or restriction of output, both of which were to become planks in the platform of the rival MFGB. Religious and cultural differences amongst the miners were of particular significance here. Mabon's conciliatory attitude towards the owners owed much to the ethical individualism of Methodism, whilst his personal authority drew upon his position as a religious leader within the community. The distinction between 'rough' and 'respectable' within the local working class was related to that between religion and irreligion, and overlapped with ethnic divisions between an indigenous élite of Welsh-speaking hewers and the mainly immigrant oncost daywagemen who were lower paid and unorganized.[20] Rank-and-file dissent, therefore, tended to originate *outside* the union and reflect social antagonisms rooted in the heterogeneity of the workforce, rather than a simple horizontal divide between leaders and men. The August 1893 unofficial hauliers' strike in South Wales may be seen in this context. It followed the formation of a separate association of 'Hauliers and Wagemen of South Wales and Monmouth' in the same year and pursued a 20 per cent increase pay claim in defiance of the sliding-scale schemes endorsed by Abraham's district unions (which represented the better-off coalface workers). Whilst the failure of the latter to support the strike contributed to its defeat, a decisive factor was the implacable hostility and sheer coercive power of the Welsh colliery owners who had formed a federation in 1890, and were at this time 'probably the best organized in the country'.[21] This serves as a reminder that the major force shaping trade union practice and the incidence and efficacy of rank-and-file dissent was conflict with capital, itself subject to varying pressures, ideologies and degrees of organization.

The sliding-scale worked rather less harshly in the other major exporting coal region of the North East where unionization was stronger prior to its introduction, but there was rank-and-file discontent, nevertheless. In Northumberland the miners' daily earnings fell from 9s 1½d in the early 1870s to 4s 4d in 1880.[22] In Durham, there was continuing independent action at the local level to secure increases outside the arbitration awards. An index of the extent of such resistance and the limited capacity of the union as an agency of control, is the high number of special circulars issued by the Durham Miners' Association during the 1880s, calling for stricter observance of the sliding-scale system. Despite these appeals, rank-and-file action reached such proportions in 1883 that irate employers demanded compensation from the union for pits made idle without 'lawful cause'.[23]

Trade union development was neither uniform nor unilinear, however. There was greater unevenness and contradiction in industrial relations in late Victorian Britain than the above analysis suggests, and a number of correctives and qualifications are needed. To place matters in perspective, it is important to realize that only 10 per cent of all workers were unionized between 1874 and 1888.[24] The trade union rank and file was not synonymous with the working class rank and file. Within the organized minority, experience was varied. Centralization and interrelated moves towards formalized collective bargaining were not universal and remained substantially incomplete prior to 1890. The development of the Boilermakers' Society cited earlier was in many respects exceptional. Elsewhere, workers in the cotton and coal industries adopted a *federal* union structure and the marked absence of organized rank-and-file movements in the spinning and weaving unions has been seen as a direct consequence.[25] The craft unions remained free from conciliation boards whilst centralized financial control was in practice combined with considerable decentralization in trade matters.[26] As long as wages and conditions were decided according to known custom and practice, there was little need or scope for policy-making or action by the Executive and the initiative stayed in local hands. A permanent bureaucracy was not established in the ASE until 1892, for example, when the newly appointed district officials received 'a frigid reception in some areas'.[27] Constitutional changes had only a limited impact upon a powerful tradition of local autonomy based on the job control exercised by the fitters and turners at the point of production. Further reinforcement came from the enormous diversity and complexity of local conditions and payment methods in engineering. This ensured the continuing importance of branch and workplace bargaining, even in the aftermath of the 1897 lockout and the 1898 national agreement through which the executive sought to increase its authority.[28]

The preferred method of craft struggle, and one which limited the opportunities for conflict between leaders and men, was unilateral regulation, supplemented by local collective bargaining of various degrees of formality but based on workshop organization.[29] Craft conditions and rates could be imposed upon recalcitrant individual firms or districts by a selective withdrawal of labour which was supported by an 'out of work' benefit paid not at the discretion of head office, but the local branch.[30] Paradoxically, the absorption of the general secretary in administration and political careerism may have provoked little concern because of the persistence of substantial local control. Even on the question of strikes, centralized control was weakened by the possession of separate branch funds sufficient to initiate if not finish a strike, from which, once started, it was difficult for the executive to withhold approval.

Since local autonomy over trade policy was yet to be challenged fundamentally, rank-and-file dissent with the ASE was muted in the 1880s. Internal union conflicts often assumed the form of disputes between the constituent localities and reflected the weakness of the executive and the absence of any common policy. This coincided with the tail-end of a favourable economic era which diminished the number of serious material grievances. The third quarter of the nineteenth century witnessed a period of unprecedented prosperity in the British imperial economy which allowed a relative equilibrium between capital and labour in the engineering industry. The employers briefly enjoyed an objective margin for manoeuvre; concessions were granted to the skilled section of the workforce without resort to sudden, drastic increases in productivity, whether through technological innovation or intensification of workload.

It would be precisely the adoption of such strategies in sections like engineering and cotton as a response to the sharpening foreign competition of the 1890s that was to inject new elements of instability. The greater intransigence of the employers, who were alarmed by the new unionism and socialism after 1889, disrupted established industrial relations, prompted a search for new solutions, and created conditions for an upsurge in rank-and-file dissent when officials proved incapable of defending the *status quo*.

There were major industries, such as building, that remained virtually exempt from change, even into the 1890s. Industrial relations continued to be run along local and informal lines. Regionalism and chronic craft sectionalism were a major obstacle to union centralization and there was no national bargaining machinery until 1904. The long parliamentary and TUC career of the Lib-Lab Stone Masons' secretary, Henry Broadhurst, seems to have provoked little overt antagonism from an apathetic rank and file. Apathy may be viewed, of course, as a passive form of dissent, but the vagaries of the building cycle, the fragmentation of the labourforce, and the absence of technological change offer a more likely explanation of rank-and-file acquiescence.[31]

Further comment is required on the operation of arbitration and conciliation machinery. Many industries were without them, the major growth occurring in the two decades prior to 1914. Conciliation boards in the earlier period were not established where the unions were too strong, as with the craft societies, nor where labour organization was too weak. Initially, and with some justification, union leaders saw their introduction as a victory for, as Alexander MacDonald pointed out in 1875: 'Twenty-five years ago, when we proposed the adoption of the principle of arbitration, we were then laughed to scorn by the employing interests.'[32]

There were sufficient examples of the employer rejecting outright, refusing to co-operate with, or actually abandoning conciliation boards to show that the latter were never a simple and successful instrument of capitalist domination. The committees of owners and workers in the hosiery trade pioneered by the Liberal employer A. J. Mundella in 1860 fell steadily into disuse and were finally abolished in 1884.[33] The boot and shoe manufacturers withdrew from the industry's remaining boards in 1894, angry at their inability to control the rank and file, and as the prelude to inflicting a crushing defeat upon the National Union of Boot and Shoe Operatives in 1895. So severe were the terms imposed that a return to the board system with all its flaws must have appeared in retrospect preferable.[34]

The majority of employers actually remained hostile to any form of arbitration which they regarded as too time-consuming and an unwarranted interference in the managerial prerogatives of property. From the employers' standpoint, reliable arbitration referees were not always easy to find. There were complaints that the lawyers available for the task were usually involved in politics and their decisions swayed by electoral calculation.[35] Employers sometimes refused to co-operate – an umpire resigned in protest at employers boycotting the Kingswood footwear board in 1894.[36] Their extreme reluctance to use the Board of Trade arbitration services established in 1896 and ambivalent response to subsequent state intervention in Edwardian industrial disputes gave credence to that sector of trade union opinion which viewed conciliation as an important gain.[37]

Where owners were confident in their ability to coerce their workforce, they did so. Representatives of the Oldham weavers would have welcomed, no doubt, the offer of arbitration during their 1878 strike. Instead, caught between militant workers and instransigent employers they presided over a bitter and unsuccessful struggle. The failure of the strike sparked off an explosion of violence directed not only against the owners but also against union property.[38] Whether this rare violent expression of rank-and-file dissent was justified is another matter. A crucial problem was the lack of support from other workers, particularly the spinners. Given the stubborn refusal of the employers to offer any kind of concession, it is difficult to see what the strike leaders could have done. The accusation of leadership 'betrayal' is misleading since it ignores the situation of power in which the strength and determination of the employers and the expectations and solidarity of the workers are crucial elements beyond individual control and subject to fluctuation over time.

Bureaucratization was a partial phenomenon prior to 1890 and its beneficial aspects need emphasis. To take an extreme but not atypical example, the sheer complexity of negotiations in cotton spinning called for the long experience and specialized knowledge displayed by leaders such as James Mawdsley, who were selected by competitive examination.[39] Reliance upon state legislation for improvements in working conditions similarly required and developed particular expertize. Union members were understandably reluctant to dispense with the services of such men, especially when the latter acquired the grey-headed veteran status.[40] Rather than an unwelcome by-product, bureaucratization has been identified as actually indispensable to the emergence of white collar unionism, since it 'destroyed paternalist relations of dependence by substituting regulation by impersonal rules which strictly excluded all forms of personal consideration between employer and clerk'.[41]

It may be mistaken to see the early trade clubs as havens of pure democracy since small-scale traditional collectives do not necessarily afford greater independence to individual members. Bureaucracy and a hierarchy of offices mean a multiplicity of organizational layers and hence spaces for counter-struggle and control. Rank-

and-file dissent, then, might find outlet within the union through the capture of local branches and opposition to central policies. It has been argued that the more tightly-knit and rigid the relations of authority, the greater the possible openings for circumventing them.[42] Formal rules require interpretation, and rather than guaranteeing unity and stability may provide the occasion and means for conflict. The union leader was never just a bureaucrat but also a representative – a dual role which involved a necessary contradiction and made some respect for democratic norms inescapable. That union membership was not compulsory and workers could always leave provided another constraint,[43] but then so did apathy which could weaken the union in the eyes of employers and public opinion ever keen to conclude that the union officials did not enjoy full support. Members' interests could sometimes suffer from insufficient or incompetent bureaucracy. A contributory factor to the rapid decline of the Dockers' Union in the 1890s, it has been suggested, was poor organization, with Ben Tillett and Tom Mann unsuited to the routine tasks of administration.[44] Bureaucratization, measured in terms of administrative cost and the proportion of full-time officials, actually tended to be higher in the 'socialist' new unions which arose after 1889 than the craft unions, but this was determined by the particular problems of recruiting casual and unskilled labour rather than organization *per se*.[45]

As applied to the trade union leadership, the thesis of 'incorporation' also requires careful treatment, especially given its functionalist connotations.[46] The situation was ambiguous, and rarely a matter of outright subordination to manipulative strategies of social control. Elected bodies like School Boards, Poor Law Guardians and local councils were the sites of class struggle, not merely a means to its solution. They afforded access to public funds, a potential for working class control and opportunities for achieving substantial social gains independent of and antagonistic to the interests of state and capital.[47] For those unions based on industries such as transport, docks and gasworks which were owned in full, or in part, by the municipal authorities, participation and influence in local politics was a necessary and valuable adjunct to industrial activity. By 1893 the gasworkers had eighteen elected members, men and women, sitting on various local bodies. In 1894 four officials of the tramwaymen were councillors, a recognition of the real gains to be won where the local authority was the employer and subject to political pressure. The Glasgow Tramways Committee enforced a maximum working week in 1891, and there were a series of concessions to the union when municipal control over trams was extended to Sheffield (1896), Manchester (1897) and Hull (1899).[48]

The social differentiation of leaders implies interests distinct from, but not necessarily antagonistic to, those of ordinary workers. Until the 1880s, at least, the major cleavage was within the class itself; between a privileged artisan stratum coextensive with craft unionism and the bulk of the labouring poor who remained unskilled and unorganized. The Lib-Lab ideology and social climbing of the senior craft officials, replete with an ambiguous class pride, may have mirrored only too faithfully the politics and pretensions of their members who constituted an aristocratic élite closer in its patterns of residence and recreation to the petty bourgeoisie than the working class proper.[49]

Inside the unions marked differences in lifestyle were only likely to become significant when these were perceived as an explanation for failure or reluctance to satisfy rank-and-file expectations. Discounting what one suspects to be perennial but subterranean individual grumblings and cynicism, the incidence and depth of rank-and-file dissent were related to changes in objective conditions and shifts in popular perception. Rank-and-file criticism was likely to be most sustained and widespread when there was not only material grievance but an awareness of alternative policies. The history of the boot and shoe industry, particularly between 1890 and 1894, provides illustration.

The formation of the National Union of Boot and Shoe Operatives (as it was later known) in 1874 was the direct outcome of rank-and-file dissent within the ancient craft society, the Amalgamated Cordwainers Association. The NUBSO was a breakaway movement instigated by new categories of worker: the riveters, lasters and finishers employed in the rapidly growing and increasingly mechanized wholesale industry.[50] The cordwainers' national leaders had sought to meet the problems of industrial and technical change by extending membership to the new men, but were frustrated by local obstruction from older, established craftsmen in the bespoke sectors. Stubborn adherence to narrow exclusivity by an entrenched élite constitutes a pattern repeated subsequently in a number of other unions; the engineers (refusal to implement the 1892 Leeds delegate meeting agreement admitting the new machinists),[51] the boilermakers (refusal to accept leadership decision in the 1890s to admit the drillers)[52] and the stevedores (hostility to the newer downstream branches, leading to near secession in 1891)[53].

Tensions within the Cordwainers Association generated two conflicting expressions of rank-and-file opinion, only one aimed at head office. The first involved the opposition of local officials to the national policy, the second was a protest against the non-implementation of that policy in branches controlled by craftsmen unsympathetic to the claims of recent recruits from the new grades. These cross-conflicts, deriving from occupational and generational differences, show how misleading it is to view dissent in terms of a horizontal dichotomy between a homogenous mass of workers and an isolated stratum of national officials. Basically, the problem originated outside the union in structural changes producing new forms of differentiation within the workforce.

The secessionist NUBSO soon built up its strength, significantly through participation in the boards of conciliation and arbitration set up in the major centres after 1875. Membership rose from 4000 in the 1870s to 19,000 by 1888.[54] But by the early 1890s technical improvements initiated by management in the face of American competition produced a groundswell of rank-and-file anger which focused both upon the conciliation agreements and the union officials still influenced by past achievement who steadfastly advocated their retention. Cumulative disillusionment with the actual experience of local boards was important but would have been less serious without the machine question and had awareness not been sharpened and channelled in particular directions by socialist militants. The latter vociferously blamed the leadership and campaigned for resistance to the new machines, the substitution of strikes for conciliation and a policy of output restriction.

The militants gained most support in Leicester, Northampton, London and Bristol. They captured the Leicester branch after local officials resigned *en bloc* in 1891, and pursued a double-pronged strategy of overturning the moderate national leadership and restricting output locally. Between 1890 and 1893 so fierce was the struggle that the union had four presidents and two treasurers, and several conciliation boards were destroyed. The general secretary, William Inskip, far from enjoying absolute powers, was unable to hold his members in check because of the depth of feeling and the lack of constitutional means for curbing the larger branches which had their own funds and full-time officials.[55]

A major complaint of the men, and one echoed by critics of the Brooklands Agreement in cotton spinning after 1893, concerned the slowness of the boards. Employers could exploit this by making unilateral changes, knowing that any official strike would be delayed pending the outcome of a protracted arbitration process. In the meantime the changes stood. A contemporary described how disputed questions were

> hanging about for six to seven months from the board to the umpire. Decisions had been given by the umpire on boots after a delay of eight or nine months. . . . New samples had been introduced at the beginning of the year, and the shoes made under protest, at a price the employers had quoted, till the end of the season. . . . The continual delay sickened the whole of them in Bristol, and although there had not been a ballot taken on the question of arbitration in Bristol, he felt sure there were over 90 per cent of the men opposed to it.[56]

The organized restriction of output engaged in as a deliberate tactic by the Leicester branch provides an example of a normally indirect and submerged form of rank-and-file dissent – sabotage. The go-slow, or 'ca' canny', properly falls into this category where the union becomes a partner in management attempts to increase productivity and if sabotage is defined as 'the clogging of the machinery of capitalist industry by the use of certain forms of action, not necessarily violent and not necessarily destructive'.[57] Usually informal, a group or individual activity, sabotage constitutes a direct and spontaneous form of workers' control and resistance to capital at the point of production. From a radical standpoint it may be seen as evidence of the permanence and irreducibility of the labour capital conflict, a method of struggle that bypasses official union structures and procedures and thus defies institutional containment.

Most union officials disapproved of the practice since it was difficult to control and like unofficial strikes could undermine the bargaining position of the union and the authority of its leaders. These anxieties were not confined to the most conservative or reactionary. At the height of mass organization in the London docks, 1889–90, Tom Mann of the Dockers' Union called repeatedly for more energetic working since go-slow tactics were discrediting the union with waterside employers already reluctant to grant the recognition that was essential if a stable labour organization was to be built, and gains not only won but defended.[58] The Northumberland Miners' Union warned its members against restricting output since successful collective bargaining depended upon the pledge of regular output.[59] But miners themselves were often opposed, either because it meant loss of earnings, or, as in Scotland during the 1880s when MacDonald's instructions to restrict output were ignored, because it was too easily disciplined by the owners.[60]

Although the retardation of British industrial productivity 1890–1913 has been cited as *prima facie* evidence of the importance and impact of sabotage so defined, not enough is known about this dimension of rank-and-file dissent partly because of deliberate concealment by those who practised it. The traditional institutional and political strengths of labour historiography are currently being supplemented in this and related areas. A recent study has argued that 'the public and visible struggle of the labour movement too often renders invisible the ocean of what it moves through: shopfloor culture'.[61] The author identifies four kinds of oppositional culture within the workplace: resistance to authority, control through the group, humour and language, distrust of theory; all suffused by an assertive masculine style. The wider-lived experience of the worker provides the context for understanding forms of resistance at work. Where work is emptied of significance from the inside by alienation 'a transformed patriarchy has filled it with significance from the outside. . . . Discontent with work is turned away from a political discontent and confused in its logic by a huge detour into the symbolic sexual realm.'[62] The wage packet becomes fetishized as a symbol of masculine achievement. *Machismo* interlocks with the tyranny of the wage form to produce patterns of rank-and-file protest and acquiescence whose origins are independent of the allegedly conservative effects of trade union organization and leadership.

The Willis study utilized oral history techniques to analyse workers' experience in one industrial Midlands town for a much later period, but offers a highly suggestive perspective for the earlier labour movement. As with sabotage, the subject matter and approach reflect a growing interest among historians in the complex and ambivalent character of popular responses to capitalism at the immediate level of the work process. But it goes further by seeking in a structuralist fashion to explore the dialectic between the factory and the family as an agency for the reproduction of gender differences. Thus it serves to highlight the importance of the sexual division of labour, and the role of women in relation to the labour movement.

On the question of women and trade unionism, the speech made by Henry Broadhurst to the 1875 Trades Union Congress is pertinent and revealing. He defined the function of trade unions as being 'to bring about a condition . . . where their wives would be in their proper sphere at home, instead of being dragged into competition for livelihood against the great and strong men of the world'.[63] The craft unions' snobbish attitude to the labourer was complemented by hostility, especially in the 1860s and 1870s, to women workers. Even in 1891 a conference of the Amalgamated Society of Tailors rejected proposals to establish a female section, a decision not reversed until 1900.[64] The Tailors, like most craft unions, had persistently opposed the employment of women which, it was believed, would undermine existing craft rates, conditions and, above all, controls. Until the mid-1890s and the impact of socialist agitation, officials and membership alike were agreed on this matter in which craft exclusiveness, patriarchal values and authentic economic fears were fused. The women's question in the clothing trades was intertwined with a number of existing problems and new developments all threatening the status of the traditional handicrafts sector; outwork, sweated labour and mechanized factory production. Union policy and opposition to it has to be seen in the context of these divisions within the workforce. Fragmentation shaped dissent and is best understood not in terms of an alien trade union bureaucracy or the activities of a labour aristocracy, but as the structured outcome of the dynamic and profoundly uneven process of capitalist development.

A reaction to the aloofness of the Tailors' Society may be read into the attempt at independent organization by female workers employed by Leeds clothing factories following an unsuccessful strike in 1889.[65] They received support from the local trades council and the socialist, Tom Maguire, a fact which confirms the significance of political intervention in overcoming sectional weaknesses and illustrates the frequently progressive role played by trades councils. Indeed, according to their most recent historian the trades councils *were* the trade union rank and file.[66] This conclusion rests upon a definition of the rank and file as an active stratum, local and militant, sandwiched between the professional labour leadership (politicians and union bureaucracy) and the mass of normally passive working people.[67] Such a precise usage is a welcome alternative to the customary vagueness but seems to underline the problematic status of the rank and file as a concept. For, in terms of what the Webbs called the trade union army, this is to concentrate upon the NCOs and what is effectively another layer of authority. The rank and file as the *majority* of workers, union or non-union, remains a somewhat shadowy presence.

The cotton industry provides the major exception to the generally low numbers of women in trade unions, 1875–1914. Approximately over half the workers in cotton spinning and manufacturing were women and there was little male opposition to their unionization. Observing that relatively fewer of all cotton disputes were unofficial in origin when compared to some industries, Keith Burgess concluded that 'the disciplined character of industrial relations reflects the dominant position of the minority of male operatives as "natural leaders" in a family economy'.[68] The formation of the independent and predominantly female Cardroom Amalgamation in 1886 may indicate, however, a degree of dissatisfaction with the established male Spinners' Union. There were also a spate of brief unofficial plant stoppages in the late 1880s and early 1890s, a reaction to managerial imposition of intensified workloads. The lower paid grades where female labour was concentrated bore a disproportionate share of the new burdens and were most involved. Yet still there was virtually no serious or organized opposition to the union, male or female, an absence perhaps also related to union structure since the 'intimacy of the rank-and-file cotton operatives' relationship with their local official – a man appointed and both closely and continuously scrutinized by an active local committee – largely prevented tension between professional agents and members from appearing in the cotton unions'.[69]

Where secessions, an important expression of rank-and-file dissent, took place in the cotton unions they were treated with relative tolerance even in the case of the small number of 'non-political' Weavers' Societies formed in North-East Lancashire between 1889 and 1906. Apparently a reaction to socialist domination of the local unions, these developments demonstrate not only the significance of political but also religious divisions in the determination of rank-and-file dissent. The breakaways show the strong influence of Catholicism and tensions with the mainly Non-conformist district union leadership. The existence of an oppositional, independent and overtly Catholic association of women weavers in Manchester suggests the intricate ways in which gender, religion and ethnicity could coincide and combine.[70]

Gender constituted an integral and important source of division, if not always antagonism, within the labour movement, modifying and reinforcing discrete occupational identities and hierarchies of labour. It seems probable that an important dimension of rank-and-file dissent, both by women and against them, remains hidden from history.[71]

The 1890s constitute a decisive and formative period in the history of industrial relations in general and the evolution of rank-and-file dissent in particular. Trends to greater concentration of capitalist ownership and control shifted the balance of power in favour of the employers. The latter, alarmed at the dual threat posed by intensifying foreign competition and domestic labour unrest (in which they detected a socialist influence), strengthened their industrial power further through federal association. An offensive was launched to subordinate trade unionism and impose industrial discipline in the name of national competitiveness. Policies of outright confrontation and judicial harassment were not abandoned but coexisted with and complemented a renewed effort, now on a vastly expanded scale, to institutionalize conflict.

The drive for increased productivity and reduced costs might involve the introduction of new machinery but invariably necessitated new working arrangements and a changed pattern of authority and power in the workplace. Continuity of production was particularly vital yet the new changes provoked vigorous resistance. A number of employers acknowledged the advantages, therefore, of a permanent and elaborate system of collective bargaining and conciliation procedures which, it was hoped, would facilitate change whilst maintaining industrial peace.

The most significant development affecting the incidence and forms of rank-and-file dissent was the creation of national and industry-wide conciliation machinery. Schemes of this kind were established successively in several key industries: cotton spinning (1893), boot and shoe manufacture (1895), engineering (1898). The terms of the agreements were highly unfavourable to labour and represent a considerable rolling-back of established workers' rights, particularly in terms of work control at the point of production. This was a marked feature of the engineering and boot and shoe industry settlements which were pushed through by employers in the immediate aftermath of massive union defeats. The NUBSO, like the ASE, was forced to give up any say in the introduction of machinery, manning ratios, discipline and general productive organization but, in addition, faced punitive financial penalties for breaches of the conciliation codes.[72]

The results of institutionalization were ambiguous and contradictory both for capital and unions. The trade unions achieved a greater permanence and authority but they had to make major concessions, and since employer recognition was explicitly conditional upon the union assuming a responsibility for enforcing industrial discipline the potential for conflict with the membership was greatly increased. If initially stifled, grassroot discontent and organization were actually stimulated in many cases and new traditions of local militancy created. Disillusionment with the operation of the conciliation schemes induced rank-and-file alienation and a heightened receptivity to radical alternatives. The links with socialism were not severed and the movement for independent working-class politics received an enormous fillip as it was realized from everyday economic experience that the Lib-Lab policies of collaboration were blatantly biased.

Conciliation procedures enhanced the authority of the trade union leader but simultaneously undermined it. For the more effectively conciliation served the cause of capital and the more complete the incorporation of the trade union leaders, the less their ability to comprehend and control the rank and file. This was particularly the case when improvements in trade were not reflected in earnings. During the boom of 1899–1901, for example, there was a wave of unofficial coal strikes by members of the MFGB, angered that the conciliation board had imposed limits on wage increases despite a sharp upswing in the price of coal.[73] This was not simply a question of wages, but factory politics. Skill-displacing technical changes, work speed-up and closer managerial supervision were ultimately matters of power and authority in the workplace. Exposed to management encroachment, workers found themselves steadily deprived of any immediate means of redress as, in response to systematic collective bargaining, power in the union was displaced upwards to a centralized, bureaucratic apex, and local initiatives discouraged. They looked in vain to the official union structures and conciliation procedures which proved unresponsive and incapable of meeting their grievances. Not surprisingly, in those industries where change was most rapid, there was a sharp increase in 'unofficial' disputes as workers resorted to direct methods and reasserted local independence.

The new system of industrial relations failed to eliminate conflict or disruption, nor could it have done so. Thus, although the spinners union officially recorded only fifteen stoppages in 1895, the masters claimed 158 in the Oldham district alone.[74] When trade recovered after 1896, the union found it difficult to restrain the rank and file and was forced to seek modifications in the Brooklands Agreement, particularly on the bad spinning issue.[75] The disillusionment and alienation of the rank and file transcended material grievances and assumed political significance with militants participating in socialist agitation for the eight-hour day.[76] Workplace experience was of central importance to the growth of rank-and-file support amongst cotton operatives for independent working-class politics, a policy opposed by their national officials.

Wherever industrial relations were institutionalized a dynamic and dialectical process ensued in which union leaders had to impose greater discipline, and dammed up rank-and-file resentment was forced to find new outlets, adopt more organized forms of struggle, and develop a thoroughgoing democratic critique of trade union structures. The paradoxical legacy, therefore, of the 1890s employers' attempt at labour containment through incorporation was rising rank-and-file militancy and ultimately an open revolt in which owners *and* union officials were the target. The workers' revolt between 1910 and 1914 signalled a serious crisis for British capitalism, precisely because it represented the rejection and failure of the recently constructed framework of conciliation and control. The trade unions were unable to act as a stabilizing agency; no longer a solution, they were part of the problem.

If the decline in real wages after 1900 and the sudden upturn in trade and employment after 1910 provided major economic impetus, this hardly offers an adequate explanation for the scale and, above all, content of the mounting industrial unrest which climaxed in the four years preceding the First World War and formed one component, perhaps the most dangerous, in the conjunctural crisis so brilliantly evoked by George Dangerfield.[77] Cumulative anger at the cumbersome and unjust operation of the institutionalized procedures for settling industrial grievances established in the 1890s and wider disenchantment with the meagre fruits of working-class incorporation were of central and linked importance.

Conciliation and arbitration boards had expanded rapidly in number from sixty-four in 1894 to 325 by 1913.[78] The centralization of union power acquired monolithic proportions as the internal authority structures of the trade unions were steadily adapted to the new demands of systematized industrial relations, with a consequent loss of accountability and rank-and-file control. The final disappearance of the lay executive was symbolic in this respect. Social differentiation of the leadership had also sharpened as the working class became more homogeneous and inward-looking on the one hand, and the union officials exposed to vastly increased opportunities for social contact with employers and the establishment on the other.[79] The growing – if hesitant and partial – moves of the state into industrial arbitration and the Liberal government's social welfare legislation created, in the absence of a professional category of social administrators, a need for the co-option of trade union expertise.[80] Another source of social displacement was the growth of labour politics and a Labour Party in secret electoral alliance with the Liberals able to offer improved prospects of parliamentary careerism to the ambitious union official.

A unique aspect of the period 1910–14 was the pervasive presence and peculiar resonance of syndicalism. The most well-known syndicalists, such as Tom Mann, Noah Ablett and Jack Wills, were working-class activists, labour's own 'organic intellectuals', who developed through their agitational and educational work new socialist and trade union strategies. As Bob Holton has demonstrated in a sympathetic and balanced work of rehabilitation, British syndicalism was not a pale reflection of its continental counterparts, nor was it as neglectful of politics as critics have alleged.[81] On the contrary, syndicalists developed penetrating insights into the corporatist trends with the Edwardian social formation, not least the 'Servile State' implications of Liberal progressivism.

In their rejection of parliamentary politics and scorn for the timidity of the Labour Party in a period of sharpening class struggle, syndicalists were opposed to all forms of external authority, whether the capitalist state and employer, or the professional labour politician and union bureaucrat. Syndicalists sought to substitute a strategy of independent rank-and-file action united and mobilized through industrial unions. They insisted upon the factory as the supreme terrain and the trade union (reconstructed and democratized) as the sole agency of revolutionary socialist transformation. An equally exclusive reliance was placed on mass working-class experience and 'direct action' (industrial militancy and civil disorder), free from any corrupting intervention or mediation by outside 'experts'.[82]

Syndicalism has been described as the 'apotheosis of proletarian autonomy'.[83] Side-stepping the issue of adequacy, its populist appeal can be readily appreciated. Aided by a strident *ouvrierist* rhetoric, it offered a comprehensive critique and a dynamic programme whose content and language spoke directly to the contemporary experience of the individual worker. Syndicalism was able to draw upon, and articulate in novel form, those older traditions of primitive democracy and control through the work process upon which popular sovereignty had once rested. The policy of workers' control, for example, had strong affinities with the traditions of local autonomy and unilateral regulation now eroded by national conciliation machinery, state intervention, capitalist rationalization and, in some cases, the degrading techniques of 'scientific management'.[84] The rejection of nationalization, a consequence of syndicalist distrust of statism in any guise, found a particularly sympathetic response amongst groups like the railwaymen and miners who were directly acquainted with the doubtful benefits of government intervention. For example, in 1912 there was a six weeks' national coal strike which the government attempted to terminate by passing the Coal Mines Minimum Wages Act. A ballot of the miners showed a small majority for continuing the strike, but the executive instructed a return to work thereby creating great dissatisfaction amongst the rank and file who felt that government interference had robbed them of 'an assured victory'.[85]

The manner in which the strike was brought to an end lent support to the syndicalist analysis and alternative offered in the *Miners' Next Step*, a pamphlet published at the end of 1911 by an unofficial miners' committee in South Wales. Its authors attacked the system of long agreements and the irresponsible powers and sectionalist policies of the moderate miners' leaders. Collective bargaining was not rejected, however, nor the need for disciplined organization since 'from the men's side we cannot permit individual bargains to be made' and 'the working class, if it is to fight effectively must be an army, not a mob'. The fundamental problem was to eliminate the 'bad side' of leadership. Through the acquisition of plenary powers and the social and economic prestige conferred by public and employer respect, the union official had become, despite good intentions, corrupted by power and no longer the servant of the workmen. The possession of power by leaders who expected unthinking obedience had as its corollary the weakness and apathy of the membership for 'sheep cannot be said to have solidarity'. The solution was thought to lie in the formation of a militant, industry-based, all-grades movement, subject to direct rank-and-file control. In a complete reversal of existing practice, negotiations with the employer were to be decentralized, but strikes centralized thus 'allowing for a rapid and simultaneous stoppage of wheels throughout the mining industry'. Nationalization was rejected in favour of workers' control which would enable 'the men themselves to determine under what conditions and how, the work should be done. This would mean real democracy in real life, making for real manhood and real womanhood'.[86]

But although syndicalism was more influential, particularly in the guise of a proto-syndicalist mood of militancy and direct action after 1910, than was once supposed, it remained a minority movement. Little headway was made either in terms of structural union reform, the substitution of new leaders, or the winning of substantial support among British workers. An article in *The Syndicalist*, 1912, virtually admitted as much when it advocated sabotage as the ideal weapon because

> it has the advantage of not requiring the active co-operation of the whole of the workers in an industry to ensure its successful application. A militant minority in the Unions can . . . demoralize an industry, and by so doing, compel the 'timid' majority to share in the benefits obtained.[87]

It is at this point that the ambiguity inherent in the usage of the term 'rank and file' becomes more clearly apparent. Central to the problem is its application both to a minority of activists distinct from the official labour leaders and to the mass of ordinary workers. The relationship between these two groups was problematic. An identity cannot be assumed; at best it existed as a partial or potential phenomenon which had to be positively struggled for and sustained, since in reality the rank and file (in the second sense) consisted of *several* rank and files, each subject to internal division. The syndicalists constituted, therefore, an alternative leadership, scattered through various industries, neither the only alternative available nor free from the necessity to compromise and the resultant democratic tensions. Ironically, Tom Mann was heckled and shouted down by unofficial leaders and strike crowds when, as an organizer of the 1911 transport strikes, he told Liverpool dockers to resume work pending negotiations with the employers. It took a week of mass meetings and all Mann's oratorical skills before the men were finally persuaded.[88]

A further source of confusion concerns the choice of a basic organizational unit within which the rank and file is to be defined. Is it the trade union, the factory, a single occupation or an entire industry? The 'rank and file' carries democratic, and hence majoritarian, connotations and yet to focus solely upon the trade union membership between 1875 and 1914 would be to ignore over 80 per cent of wage earners who were not unionized. It has been shown that certain kinds of dissent from trade union policy and practice emanated from or concerned non-unionists. Indeed, refusal to join a union, or disaffiliation, constitute one important aspect of dissent. It has also been argued that when applied within the trade union, the term 'rank and file' can be seriously misleading if it implies a simple dichotomous conception of union power in which a 'massified' membership confronts a monolithic bureaucratic leadership. The advent of large, national unions and the profound unevenness of the British economy and hence of the workers' experience and consciousness, made for a heterogeneous and frequently divided membership. The complex and multiple forms of rank-and-file dissent, individual or collective, constitutional or unofficial, have to be studied in this context. Historical knowledge remains incomplete, however, in this area and awaits the results of micro-studies informed by a 'totalizing' approach. In the meantime, it seems that rank-and-file dissent was determined not only by the growing differentiation of leaders and the centralization of union power but also stratification within the rank and file itself, a product of complex economic, political, cultural, ethnic and gender divisions embracing but extending beyond the workplace.

References

1   S. & B. Webb, *Industrial Democracy*, (1902), p. 36.
2   *Ibid.*, p. 8.
3   K. Burgess, *The Origins of British Industrial Relations*, (1975), p. vii.
4   S. & B. Webb, *The History of Trade Unionism* (1920, reprinted 1950), p. 318.

5 R. Michels, *Political Parties* (1915, reprinted and translated, New York, 1952), particularly pp. 333–57.

6 R. Hyman & R. H. Fryer, 'Trade Unions: Sociology and Political Economy,' in (ed.) T. Clarke & L. Clements, *Trade Unions Under Capitalism*, (1977), p. 57.

7 S. & B. Webb, *Industrial Democracy*, p. 28.

8 *Ibid.*, p. 30.

9 See R. Harrison, *Before the Socialists*, (1965), especially ch. 1, pp. 26–33.

10 S. & B. Webb, *The History of Trade Unionism*, pp. 255–63.

11 *Ibid.*, p. 317.

12 *Ibid.*, p. 325.

13 P. S. Bagwell, *Industrial Relations*, (1974), p. 31.

14 *Ibid.*

15 J. H. Porter, 'Wage Bargaining under Conciliation Agreements,' *Economic History Review*, 23, 3, (1970). See also V. L. Allen, 'The Origins of Industrial Conciliation and Arbitration,' *International Review of Social History*, 9, (1964).

16 In 1874 an article by Lloyd Jones published in the *Bee-Hive* warned 'working men of the danger there is in a principle that wages should be regulated by market prices . . . a mode of action most detrimental to the cause of labour' and urged the stipulation of a minimum wage. S. & B. Webb, *Ibid.*, pp. 340–1.

17 This is the argument of H. A. Clegg, A. Fox & A. F. Thompson, *A History of British Trade Unions Since 1889*, Vol. 1, (1964), p. 23.

18 V. L. Allen concluded that trade unionism in South Wales mining actually ceased to exist for twenty years. *op.cit.*, p. 253.

19 K. Burgess, *op.cit.*, p. 196.

20 *Ibid.*, pp. 168–71, 197.

21 *Ibid.*, p. 211.

22 S. & B. Webb, *op.cit.*, p. 347.

23 K. Burgess, *op.cit.*, p. 196.

24 H. A. Clegg, *et al.*, *op.cit.*, p. 2.

25 H. A. Turner, *Trade Union Growth and Policy*, (1962), p. 318. He notes that the only exception prior to the First World War, were *ad hoc* rank-and-file committees which opposed 'not the *caution* of union leaders, but the militancy of their industrial policy'.

26 H. A. Clegg *et al.*, *op.cit.*, p. 8.

27 *Ibid.*, p. 143.

28 J. Hinton, *The First Shop Stewards Movement*, (1973), p. 81.

29 'Memorials', deputations, shop meetings; the weapons of ca' canny, refusal to teach apprentices or to set up tools for handymen; joint action by members of different sectional societies, and by unionists together with non-unionists – all these forms of workshop bargaining, organization and activity were practised in mid-Victorian times.' *Ibid.*, p. 78.

30 H. A. Clegg *et al*, *op.cit.*, pp. 8–9.

31 K. Burgess, *op.cit.*, pp. 138–9.

32 S. & B. Webb, *op.cit.*, p. 338.
33 S. & B. Webb, *Industrial Democracy*, p 187.
34 H. A. Clegg *et al.*, *op.cit.*, pp. 201–02.
35 S. & B. Webb, *op.cit.*, p. 190 fn. 1, p. 240.
36 *Ibid.*, p. 188.
37 For the respective attitudes of employers and the state see R. Davidson, 'The Board of Trade and Industrial Relations 1896–1914,' *Historical Journal*, 21, 3, (1978); see also R. Hay, 'Employers and Social Policy in Britain: the Evolution of Welfare Legislation, 1905–14,' *Social History*, 4, 1, (1977).
38 K. Burgess, *op.cit.*, p. 275.
39 See S. & B. Webb, *op.cit.*, pp. 196–203, where specimen examination questions are quoted.
40 Noting that dismissal of general secretaries was rare, V. L. Allen offered as one explanation 'the strong feeling within organizations against dismissing men who have passed their best, who have grown old and inadequate'. *Power in Trade Unions*, (1954), p. 231.
41 D. Lockwood, *The Blackcoated Worker*, (1958), p. 141.
42 A. Giddens, *Central Problems in Social Theory*, (1979), p. 147.
43 'A trade union leader who is in continual fear of losing his members will inevitably take steps to satisfy their wants . . . A falling membership is a much greater stimulant than a strongly worded resolution'. V. L. Allen, *op.cit.*, p. 63.
44 H. A. Clegg *et al.*, *op.cit.*, p. 89.
45 In 1898 administrative costs accounted for 81 per cent of all expenditure in the case of the dockers compared with 7 per cent in the ASE. *Ibid.*, p. 95.
46 See G. S. Jones, 'Class Expression versus Social Control?' *History Workshop Journal*, 4, (1977).
47 S. Yeo, 'State and Anti-State: Reflections on Social Forms and Struggles from 1850,' in (ed.) P. Corrigan, *Capitalism, State Formation and Marxist Theory*, (1980), p. 136.
48 H. A. Clegg *et al.*, *op.cit.*, pp. 88–9.
49 Referring to the *laissez-faire* politics of the trade union leaders, the Webbs remarked that 'up to 1885 they undoubtedly represented the views current among the rank and file'. *The History of Trade Unionism*, p. 374.
50 H. A. Clegg *et al.*, p. 25.
51 *Ibid.*, p. 143.
52 *Ibid.*, p. 132.
53 J. Lovell, *Stevedores and Dockers*, (1969), pp. 142–5.
54 H. A. Clegg *et al.*, *op.cit.*, *ibid.*
55 *Ibid.*, pp. 109–200.
56 S. & B. Webb, *Industrial Democracy*, pp. 187–8.
57 Written in 1920 by W. Mellor, and cited by G. Brown, *Sabotage*, (1977), p. xi.
58 J. Lovell, *op.cit.*, p. 125.
59 P. N. Stearns, *Lives of Labour*, (1975), p. 301.

60 F. Reid, 'Keir Hardie's Conversion to Socialism,' in (ed.) A. Briggs & J. Saville, *Essays in Labour History 1886–1923*, (1971), p. 25. The presence of cheap Irish immigrant labour was also an obstacle here.
61 P. Willis, 'Shop-floor Culture, Masculinity and the Wage Form,' in (ed.) J. Clarke, C. Critcher & R. Johnson, *Working Class Culture*, (1979), p. 197.
62 *ibid.*, p. 196.
63 H. A. Turner, *op.cit.*, p. 185.
64 H. A. Clegg *et al*, pp. 137–8.
65 *Ibid.*, p. 183.
66 A. Clinton, *The Trade Union Rank and File: Trades Councils in Britain 1900–40*, (1977).
67 *Ibid.*, p. 1.
68 K. Burgess, *op.cit.*, p. 252.
69 H. A. Turner, *op.cit.*, p. 224.
70 *Ibid.*, p. 315, fn. 1.
71 See Anna Davin, 'Feminism and Labour History,' in (ed.) R. Samuel, *People's History and Socialist Theory*, (1981).
72 H. A. Clegg *et al.*, p. 202.
73 K. Burgess, *op.cit.*, p. 209.
74 *Ibid.*, p. 288.
75 *Ibid.*
76 *Ibid.*, pp. 282–3.
77 G. Dangerfield, *The Strange Death of Liberal England*, (1935).
78 H. Browne, *The Rise of British Trade Unions 1825–1914*, (1979), p. 94.
79 See G. S. Jones, 'Working-class Culture and Working-Class Politics in London, 1870–1900: Notes on the Remaking of a Working Class,' *Journal of Social History* (1974).
80 E. J. Hobsbawm, *Labouring Men*, (1964), p. 338. 37 per cent of disputes dealt with under the 1896 Conciliation Act were entrusted to working-class mediators and umpires. R. Davidson, *op.cit.*, p. 586.
81 R. Holton, *British Syndicalism*, (1976).
82 *Ibid.*, p. 19.
83 R. Michels, *op.cit.*, p. 298.
84 Scientific management techniques were adopted by Armstrong-Whitworth before 1900. E. J. Hobsbawm 'Custom, Wages and Work-load,' *op.cit.*, p. 360. See also G. Brown, *op.cit.*, Part 3, 'Taylorism'.
85 R. Page Arnot, *The Miners: Years of Struggle*, (1953), p. 110.
86 Unofficial Reform Committee, *The Miners' Next Step, Tonypandy 1912*, (reprinted 1972).
87 G. Brown, *op.cit.*, p. 28.
88 R. Holton, *op.cit.*, p. 95.

4

Strikes 1870–1914

James E. Cronin

'Striking has become a disease, and a very grave disease, in the body social,' intoned George Phillips Bevan at the beginning of his learned lecture on strikes to the Royal Statistical Society on 20 January 1880.[1] Worse still, the disease 'as yet shows no sign of having run its course,' and the concerned statistician could not bring himself 'To believe in any speedy cure,' whether 'by legislative measures or any one course of action'. Bevan's subject was the record of industrial disputes during the 1870s, which he compiled in a most thorough and useful fashion, and his judgement on this particular era in industrial relations was endorsed by George Howell, who also had recourse to the metaphor from pathology. 'This was a period of strike epidemics, not to occur again, let us hope,' wrote Howell on the very eve of the next such epidemic in 1889.[2]

The figures produced by Bevan, and reproduced as part of Table 4.1 (p. 76), are indeed impressive; impressive enough to suggest that the 1870s probably were the years when strikes became the dominant form of workers' collective activity. Though the labour market was buoyant in 1870 – unemployment was only 3.9 per cent, compared with 7.9 per cent in 1868 and 6.7 per cent in 1869 – only thirty strikes were recorded. The figure tripled in 1871 to ninety-eight, and more than that again in 1872, when 343 disputes were noted. (See also Figure 1.)[3] The levels remained high through the 1870s, as what Thomas Wright called 'the alternation between "flushes" and "crashes" ' shifted the balance of tactical advantage back and forth, and so prompted first workers and then employers to press their advantage to the fullest.[4] Indeed, the strike wave of the early 1870s was probably the first of those major explosions of militancy and union organization that have characterized the subsequent history of British industrial relations.[5] Like the waves of 1889–90, 1911–13, and 1919–20, it represented not merely an escalation of overt conflict between workers and employers, but also a shift towards more inclusive organization of less skilled workers, together with an upsurge of rank-and-file activism, a rejection of the cautious advice of established officials, and a renewed emphasis upon the efficacy of strike activity.[6] Like later insurgencies, too, it was followed by a substantial counter-attack by employers which succeeded in beating back workers' organization from its furthest and weakest extensions, but which did not manage to turn the clock back to the state of organization existing prior to the strike wave. The modes used to re-establish order within 'the industrial relations system' also exhibited marked similarity during these successive counter-offensives: an odd mix of employer attempts to inflict symbolic defeats upon key groups of workers, together with efforts on the part of union leaders, state officials and enlightened employers to elaborate restrictive conciliation schemes and procedures for resolving disputes.[7]

Despite certain earlier prefigurations, it seems reasonable to regard this pattern as basically novel to the era beginning in 1870. The essence of this new pattern was the advance of worker organization from a very modest position in 1870 – about 250,000 trade unionists were affiliated to the TUC in that year – to the point where, in 1920, the bulk of the manual workers, skilled and unskilled, were organized in trade unions whose strength exceeded eight millions. This massive achievement, which has yet to be properly appreciated, was accomplished by aggressive worker activity at the point of production which, at its core, involved the strike.[8]

In this sense, the strike truly came into its own as a form of collective organization in the 1870s. To be sure, strikes were an element, and an increasingly important one, in the arsenal of tactics used for popular mobilization prior to this, and it is clear that, as Charles Tilly argues, there was an earlier shift toward modern forms of contention well before 1850.[9] Certainly, there were strikes before 1870, but what records exist suggest they were far more defensive in character, and less successful, than those after that date.[10] More significantly, there is a disjuncture in pupular agitation around the Second Reform Act of 1867. Though the movement for reform involved many workers and their trade societies, it was conducted with the political tactics developed by the advocates of Catholic Emancipation in the 1820s and reformers of the early 1830s, refined by the Anti-Corn Law League, and the Chartists. Like the social movements of 1828–31, the reform agitation of 1865–7 did not much rely upon strikes as vehicles for mobilization, nor were indus-

Table 4:1 *Strikes and Strikers in Britain, 1870–1914*

	A (Bevan)a	Strikes B (Webb)b	C (Official)c	Strikers C (Official)c
1870	30			
71	98			
72	343			
73	365			
74	286			
75	245			
76	229	17		
77	180	23		
78	268	38		
79	308	72		
1880		46		
81		20		
82		14		
83		26		
84		31		
85		20		
86		24		
87		27		
88		37	517	119,000
89		111	1211	337,000
1890			1040	393,000
91			906	267,000
92			700	357,000
93			782	599,000
94			929	257,000
95			745	207,000
96			926	148,000
97			864	167,000
98			711	201,000
99			719	138,000
1900			648	135,000
01			642	111,000
02			442	117,000
03			387	94,000
04			354	56,000
05			358	68,000
06			486	158,000
07			601	101,000
08			399	224,000
09			436	170,000
1910			531	385,000
11			903	831,000
12			857	1,233,000
13			1497	516,000
14			972	326,000

Notes and Sources:
a *Derived from various newspapers and reports by G.P. Bevan, 'The Strikes of the Past Ten Years,' Journal of the Royal Statistical Society, (March 1880), p. 37.*
b Collected from strikes mentioned in *The Times* by S and B. Webb, *The History of Trade Unionism* (New York, 1920), p. 347n.
c Based on the *Reports on Strikes and Lockouts*, published by the Board of Trade, 1888–1914.

trial tactics seen as having much capacity either for influencing the authorities or for achieving much on their own.[11] The movement surrounding the Second Reform Act was accompanied, however, by the last substantial outbreak of food riots in the south – in Deptford and Greenwich, as well as in more rural areas such as Oxford and Devon. As a form of collective action, the food riot was certainly not predominant, but it was nonetheless at least viable in the mid-Victorian era. In an incident that reads like something from the eighteenth century, 500 women in Durham were moved in 1872 'to parade through the streets with banners, fire-irons, shovels and trays, "with which they continued to beat, making wild and unearthly music," ' protesting the cost of meat, milk and potatoes. The ostensible leader of the women threatened to burn in effigy any other woman who bought food at what were thought to be excessive prices. Community organization was strong enough, its 'moral economy' meaningful enough, to make the threat effective, and the movement spread to other colliery villages in the county.[12]

Despite their occasional recurrence, most notably during the First World War, food riots did tend to disappear. Whether this reflected a maturation of protest is difficult to determine. One key factor seems to have been the decline in agricultural prices in the Great Depression, which reduced food costs by about 40 per cent from 1877 to 1896. Even when prices began to rise again after 1905, the cost of food remained relatively stable and thus came to constitute a smaller proportion of workers' expenditure than it had before. The effect, it appears, was to shift attention from consumption to wages and conditions of employment, and to relocate protest from the market to the place of work.

Though food riots became fewer, other types of riot continued to occur after 1870, and quite a substantial number took place in urban, industrial centres. Still, the pattern was for the number of such outbreaks to decline, and for riots and strikes to become distinct, and ultimately antithetical, modes of action. (The exception, of course, was the continuation through 1914 of riots against the use of police and troops to protect blacklegs during strikes.) Thus, of 452 riots counted up between 1865 and 1914, 292 occurred in the quarter century ending in 1890, and only 160 in the next twenty-five years – a decrease of over 40 per cent. More specifically, of the seventy-four situations in which riots were associated with strikes, fifty-six took place before 1895, but only eighteen from then until

1914.[13] The gradual replacement of riots by strikes was noted explicitly by Thomas Brassey in the late 1860s, and the change was most welcome: 'The conduct of the trade unionists, while out on strike, will probably be as much superior to that of the rioters in the manufacturing districts in the early part of the present century as the discipline of the standing army is to that of the guerrilla band.'[14] No doubt when George Potter claimed in 1871 that, 'instead of violence accompanying strikes as once it too often did, outrage of any kind is now the exception, and is so rare as to be scarcely that,' he had an interest that was more than historical, but his claim was only somewhat premature.[15]

All this suggests that by 1870 British workers had become quite proficient in the waging of strikes in spite of sustained opposition from the articulate public, and persistent difficulties with the courts. The legal status of strikes and picketing remained precarious at least until 1906, and despite the reform of 1875, but by the 1870s unions were quite fluent with the law, and adept at tailoring their actions to suit its restrictions.[16] And if the 'public' were still predominantly hostile to strikes, there were some notable cases where they did support strikes, as in the engineers' strike of 1871 and the dockers in 1889, and, perhaps more importantly, they came to accept the inevitability of strikes. The shift in the discourse about strikes is evident in many forums, but nowhere more obviously than among social scientists. The famous investigation of the National Association for the Promotion of Social Science in 1859 smacks of a sense of wonder, discovery and novelty; while Bevan's paper to the Royal Statistical Society is greeted with a chorus of arguments that have obviously been rehearsed many times over.[17] Even political economists were forced gradually to amend their arguments in the face of workers' sustained preference for behaviour that was economically 'irrational'.[18] With justice, George Howell could assert in 1879 that: 'The right to strike is not . . . seriously disputed.'[19]

Having thus 'learned the rules of the game', British workers after 1870 took rapidly to organizing and to its necessary concomitant, strikes. Thomas Wright, 'The Journeyman Engineer', perceived this essential thrust to working-class activity as early as 1871:

> Average English workmen are not so political as continental, and especially French, workmen are . . . They have not the type of mind for which theoretical or philosophical politics have fascination . . . their political thoughts and aspirations, though they scarcely recognize them as being

strictly political, turn exclusively upon improving the position of labour in relation to capital. And this they seek to accomplish by direct action – as, for instance, by strikes and the strengthening of trades unions – and not by the establishment of entirely new social systems.[20]

The history of both unionism and strikes from 1870 through the war is concerned, therefore, with the spread of each, downwards and outwards (and occasionally upwards),[21] to progressively larger sections of the working class. This extension is revealed graphically in Figure 1 (above), which depicts the number of strikes, strikers and trade union members from 1870 to 1914. Two questions are immediately suggested by these graphs: first, why the general upward trend in organization and, to a lesser extent, strikes and strikers? and second, why is so much of the progress along the trend concentrated in so few years, 1871–3, 1889–90, 1910–13? It should be pointed out, to begin, that these two critical questions have received surprisingly little attention from those who study labour, and that, of the two, the first and most important has been discussed least of all.

Several reasons can be adduced for this neglect of the great transformation in the state of labour. First, because the change cut across industries and localities, its analysis requires a willingness to synthesize and theorize that is difficult in itself and that, in addition, runs against the instinct and training of most labour historians. Ordinarily, the study of labour is chopped up into the history of one or another industry or union, and such history revels in the local and particular. It is often confined as well to rather narrow bands of time, which makes it easier to catch the ebb and flow of conjuncture, but harder to capture and analyse the secular, and presumably structural, transformations.

The second factor retarding such analysis is simpler, and that is that many of the most notable and spectacular incidents in labour history do not fit in well with this overall pattern. Successful strikes tend to be shorter, less violent, and often less noticeable than those prolonged tests of strength, often spilling over into violence, that have received most attention. Thus, the average duration of strikes during the wave of 1871–3 was between $2\frac{1}{2}$–3 weeks, but it was more than double that in 1878–9, when employers took advantage of the slump to reduce wages and, in some cases, to attempt to crush the unions altogether. Inevitably, the bitter contests of the latter years live longer in the popular memory, and in the rendering of labour history, than the multitude of strikes that ended in victory or compromise.

It is also the case that certain kinds of strikes draw a great deal of attention because of the nature of the issues involved, and that these do not necessarily follow the secular trend at all. Disputes over the introduction of new machinery, for instance, have occurred in a far less predictable pattern than other strikes, yet have attracted a great deal of analysis because they affect the entire future organization of particular branches of industry. This randomness is obviously linked to the pace and direction of technological innovation, and varies a great deal between industries. In engineering during the nineteenth century, fights over the effects of new machinery and attendant changes in earnings, manning and work routines came in 1851–2 and 1897–8 i.e., at the beginning of economic booms which simultaneously increased the leverage of the men, and heightened the incentive of employers to reap the benefits of new methods of production.[22] In cotton, on the other hand, the major strikes over machinery came in the long downswing of 1820–47: in Manchester in 1829 and Glasgow in 1837. After that, most strikes came over wages and, before 1870, over unionism itself.[23] The boot and shoe makers, by contrast, fought against the use of new sewing machines in Northampton in 1857–9 and again in London in 1895. Glass and bottle makers struck over new presses in 1876–7, dockworkers opposed the introduction of steam cranes in the 1890s and after, compositors struck for control over work and machinery in 1911, engineers fought repeatedly over apprentices and piecework, and shipbuilders over who should be allowed to work on the new, iron ships after 1890.[24] Seldom, however, were such movements particularly successful, for the opposition to technical progress was unlikely to win allies, and the very introduction of machines ordinarily created a pool of workers who stood to gain by working them and who were unlikely to join struggles over the issue.[25] On the other hand, the prosperous conditions that stimulated innovations also increased the demand for labour and often negated the effects upon workers of the introduction of machinery. This contradictory conjuncture thus strengthened the hands of workers, made skilled hands scarce, and so made the victories achieved by employers in strikes over machinery difficult to enforce. The classic case is, of course, engineering, where events seemed to conspire to recreate workshop power for the men and thus necessitate the 1922 replay of the 1897–8 strike.[26]

Finally, it should be noted that disputes over technical change tended to decrease over time. As early as 1870, Potter declared that, 'Strikes against the use of machinery, once so frequent, are become rare to obsoleteness'. This is perhaps too strong, for the issue was a recurring one, but the statement was not wildly inaccurate.[27]

A third factor discouraging investigation into the long-term growth in strikes and unionism may be briefly mentioned. That is the marked tendency among British historians of labour to emphasize elements of continuity over those of change, to denigrate and minimize the genuine achievements of labour, and to stress the strength of tradition, sectionalism and conservatism among workers rather than the secular increase in class awareness and organization. As Royden Harrison has noted sarcastically, 'In certain quarters it is imagined that to explain why the British working class is not revolutionary is the only worthy object of historical inquiry'.[28] Harrison's irony is directed at historians on the Left, whereas in fact those most insistent on the gradualism and moderation of labour would seem to approach the problem from a somewhat different perspective. Nevertheless, the effect of all such writings has been to divert attention from what would seem from the evidence reviewed here to be a quite dramatic shift in the balance of power within industry.

What, then, does account for the great expansion of organization and of workers' propensity to strike? First, we must attend to the formulation of the question. The norm for analysis in labour history has been to focus on the accumulation of grievances, as if the relationship between the extent and character of oppression and the resistance to it was uniformly close and direct. By now, the sum of research on collective action showing the importance of strength and resources for mobilization ought to allow us to modify that approach considerably, so that the key question becomes not, 'why did workers fight?' but rather, 'what allowed or facilitated their translation of grievance into protest?' It is important, secondly, to recognize that, because the transformation in organization and strikes occurred throughout industry, the critical factors should themselves be effective at a broad societal leval. What we are seeking, therefore, are changes of a structural nature in economy and society that combined to enhance the collective capacity of working men and women to organize and resist.

Before 1870, the social reach of unionism and of strikes was very narrow. Not without reason were unions in this period attacked as the province of the skilled and best paid of workers. 'It is notorious,' one hostile observer wrote, 'that strikes and combinations have been most common amongst those portions of the working population whose wages are highest.'[29] By 1914, this was no longer true in any sense: organization and strike-proneness had spread decisively to the semi- and unskilled. The change is recorded in both the geography and the industrial distribution of strikes. In the 1870s, medium-sized towns exhibited the highest strike rates: Barnsley came just after London in the list of strike locations; Manchester saw fewer than Dundee or Merthyr; Sunderland outpaced Birmingham, Bradford, Bristol and Belfast. A similar pattern can be observed during the explosion of the 'New Unionism' and at the turn of the century. This clearly reflected the coming to union organization of operatives in basic industry located in these urban centres of modest size. The pattern shifted slightly after 1900, as many transport and service workers in the large provincial cities and in London finally succeeded in building stable unions and so were able to launch effective strikes. These geographical patterns were manifestations of the continued extension of organization, from the craftsmen in the largest cities to the operatives in the factory towns and the miners in their mining villages back to the least skilled workers in the service sectors in the big cities.[30]

The industrial distribution of strikes is similarly broad from 1870 onwards, and seems to broaden further in the years approaching 1914. The militancy of 1871–3 touched at its peak agricultural workers, dockers, and other unorganized groups. Even among the engineers, the unorganized played a major role, as in Newcastle in 1871, when no more than 10 per cent of the strikers were ASE members. From then until 1914, strike propensity was surprisingly evenly spread out in 'the staple industries', as Bevan had noted for the 1870s. Though some groups, like the miners, were more prone to strike (for reasons that have been discussed many times over), the really marked divergence between industries visible since the 1920s was much less clear before 1914. And the changes that do occur before 1914 – the slight decline in strikes among builders, the increase among transport workers – confirms the tendency for the differences between industries and between skilled and unskilled to lessen somewhat as organization advanced.[31]

So while strikes occurred and organization deepened among the skilled, the truly novel phenomenon was the enrolment of those

without craft skills into the labour movement, and it was this that
accounted for the massive growth in unions and in strike activity
throughout the pre-war era. Three sets of factors seem most compel-
ling as explanations of this change. First, there was crude demogra-
phy: the ranks of the semi-skilled and unskilled increased substantially after 1870. This was intimately linked with a second factor: the
pattern of industrial development led to increased demand for semi-
skilled, as opposed to skilled, labour, and this demand was filled
largely, though not exclusively, by an upgrading in the status of
unskilled or casual labour. Third, the social ecology of mid-
Victorian cities slowly gave way to a more socially segregated pattern of residence during the massive urban growth of 1870–1914.
The effect was to create a physical space for the development of a
strong and distinctive working-class culture sustained by, and itself
helping to sustain, a broad array of social and political institutions
that together added substantially to the resources which workers
could mobilize on their own behalf.

To document these changes to any substantial degree would
necessitate extensive discussion, but one might nevertheless suggest a
few reasons for believing them to have been both real and significant.
The growth in the ranks of the semi- or unskilled is well-known, and
resulted from an expansion of the number of non-apprenticed workers in trades like engineering, printing, iron and steel, from the
development of new industries that required a small number of
skilled men for maintenance and much larger numbers of unskilled
workers for production, and from the enhanced economic importance of transport, communication and service.[32] From 1890, the
rate of increase of the workforce in these industries exceeded that of
manufacturing industry, and added greatly to the amount of stable
semi-skilled employment. Even within manufacturing, there was a
steady increase in the size of plant, the ratio of capital per worker,
and in industrial concentration. However retarded the modernization of British industry, the trends were visible and important, both
in new industries and in old staple trades, like mining and cotton.[33]

In terms of labour, the net result of such changes was to make
work more regular and predictable, as well as more tightly controlled and supervized. Scientific management remained more of an
ideology than a reality, but even that revealed a greater attention on
the part of management to the affairs of production.[34] In some cases,
this led to sharp conflicts with the skilled workers, as in engineering,

but other factors combined to make such confrontations the exception. First, the process of 'deskilling,' as it has been called, occurred more at the level of the class or the entire population than the individual, for individual artisans were kept employed in superior grades or work, in the toolroom or in specialized production rather than displaced. This was guaranteed by the timing of the change in particular, for the diffusion of new equipment could be achieved only during periods of high demand and investment, which meant that labour shortages were also acute.

The skilled were therefore challenged, but by no means defeated or eliminated.[35] The evolution of industrial structure affected the unskilled in an equally contradictory fashion. Jobs came to approximate the norm of factory work, with greater distance between master and men, more bossing and discipline and, ordinarily, a more intensive pace of production. But the greater regularity, rationality and stability of employment provided the material underpinnings for organization and resistance. It took time, naturally, for new unskilled factory hands to acquire what Hobsbawm has termed the 'habit of solidarity', and in particular for workers in transport and government service to evolve forms of organization appropriate to the scale and style of their employment, and to the combined strength of their employers, but by 1914 the process was well advanced.[36]

The impact of developments in the spatial relations of classes is difficult to assess with precision, but seems to have worked in most cases to facilitate militancy. The pattern varied a good deal from place to place, depending upon the nature of local transportation systems, housing and labour markets, but in general it appears that, from 1870–1914, working-class communities acquired a degree of stability and homogeneity such as to allow for the elaboration of a robust, and partially autonomous way of life.[37] Intimately linked to this culture, or these locally rooted sub-cultures, were networks of formal and informal institutions, from adult classes to the friendships of the street and the pub. The emergence of this working-class social and cultural presence in the cities of late Victorian and Edwardian Britain has been documented by several historians, and was, of course, much discussed by contemporaries as well. In both instances, commentary has tended to stress the problems with this new culture – its patriarchal, hierachical and complacent aspects being deplored by historians, its paganism, cynicism and insularity being attacked by contemporaries. Neither perspective, it can be argued, sufficiently emphasizes the novelty of the development, or the implications for politics and other forms of collective action, for these increasingly solid communities represented a substantial increment to the strength of labour.[38]

The strengthening of independent working-class communities seems to have occurred throughout the country, though the precise set of processes involved varied a good deal. In mining communities, the major factor seems to have been the gradual slowing down of migration, which eliminated much of the instability and heterogeneity common during periods of rapid demographic expansion.[39] For older industrial centres, the process differed. Urban growth after 1870 seems to have centred in the larger towns and cities, rather than in those medium-sized towns that housed so many of the mills of the first industrial revolution. As cities grew, the local 'urban villages' centred on a factory and presided over by a paternalistic employer, described so well by Patrick Joyce in Lancashire, were submerged in the larger agglomerations of working-class residence that were housing the growing industrial population.[40] In London, the key seems to have been the spreading out of working-class families into newer settlements from Hackney to the north and from the Thames south.[41] The classic case was Battersea, a centre of Labour voting, trade union membership, and left-wing support, but other areas followed not dissimilar paths.[42]

At the point of production and in their communities, therefore, British workers found new sources of strength from 1870 to 1914, and this was particularly important for those who did not possess a certified and marketable skill with which to bargain. When these new resources were combined with a favourable economic conjuncture – i.e., a tight labour market – the common result was an outbreak of union activity and strikes. Obviously, a great deal remains to be said about these structural determinants of the balance of power between classes – the role of the state in particular could use further explication – but the foregoing must suffice for present purposes.[43]

If secular trends in the structural evolution of economy and society lay behind the great changes in industrial relations, it is nonetheless the case that the pace of development varied considerably from year to year. Both the growth of organization and the increase in strikes were concentrated in three 'great leaps', in 1871–3, 1889–90, and 1911–13. What caused this distinctive clustering of forward movements? The vagaries of the trade cycle are no doubt part of the answer: each of the strike waves occurred when the labour market was most favourable to workers. The wild boom of 1871–3 saw unemployment in the organized trades well below 2 per cent; in the same industries only 2.1 per cent were out of work in 1889–90, compared with 10.2 per cent just two years before; in 1911–13, unemployment averaged just under 3 per cent, whereas double that were out of a job in 1908–9. Clearly, a favourable labour market was something of a precondition for launching a wave of militancy.[44]

A slightly broader view of economic conjuncture suggests a further feature common to these moments of insurgency. If one considers not simply the classic trade cycle of 7–10 years, but also the long waves of roughly half a century through which capitalist development seems to pass and progress, it becomes clear that strikes and organization have tended to come during short-term upswings near the end of each phase of the long wave. The first great British strike wave in 1871–3 came during the speculative climax of the mid-Victorian boom; the 'New Unionism' broke through during the flurry of trade just before the last trough of the Great Depression; and the 'labour unrest' swept Britain near the end of the long Edwardian prosperity. This quite marked pattern suggests a very intimate relation between the '*langen Wellen der Konjunktur*,' as Kondratiev called them, and labour militancy. It seems, in addition, that long waves are connected with the structural evolution of economy and society which brought about the enhanced capacity for workers' collective action after 1870.[45]

Perhaps the best way to show these links and mediations is to describe briefly the most salient feature of each major outbreak of strikes. Unfortunately, we must begin with what is surely the least well-documented of such episodes, the militancy of 1871–3. According to Bevan's count, the number of separate strikes increased from a mere thirty in 1870 to about 350 for 1872 and 1873, an increase of well over ten times. Of these, however, very few find their way into George Howell's list of 'Great Strikes' or a similar list compiled by the Board of Trade in 1889, so our knowledge of most remains scanty indeed. The best-known is the engineers' nine-hours' strike on the North East in 1871, which seems to have been a stimulant to other workers. Several features stand out in the various accounts of that struggle: the quality of the men's leadership, particularly John Burnett; the fact that most of the strikers were not members of the union; the recalcitrance of the owners and the public support generated by the workers. The demand for a shorter working day was extremely popular, and was widely emulated by workers in other industries. The initiative of the unorganized was also characteristic of the movement elsewhere, and the two often came together, as when 'a massive strike wave' swept Sheffield in 1872, bringing over 1200 smelters into the union around the demand for a shorter working week. The strikes in general reflected a broad attempt to organize unions, and membership in TUC-affiliated societies grew from about 250,000 in 1870 to almost 1.2 million in 1874. The growth was particularly concentrated in heavy industry, like engineering and metal working: the ironworkers grew from a mere 476 members in January 1869 to over 35,000 in 1874.[46]

It seems that unions and strikes, though still strongest in the older, skilled trades, were spreading into basic industry. (See Table 4:2.) Unskilled 'boys' in shipbuilding, gas-stokers, building labourers, dockers, even agricultural labourers, formed unions and/or struck in the early 1870s in what was by then the furthest extension of organization ever achieved. In 1874, the National Union among agricultural workers claimed 100,000 members in approximately 1000 branches. Among the miners, it was the South Wales coalfield, which was newer than other fields, rapidly expanding, and previously less well-organized, that was the centre of mining militancy. Generally, the strikes of 1871–3, whether in industry or the older trades, were short, small, and successful, pushing organization to its furthest limits.[47]

Inevitably, the depression of the late 1870s destroyed much of what was gained by 1874. Union membership was halved, but still remained almost twice as high as it had been in 1870. The footholds of unionism in agriculture, on the docks, and among other unskilled workers were lost, but advances made within industry were more stable. Overall, therefore, this foray into organizing beyond the skilled trades produced mixed results. One obvious weakness was ideological and strategic. The extension of organization downward and outward within the working class was not accompanied by a new set of political ideas, by novel strategic thinking or what might be termed a new philosophy of labour. Yet clearly the outlook and style of the established unions were not well suited to the needs of the mass of workers.

The inability to maintain the gains of 1871–3 showed the inade-

Table 4:2   *Major Participants in Strikes, 1871–3*

Industry or occupation	Number of strikes
Agricultural labourers	3
Bakers	17
Boilermakers	8
Bricklayers	14
Building operators	20
Carpenters and joiners	65
Colliers	87
Cotton hands	19
Dock labourers	15
Engineers and fitters	37
Flax, linen and jute hands	24
Ironworkers	44
Masons	31
Nail and chain makers	14
Navvies	5
Painters	8
Plasterers	9
Plumbers	81
Printers and compositors	10
Quarrymen	16
Railway and telegraph employees	13
Shipbuilders	28
Shoe and boot makers	48
Slaters	11
Tailors	24
All others	232
Total	806

Source:
G.P. Bevan, 'The Strikes of the Past Ten Years,' *Journal of the Royal Statistical Society* (1880), pp. 39–41.

quacy of the old unions and the old ideas for the new era of mass organization. In this sense, the Great Depression was a great teacher of labour. The defeats of 1878 prompted changes in the cotton unions, the fall in product prices gradually disabused the miners and others of the fondness for sliding-scales, the railwaymen slowly discovered the need for an 'all-grades' strategy, even the engineers toyed repeatedly (if unsuccessfully) with plans for opening membership more broadly, and, most obviously, a new generation of activists came quickly to the conclusion that a broad, inclusive strategy was the key to organizing the unskilled. These ideas and this strategic perspective crystallized in the 'New Unionist' explosion of 1889, but the antecedents go back to the 1870s. It is no doubt true, as George

Howell wrote in 1902, that very quickly the novelty of the New Unionism wore off, that the new unions took on characteristics of the old, and vice versa, but the net effect of the movement was nevertheless a major shift in the nature of the labour movement.[48]

Once again, in 1889–90, union membership jumped – from 817,000 in 1888 to 1,470,000 in 1890; the number of strikes increased a comparable amount, from 517 in 1888 to 1211 in 1889 and just over one thousand in 1890; while the workers involved grew by still more, from 119,000 in 1888 to just under 400,000 in 1890. As in 1871–3, strikes were relatively short and extremely successful. In 1889–90, 312,000 workers achieved clear-cut victories in strikes, a further 254,000 some sort of compromise, while only 143,000 experienced defeat. This is quite a remarkable record, for it is a commonplace in industrial relations that neither side is ordinarily anxious to claim or concede victory or defeat. The industrial spread of strikes was even broader than in 1871–3, with much increased participation by transport workers and by workers in metal, engineering and shipbuilding and somewhat reduced activity among the mostly skilled building trades. The shift toward heavy industry and toward the less skilled was thus further accentuated. Most significantly, the 1890s witnessed the first large-scale organization of women workers, mostly in textiles, but also in teaching and other white-collar occupations.[49]

Predictably enough, the wave of 1889–90 was followed by an employers' counter-attack that began during the depression of 1892–3 and continued through the decade. The reaction was notable in several respects. First, it led to some of the most bitter, and occasionally violent, confrontations in the history of labour, among dockers, miners, engineers, quarrymen, boot and shoe makers, and others. Second, the employers' side took the initiative in evolving new forms of organization with which to prosecute their aims. The Shipping Federation and the Engineering Employers gave the lead in organized strike-breaking, while individual companies pursued the legal attack on unions culminating in Taff Vale. The advance in workers' organization thus prompted counter-organization among employers that tipped the balance of forces back in their direction. Third, despite the strength of the attack upon labour, union membership remained relatively stable through the 1890s, and even began to creep up again after 1896. This was no doubt due to the much improved labour market in the late 1890s, but whatever the cause, it meant that unions kept more of the gains resulting from the 'New Unionism' than they had from the 1871–3 strike wave. The mass organization of industry was gradually taking hold.[50]

The further development of unions and strikes was greatly hindered after 1900 by the combined effects of legal restrictions, which lasted until 1906, strong employer organizations, and an uncertain economic climate. The underlying structural weakness of the British economy meant that the upswing beginning in 1896 was much weaker than in other countries, and unemployment from 1901–10 was on average double that of 1896–1900. The numbers unemployed were below 3 per cent during 1898–1900, but consistently above that every year after, until the war. Faced with such disadvantages, union strength stagnated, and even declined slightly from 1900 until 1905. The legislation of 1906, and a reasonably strong demand for labour, allowed a jump in that year, but membership declined again from 1907–09. By 1910, membership had crept over the $2\frac{1}{2}$ million mark, from which point a rapid rise ensued. Over 1.5 million new members were added during the next three years as organization was consolidated and extended among transport workers – dockers and railwaymen primarily – and in basic industry.

The 'labour unrest' of 1911–13 was thus, in the first instance, a qualitative breakthrough in the extent of organization achieved in the teeth of tremendous and quite unrelenting employer opposition. Inevitably, such a movement had to be led by the rank and file, and often even took the form of a rebellion against the union leaders. Not without reason did Sydney Buxton, President of the Board of Trade, complain in 1911 about 'the serious diminution in the control which the leaders of the men used to exercise over their rank and file'. It was also left to the rank and file and to various militants to articulate a new philosophy of mass unionism and direct action. Whether a great many workers grasped the key tenets of syndicalism or not, the syndicalist approach resonated well with the mood of the men and helped to express its essential thrust. The rebellion within the labour movement against the leaders can in a sense be viewed as the critical, preliminary skirmish in the struggle for another, qualitative advance of organization.[51] The nature of strikes during 1911–13 confirms this general picture. The spread of unions and of the capacity to strike is revealed in the mass character of disputes and in their industrial incidence. The size of the average strike increased from 350 during 1889–92 to 780 workers during 1910–13. As in

1889–90, these strikes were immensely successful: 1,135,000 strikers (44 per cent) winning outright victories against employers, 1,080,000 (42 per cent) being involved in compromises and only 363,000 (14 per cent) experiencing clear-cut defeats. The pattern of participation revealed a further shift away from skilled craftsmen towards the newer, more 'proletarian' workers in industry and transport, with miners, dockers, railwaymen, and textile workers especially prominent.[52]

The transformation wrought by these waves of organizing and strikes by 1914 is perhaps best revealed by the changed role and attitude of the government. The government had become interested in fostering industrial peace in the late 1880s, appointing the Royal Commission on Labour of 1889–92, setting up a Labour Department at the Board of Trade just after this, intervening in the 1893 coal dispute, and legally fostering conciliation from 1896 onward. Faced with employer resistance, and not pressed on by any crisis in industrial relations, such efforts languished from about 1897 to 1910. The wave of strikes that broke out in 1911, however, brought government back into the field for good. Troops were sent to Wales in 1910, to Liverpool and other ports in 1911; Lloyd George got involved directly in 1911–12 with the railwaymen and the miners; and throughout the turbulence the government's chief conciliator, George Askwith, was kept continually busy. The net effect of government intervention was problematic – its protection of blacklegs angered workers and assisted employers, but Lloyd George's efforts to mediate were resented almost as much by the employers. By 1913, the government was disillusioned with the results of its efforts, and the outcome of the contests on the docks and the railways remained in doubt, the possibility of major disputes in 1914–15 looming just over the horizon. It is especially unclear just what role government would have played in such confrontations, but is seems unlikely they would have been able to withdraw. By 1914, workers were organized in all the major industries, and their combined action could have dramatic consequences. Government could no longer remain aloof from the day-to-day conduct of industrial relations.[53]

Though the First World War is beyond the scope of this essay, it should be noted, at least by way of postscript, that its initial effect on workers was to spread their organization even further and deeper than it had been in 1914. The battle to establish collective bargaining had therefore been won by 1918, and the conduct of industrial

Figure 1: Strikes and Union Organization, 1870-1914

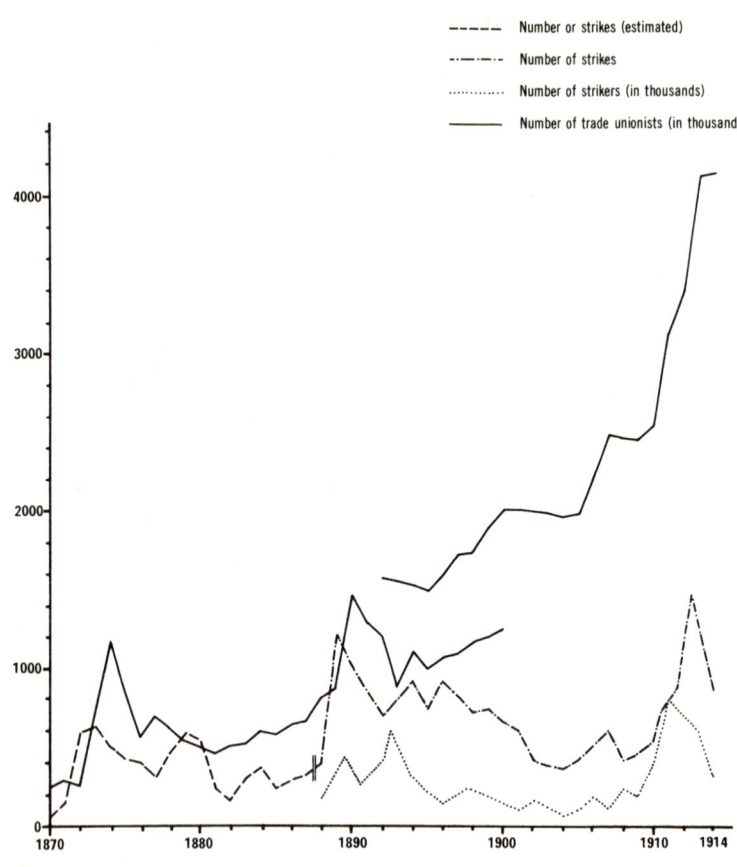

----- Number or strikes (estimated)

-·-·-·- Number of strikes

············ Number of strikers (in thousands)

——— Number of trade unionists (in thousands)

Sources

Data on strikes and strikers based on Table 1, as explained in note 3.

Data on union membership drawn from official statistics. The earlier and lower totals refer to the membership of TUC affiliated unions, the later and higher ones to total trade union membership.

relations permanently altered.[54] This was what the great waves of militancy of 1871–3, 1889–90 and 1911–13 had been about, although on the surface the demands usually concerned wages, piecework, apprentices and similar narrow, 'economistic' issues. The real issue was power, which is, of course, the essence of the entire history of strikes.

References

1 G. P. Bevan, 'The Strikes of the Past Ten Years,' *Journal of the Royal Statistical Society*, 93, (March 1880), pp. 35–54.

2 George Howell, 'Great Strikes: Their Origin, Costs, and Results', *Co-operative Wholesale Societies Annual 1889*, p. 310.

3 In this figure, estimates of strike activity have been made from 1870–87 by combining data from Bevan and the Webbs with the published reports of the Board of Trade from 1888. These are only estimates, derived from extrapolation of the post-1888 data backwards and based upon the ratios between the three sets of figures for overlapping years. They are probably quite reliable for year-to-year fluctuations, but the general levels may be distorted slightly by the use of the Webbs' narrow sample. Still, the results tally with other, more impressionistic evidence available.

4 Thomas Wright, 'On the Condition of the Working Classes,' *Fraser's Magazine*, (October 1871), p. 427.

5 The importance of strike waves in labour history is stressed generally by E.J. Hobsbawm, 'Economic Fluctuations and Some Social Movements since 1800,' in *Labouring Men*, (1967); and for Britain in J. Cronin, *Industrial Conflict in Modern Britain*, (1979), pp. 45–73.

6 One implication of this recurring pattern is that the tension between entrenched union leaders and rank-and-file activists is a long-term, indeed structural, aspect of labour history, not peculiar to any particular moment but to those various periods when workers on the shop floor perceived a possibility of advance beyond what the leaders have come to expect. Ideological factors, generational differences, degrees of bureaucratization, and government policy all help to condition and mediate this tension, but its roots seem to me to go much deeper. The evidence for this view is scattered widely throughout the record of labour history, but one might begin the study of the unofficial character of virtually all insurgencies with George Howell. He claimed in 1890 that: 'It is perhaps a bold thing to say, but the statement can be made with considerable confidence, that in 90 per cent of the strikes which take place, the men directly concerned are the instigators and promoters, and that the union is the brake on the wheel which prevents too great precipitation, and liability to consequent failure.' (See J. Howell, *The Conflicts of Capital and Labour*, (2nd. ed., 1980) p. 211.) The echoes with more recent complaints are striking.

7 The persistent preference for conciliation in the British system of industrial relations has been noted by Frank Wilkinson, 'The Development of Collective Bargaining in Britain to the Early 1920s,' paper presented to the Shop Floor Bargaining Seminar, King's College Research Centre, Cambridge (March 1981). See also J. H. Porter, 'Wage Bargaining under Conciliation Agreements, 1870–1914,' *Economic History Review*, 23, (1970), pp. 460–75; and R. Davidson, 'Social Conflict and Social Administration: The Conciliation Act in British Industrial Rela-

tions,' in (ed.) T. C. Smout, *The Search for Wealth and Stability*, (1979).

8   For the most recent overview, see E. H. Hunt, *British Labour History, 1815–1914*, (1981).

9   Charles Tilly, 'Britain Creates the Social Movement,' in (ed.) J. Cronin & J. Schneer, *Social Conflict and the Political Order* (1982), pp. 21–51.

10 See the listing of past strikes and their results in the table produced in the *Report on the Strikes and Lockouts of 1888*, by the Labour Correspondent of the Board of Trade, C. 5809, *Parliamentary Papers* (1889) LXX, C. 5809, pp. 21–9. The most impressive collection of evidence on early strikes is C. R. Dobson's list of 383 disputes from 1717–1800 in *Masters and Journeymen. A Prehistory of Industrial Relations 1717–1800*, (1980). Whether such an account demonstrates the continuity of patterns of protest may be doubted, but it does suggest that the impulse to strike is deeply structured into the historic relation between employer and employee.

11 See Tilly, 'Britian Creates the Social Movement,' on the virtual absence of strikes in 1828–31. The first serious attempt to integrate the strike into a social movement seems to have come in the second phase of Chartist agitation in 1841–2. See I. Prothero, 'William Benbow and The Concept of the "General Strike",' *Past and Present*, no. 63, (1974), pp. 132–71; see also Brian Brown, 'Lancashire Chartism and the Mass Strike of 1842: the Political Economy of Working Class Contention,' Center for Research on Social Organization, Working Paper 203 (University of Michigan, 1979).

12 Donald C. Richter, 'Public Order and Popular Disturbances in Great Britian, 1865–1914,' (University of Maryland, Ph.D. Thesis, 1965), pp. 30–1; Robert Storch, 'Popular Festivity, Social Protest and Public Order: The Devon Food Riots of 1867,' (Pacific Coast Conference on British Studies Meeting, Los Angeles, April 1979).

13 Figures derived from Richter, 'Public Order and Popular Disturbances,' pp. 85 & 260. Unfortunately, Richter follows Bevan's practice of almost a century before of not explaining his precise method of counting up incidents. Still, his figures are corroborated by other evidence of a less quantitative sort, and are in any event meant as an index, not as a comprehensive accounting.

14 Thomas Brassey, quoted in George Potter, 'Strikes and Lockouts from the Workman's Point of View,' *Contemporary Review* 15, (1870), pp. 34–5.

15 G. Potter, 'Trades Unions, Strikes, and Lockouts. A Rejoinder,' *Contemporary Review*, 17, (1871), p. 535.

16 See W. Hamish Fraser, *Trade Unions and Society*, (1974), pp. 185–97, for a brief survey of the law regarding strikes. See also John Orth, 'Striking Workmen before the Courts, 1859–71,' (University of North Carolina, School of Law, unpublished paper, 1980).

17 National Association for the Promotion of Social Science, *Trades' Societies and Strikes*, (1860); the comments on Bevan follow his paper in the *Journal of the Royal Statistical Society*, (March 1880), pp.

55–64. On the public support for the Newcastle engineers, see John Burnett, *Nine Hours' Movement. A History of the Engineers Strike in Newcastle and Gateshead*, (1872); and, more recently, E. Allen *et al.*, *The North-East Engineers' Strikes of 1871: The Nine Hours' League*, (1971).

18 Fraser, *Trade Unions and Society*, 167–84. See also S. Pollard, 'Trade Unions and the Labour Market, 1870–1914,' *Yorkshire Bulletin of Social and Economic Research*, 17, (1965), pp. 98–112, which makes a rather pessimistic argument on the ability of unions to increase labour's share of national income.

19 G. Howell, 'Strikes: Their Costs and Results,' *Fraser's Magazine*, 20 (1879), p. 767.

20 Thomas Wright, 'The English Working Classes and the Paris Commune,' *Fraser's Magazine*, 4 1871), p. 62.

21 On the beginnings of organization among teachers, shop assistants, government workers and others in white-collar jobs after 1880, see Hunt, *British Labour History*, p. 302.

22 K. Burgess, *The Origins of British Industrial Relations*, (1975), 2 and *passism*.

23 G. Howell, 'Great Strikes,' 275–85; H. A. Turner, *Trade Union Growth, Structure and Policy*, (1962); and Joseph White, *The Limits of Trade Union Militancy*, (1978).

24 *Report on Strikes and Lockouts in 1888*, pp. 23–5; P. Stearns, *Lives of Labor* (1975), Part II; Jonathan Zeitlin, 'Craft Control and the Division of Labour: Engineers and Compositors in Britain, 1890–1930,' *Cambridge Journal of Economics* (1973) III, pp. 263–74; and J. F. Clarke, 'Workers in the Tyneside Shipyards in the Nineteenth Century,' in (ed.) N. McCord, *Essays in Tyneside Labour History*, (1977), 109–31.

25 P. Stearns, in 'Measuring the Evolution of Strike Movements,' *International Review of Social History*, 9, (1974), pp. 1–27, and in *Lives of Labor*, pp. 308–10, makes this point generally and it is confirmed in detail in A. L. Levine's review of strikes over technology in *Industrial Retardation in Britain*, (1967).

26 If employers had been able to take full advantage of the victory over the ASE in 1898 and introduce machinery on a wider scale, productivity would surely have increased in engineering, whereas in fact it virtually stagnated. See, in particular, E. H. Phelps Brown, with M. H. Browne, *A Century of Pay*, (1968), pp. 174–95. The proportion of semi-skilled did, of course, continue to increase, but not as rapidly as would have been possible on technical grounds alone. See J. Hinton, *The First Shop Stewards' Movement*, (1973), pp. 61–3.

27 G. Potter, 'Strikes and Lockouts from the Workman's Point of View,' p. 50.

28 R. Harrison, *The Independent Collier*, (1978), p. 1.

29 Quoted in Potter, 'Trades' Unions, Strikes, an Lock-Outs,' p. 529.

30 Bevan, 'The Strikes of the Past Ten Years,' p. 45; Lynn H. Lees, 'Strikes and the Urban Hierarchy in English Industrial Towns, 1842–1901,' in (ed.) Cronin & Schneer, *Social Conflict* (1982), pp. 52–72.

31   Bevan, 'The Strikes of the Past Ten Years,' pp. 39–42; Cronin, *Industrial Conflict*, pp. 159–161; and, on mining in particular, pp. 179–83.

32   Peter Stearns, 'The Unskilled and Industrialization: A Transformation of Consciousness,' *Archiv für Sozialgeschichte* (1976), 16, 249–82, is a useful comparative overview.

33   Hunt, *British Labour History*, pp. 312–13, 331–2. The contrast with the mid-Victorian mix between skilled and casual labour is especially marked. See R. Samuel, 'The Workshop of the World: Steam Power and Hand Technology in mid-Victorian Britain,' *History Workshop*, 3, (1977), pp. 6–72.

34   E. Hobsbawm, 'Custom, Wages, and Work-Load,' in *Labouring Men*, p. 406.

35   On skill in general, see Charles More, *Skill and the English Working Class, 1870–1914*, (1980).

36   The situation on the railways posed particularly difficult problems. See G. Alderman, 'The Railway Companies and the Growth of Trade Unionism in the Late Nineteenth and Early Twentieth Centuries,' *Historical Journal*, 14, (1971), pp. 129–52; P. S. Gupta, 'Railway Trade Unions in Britain, c. 1880–1920,' *Economic History Review*, 19, (1966); and, of course, P. S. Bagwell, *The Railwaymen*, (1963).

37   In general, see R. Dickinson, *The West European City*, (1961), pp. 463–4; J. P. McKay, *Tramways and Trolleys: The Rise of Mass Transport in Europe*, (1966), pp. 205–25; (ed.) S. D. Chapman, *The History of Working-Class Housing*, (1971); John Burnett, *A Social History of Housing*, (1978); and J. R. Kellett, *The Impact of Railways on Victorian Cities*, (1969).

38   See, for both reactions, S. Meacham, *A Life Apart. The English Working Class*, (1977); Gareth Stedman Jones, 'Working-Class Culture and Working-Class Politics in London, 1870–1900,' *Journal of Social History*, 7, (1974), pp. 460–508; and R. Roberts, *The Classic Slum*, (1971). For the beginnings of a critique, see J. Cronin, 'Labour Insurgency and Class Formation. Comparative Perspectives on the Crisis of 1917–1920 in Europe,' *Social Science History*, 4 (1980), pp. 125–52.

39   C. Storm-Clark, 'The Miners, 1870–1970: A Test Case for Oral History,' *Victorian Studies*, 15 (1971); Cronin, *Industrial Conflict*, pp. 180–3.

40   P. Joyce, *Work, Society and Politics. The Culture of the Factory in Later Victorian England*, (1980). Whether Joyce has exaggerated the degree of paternalism and supra-class politics of 1850–80 or not, his description of the change after 1880 seems very accurate. As he explains: 'Both industry and the town were by the end of the nineteenth century taking on their modern forms, forms marked by the mutual ignorance and antagonism of the classes.' And again: 'The changing ecology of the factory town, and the increased degree of organization and commercialization in popular culture combined to enlarge the scope of people's lives, and break the hold of the old communities of work, religion and politics on their daily lives.' (p. 342) There is

obviously a need for more local, provincial studies of such developments. The ideal would be a study that combined the technical sophistication of R. M. Pritchard's *Housing and the Spatial Structure of the City*, (1976) with the interpretative subtlety displayed by Joyce.

41 Harold Pollins, 'Transport Lines and Social Division,' in (ed.) R. Glass, *London: Aspects of Change*, (1964), pp. 34–46.

42 See Chris Wrigley, 'Liberals and the Desire for Working-Class Representatives in Battersea, 1886–1922,' in (ed.) K. D. Brown, *Essays in Anti-Labour History*, (1974), pp. 126–58.

43 On the state, see the contributions by Wrigley and Davidson in this volume, chs. 7 and 8.

44 These statistics were taken originally from the Department of Employment and Productivity, *British Labour Statistics: Historical Abstract, 1868–1968*, (1971). They also appear, together with extensive strike statistics, in Cronin, *Industrial Conflict*, pp. 206–38.

45 J. Cronin, 'Stages, Cycles, and Insurgencies: The Economics of Unrest,' in (ed.) T. Hopkins & I. Wallerstein, *Processes of the World System*, (1980).

46 See Table 1 for details, as well as Bevan, 'The Strikes of the Past Ten Years'; Howell, 'Great Strikes,' and the *Report on Strikes and Lockouts in 1888*. On the iron and steel workers, see N.P. Howard, 'Cooling the Heat: A History of the Rise of Trade Unionism in the South Yorkshire Iron and Steel Industry, from the Origins to the First World War,' in (ed.) S. Pollard & C. Holmes, *Essays in the Economic and Social History of South Yorkshire*, (1976), pp. 59–73.

47 On shipbuilding, see J. F. Clarke, 'Workers in the Tyneside Shipyards in the Nineteenth Century,' in (ed.) N. McCord, *Essays in Tyneside Labour History*, pp. 109–31; on agricultural workers, see Howell, 'Great Strikes,' pp. 301–03; and R. Groves, *Sharpen the Sickle! The History of the Farm Workers Union*, (1949), pp. 39–92.

48 G. Howell, *Labour Legislation, Labour Movements, and Labour Leaders*, (1902). More generally, see Hunt, *British Labour History*, pp. 304–15, where the contrast between the 'New Unionism' and the old is reviewed. Hunt generally opts for the 'revisionist' perspective which minimizes the difference between the two, but the evidence he marshalls nevertheless makes clear that the labour movement was very different after 1889 than before.

49 See S. Lewenhak, *Women and Trades Unions*, (1977); and Hunt, *British Labour History*, pp. 299–300.

50 See E. Wigham, *Power to Manage*, (1973), pp. 29–62 on the Engineering Employers' Federation; and J. Saville, 'Trade Unions and Free Labour: The Background of the Taff Vale Decision,' in (ed.) A. Briggs and J. Saville *Essays in Labour History*, (1967), pp. 317–50, more generally.

51 Buxton, quoted in C. J. Wrigley, *The Government and Industrial Relations in Britain 1910–1921*, (1979), p. 5. On rank-and-file movements and syndicalism, see B. Holton, *British Syndicalism, 1900–1914*, (1976); and R. Price, *Masters, Unions and Men*, (1980), pp. 238–67.

For the view that the unrest was a matter of the trade cycle and little else, see H. Pelling, 'The Labour Unrest, 1911–1914,' in *Popular Politics and Society in late Victorian Britain*, (1968). See also E. H. Phelps Brown, *The Growth of British Industrial Relations, 1906–1914* (1959).

52   The general pattern of strikes is most clearly indicated in G. R. Askwith, *Industrial Problems and Disputes*, (1920).

53   Chris Wrigley, *David Lloyd George and the British Labour Movement*, (1976), ch. 3; and also chs. 7 and 8 of this volume.

54   For a useful introduction to industrial relations after 1918, see W. R. Garside, 'Management and Men: Aspects of British Industrial Relations in the Inter-War Period, in (ed.) B. Supple, *Essays in British Business History*, (1977), pp. 244–67.

5

Employers and Managers: Their Organizational Structure and Changing Industrial Strategies

W.R. Garside and H.F. Gospel

The role of the employer and manager in the history of British industrial relations is a rather neglected subject. For the most part, labour historians have focused on the organization and strategies of trade unions; where they have written more broadly about the development of industrial relations this has been largely from the trade union standpoint. Historians of British business, for their part, have concentrated on the organizational and commercial aspects of the business enterprise and have tended to neglect the labour and industrial relations side of business growth and development. Yet *a priori* it might be argued that employers and managers should be given as much attention as workers and trade unions in any history of industrial relations. More empirically, we argue in this chapter that the employers, with their considerable power resources, have played a major role in shaping the British industrial relations system and that trade unions on the whole have reacted to employer initiatives.

There are a number of possible explanations of the relative neglect of the employer–manager side of industrial relations. First, the majority of students of labour history have probably been sympathetic towards, and have preferred to study, trade unions. Second, employers' organizations and firms have tended in the past to be more secretive than trade unions, and less willing to allow access to their records on labour matters. Third, the study of employers' industrial relations policy is plagued with problems of collecting material, for generalization would seem to necessitate drawing on the records of a large number of individual firms as well as on the more conventional sources of labour history.

A further possible reason for the neglect of employers is the notable absence of any systematic body of theory relating to the industrial relations activities of business management compared with that available for the trade unions. Certainly the neo-classical economic theory of the rational profit-maximizing entreprenuer has not proved very useful for examining the actual behaviour of employers. More recently, however, this gap has started to be filled, and economists, sociologists and historians have begun to develop theories of structure and typologies of strategy which could be of use to the historical study of employers. Recent work on the broad administrative structure and organization of business enterprises suggests several lines of approach for examining the structure and organization of management in industrial relations.[1] Much of the work on strategy has centred on the notion of methods of control over workers and work processes. One early typology was that developed by Woodward who identified three basic types of managerial control – 'personal', through direct supervision and the development of managerial hierarchies; 'administrative', based on more impersonal rules specifying required behaviour; and 'mechanical', embedded in machinery and production processes.[2] In the USA, Braverman, writing generally about the development of capitalism, has stressed particularly the way in which employers have constantly sought to reorganize, subdivide, and deskill work.[3] The emphasis was thus placed on the use by employers of technology and work organization to control the labour process. A further American study by Edwards has emphasized the gradual development of employer strategies from 'simple' control by foremen, and by relatively unsophisticated piecework systems, through 'technical' control via machines and methods of work organization, to a 'bureaucratic' stage where employers seek to develop elaborate systems of hierarchies, rules and procedures to control workers.[4] Finally, Friedman in the British context has talked about the strategies of 'direct' control by coercion and close supervision and 'responsible autonomy' where workers are given more say and treated in a more co-optive manner by employers.[5] These various strategies have been placed by their authors in the context of different technologies, labour and product markets, and stages of economic development.

Such conceptual frameworks, though of potential value to historians, cannot be developed in any great detail here, except in so far as later we consider the development of management organization and structure, and the various operational strategies used by employers to control workers and to contain trade unions. The principal

purpose of this essay is twofold: to shift the focus to the employer–manager side of industrial relations, while drawing mainly on
the existing literature of labour history and industrial relations, and
to emphasize the formative role employers and managers played
before 1914 in determining the system of industrial relations in
Great Britain for decades to come.

It is important to understand how employers have organized themselves for the purposes of labour management and industrial relations. This is because stategies are only really intelligible in the
context of organizational structures, and vice versa.

It is customary to think of the nineteenth-century entrepreneur
himself directly employing, supervizing, and controlling his workforce and dealing with trade unions. This was indeed common, but
during the period covered by this essay many entrepreneurs left the
tasks of labour management and industrial relations to others, in
particular to subcontractors, foremen and employers' organizations.
For internal labour management it was usual from the early period of
industrialization onwards to rely on a system of subcontracting.
Under this form of organization, the entrepreneur provided the locus
of production and the machinery, supplied raw materials, and
arranged for the sale and distribution of the product. But the actual
production was under the control or one or more subcontractors
who hired the workers, paid them their wages, supervized the work
process, and received a rate from the entrepreneur for the finished
goods. For the entrepreneur the advantages of subcontracting were
that many of the risks and troubles of production and labour
administration could be transferred to others. For the subcontractor,
the system allowed a man, usually a skilled craftsman or an experienced worker, to operate as a small entrepreneur and to make a
profit out of the difference between the price of his contract with the
capitalist and the wages he paid to the workers.

According to one late nineteenth-century observer, subcontracting was 'practically ubiquitous'.[6] It was prevalent in the building and
civil engineering industries. It was by the subcontract system that the
canals, railways, and large factories and buildings of the nineteenth
century were built. It was widespread in coalmining where the mine
owner usually sank the pit and installed machinery, but where a
subcontractor, or 'butty' as he was often called, would recruit the
miners and organize the labour process. Even in factory industries,

where work was concentrated under one roof, subcontracting was common. It was extensively used in the iron and steel trades; it was to be found in engineering factories; and it was common on a smaller scale in the metal workshops of the West Midlands. In other industries, such as textiles, a related form of labour management, the helper system, existed. Here skilled craftsmen hired their own helpers, supervized them, and paid them out of their wages. Though they had more restricted managerial functions than subcontractors, these master craftsmen relieved the entrepreneur of many labour management functions such as directly recruiting, supervizing, disciplining, and paying large numbers of workers.

The importance of subcontracting began to decline from the late nineteenth century onwards. Different factors operated in different industries, but for the most part the intensification of foreign competition and the need to introduce new machinery and methods of working forced entrepreneurs to cut out the middleman and themselves to introduce more direct forms of management. However, it did not die out altogether and continued well into the twentieth century in industries as diverse as coalmining and vehicle building and remains important today in the construction trades.[7]

Foremen, direct agents of the entrepreneur, had long existed and had often operated side-by-side with the subcontractors. But from the late nineteenth century, they came to take over many of the functions of the subcontractor. The foreman of the late nineteenth and early twentieth centuries, his position symbolized by his bowler hat and watch chain, played a key role in the planning of production, hiring and firing of workers, allocation of work, labour discipline, and the fixing of wages. The foreman was a pivotal character in labour relations at the time, in practice the master on the shopfloor, and the source of many employment rules.[8]

The considerable power of the foreman was to continue largely unchanged up to the First World War and beyond. But in many industrial situations his domain probably reached a peak in the late nineteenth century, and even in the pre-war years there were signs of a gradual diminution of his power and authority. Where trade unions were strong, union rules and collective agreements placed restrictions on his right to hire and fire, to organize work, and to fix rates. However, as much if not more, the reduction in the foreman's power and discretion came because of other pressures on management and the perceived need to develop alternative organizational structures. Influenced by competitive pressures, technological change, and new management ideas, especially in the fields of engineering and accounting, some larger firms were beginning before the war to rationalize their management structures. Higher management saw the need to monitor and discipline their foremen so that they in turn would more closely control those whom they supervized. In some larger firms there was a slow trend to shift various functions away from foremen to central bureaux. Thus selection and dismissal, production planning and quality control, and wage administration started to be parcelled out to specialist departments. In the latter instance the spread of more sophisticated piecework systems resulted in some diminution of the foreman's function of 'driving' control and his ability to regulate wage rates.

An important development in managerial hierarchies before the war was the emergence of the first 'welfare' and 'employment' departments. A few large firms such as Rowntrees, Jacobs, Carrs, Peek Freans, Metal Box, Boots, Reckitts, Colmans, and Lever Bros. had appointed full-time 'welfare workers' employed to deal not only with working conditions and recreational facilities, but also with recruitment, factory discipline, wages, and even trade union negotiations. As early as 1906 the large engineering firm of Renold Chains had established an employment department. Together, these constituted the predecessor of modern personnel and industrial relations hierarchies, though by 1914 there were still fewer than one hundred such specialists.[9]

External to the firm, entrepreneurs also relied on employers' organizations for certain aspects of labour management, in particular for dealing with trade unions. Employers' associations proved to be a main defence against emergent trade unionism in the workplace, as well as an increasingly important source of formal rules governing employment relations. Such organizations had a long history, for as Adam Smith pointed out, 'Masters are always and everywhere in a sort of tacit but constant and uniform combination not to raise the wages of labour above their actual rate . . . Masters too sometimes enter into particular combinations to sink the wages of labour even below this rate'.[10] In the final quarter of the nineteenth century, however, there was an increase in the number of employers' organizations and in their stability, and national federations were established in some of the main British industries, such as cotton, shipbuilding, shipping, footwear and engineering. In part these organizations were a response to the rise in trade union membership and to the 'New Unionism' of the late 1880s. But they were also a reaction to the economic pressures of the time: for as competition intensified and as profit margins were squeezed, employers sought either to take wages out of competition between themselves where this was feasible, or to reduce production costs by keeping a closer control over all aspects of labour costs and by ridding themselves of the practices of the craft unions which impeded the introduction of technological change. In the year immediately before the war there was a further growth in the number and activity of employers' organizations, largely in response to the rise in union membership and the labour conflict of 1910–13. Official figures show that in 1895 there were 336 employers' organizations, by 1898 the number had risen to 675, and by 1914 had increased again to 1487.[11]

Thus, by the First World War the internal and external structure of management organization had taken shape. Internal to the firm the organization of industrial relations management was still very simple, though more bureaucratic systems were beginning to replace the *ad hoc* informal methods of the nineteenth century. External to the firm employers' organizations played an important role in industrial relations and facilitated the development of more sophisticated procedural and substantive strategies.

The organizational developments described above must be seen against the background of a number of major trends: the intensification of international competition during the late nineteenth and early twentieth centuries; the concentration of capital in ever larger companies, and the drive to accumulate more capital; and the spread of trade union membership to new areas of employment. They represented, however, only part of the employers' reactions to the rise of labour and to changing economic circumstances.

The contrast between a relatively large number of sellers in the labour market organized in trade unions and seeking to maximize the basis of their subsistence against the opposition of a smaller number of capital-owning employers equally determined to reduce costs and increase profits lay at the heart of the power struggle within British industrial relations. Employers had long sought to assert their dominance and authority within that power struggle either by opposing organized labour completely or by seeking purposefully to contain and channel its influence. Before the 1890s, employers in general came to recognize that collective bargaining, in essence an institutionalization of industrial conflict, could effectively diffuse the 'tyranny' of the unions if it operated to establish or reimpose managerial authority, so vital in a hostile market environment. To some extent the employers were helped by developments within the trade union movement itself. Although in the mid-nineteenth century employers had readily resorted to the lock-out and to intimidation and strike-breaking to resist workers' demands and to undermine the trade unionist's right to combine,[12] union leaders in later decades came increasingly to recognize the dangers of confrontation and the advantages of co-operation as a means of safeguarding not only the interests of predominantly skilled craftsmen or labourers but also the very survival of the unions themselves. In the 1880s the boilermakers refunded to their employers losses incurred as a result of unofficial strikes or bad workmanship. Officials in building, cotton, coal, iron and engineering increasingly came to assume disciplinary and production functions rather than pose a challenge to the existing relations of production.[13] As a result many employers, with the notable exception of those in railways and shipping, proved more willing than before to enter into various forms of conciliation, arbitration and collective bargaining when they seemed to promise industrial peace, regularity of production and flexible costs of production. The establishment of permanent employers' organizations led to the development of new collective bargaining machinery in a number of industries in the 1890s: these included the 1893 Brooklands Agreement in cotton spinning; the Wages Conciliation Board of the same year in coalmining; the 1895 Terms of Settlement in the footwear industry; and the more famous 1898 Terms of Settlement in engineering. These were followed by similar agreements in building in 1904 and ship building in 1908.[14] The initiative for these agreements came mainly from the employers' organizations which saw them as a means of reasserting managerial prerogatives, constraining trade union activity, and bringing order and stability into their industries.[15]

With product prices falling between 1873 and 1896 employers succeeded in important instances in having industrial relations governed primarily by consideration of the state of trade. The majority of employers and contemporary arbitrators shared the conventional view of political economy, namely that selling prices and market conditions (but not profits) should be the principal determinants of an employer's ability to concede wage demands.[16] Thus the emphasis put upon adjusting wage rate changes in the coal and iron industries according to a sliding-scale of prices allowed employers to respond quickly to changing competitive conditions (a major consideration in the iron industry where idle capital equipment was extremely costly). Fairly rapid and automatic adjustments in total costs could be achieved without necessarily incurring industrial conflict, while employers gained directly in periods of stable or falling prices from any rises in productivity. Employers in cotton textiles, faced with intense international rivalry after 1873, encouraged negotiations with workers' representatives as a way of gaining their support for reductions in unit costs (by increasing work loads) and for the determination of wages according to a mutually acceptable criterion such as the 'standard margin' which could be adjusted regularly to meet the demands of the market.[17] Conciliation, arbitration and selling-price sliding-scales therefore provided employers with the ability to secure long-term wage agreements (incorporating procedural safeguards against disrupted output through direct action) without being obliged to discuss anything outside the realm of wages and prices which might encroach upon their authority.

By the end of the 1880s, however, employers were searching for new patterns of industrial relations. The concessions obtained from employees during the previous two decades, secured largely through their surrender of a separate or special interest in the determination of wages, were often in themselves insufficient to counter new pressures in product and labour markets. Increased competition from technically advanced rivals, especially the United States and Germany, and a cluster of innovations over a wide range of industries including engineering, printing, footwear and clothing threatened existing work practices and wage levels. The squeeze on profit margins during the Great Depression intensified the drive for higher productivity and greater flexibility in methods of work. But the worsening economic and competitive climate coincided with demands for unionism and collective action among the unskilled workers in 'new' unions and for the enforcement of customary notions of 'a fair day's work for a fair day's pay'.

It is no coincidence, therefore, that the 1890s witnessed the growth and consolidation of employers' organizations and federations. The change in the attitude of employers was seen most dramatically in their counter-offensive against 'New Unionism'. They resented what they clearly saw as intimidation, unlawful boycotting and, more especially, the direct challenge by trade unionists to management's right to employ labour – union or non-union, apprenticed or non-apprenticed – as it thought best. Substitute labour was readily employed to defeat strikes in the gas and shipping industries. The Shipping Federation was particularly successful in the early 1890s in using 'free labour' to counteract militancy in the docks,[18] though it was easier to score successes in an industry overstocked with casual labour than it was in more skilled ones such as mining and textiles. The National Free Labour Association, established by employers in May 1893, organized strike-breaking campaigns in the engineering, railway, shipbuilding, and iron and steel industries in a determined effort to defend the existing power structure against an increasingly militant trade union movement. Its success down to 1906, though more psychological than real, nevertheless illustrated the extent to which employers were willing to forego their traditional autonomy and engage in collective action when managerial authority was openly challenged.[19] The overall effects of free labour tactics on industrial relations throughout industry, however, ought not to be exaggerated. Their significance really lies in the context in which they were adopted and pursued.

The employers' offensive was not confined to strike-breaking or directed only towards new and relatively weak trade unions. Exasperation mounted within the craft trades as employers sought to rid themselves of irksome trade union restrictions on output, the supply of labour and methods of work. As described above, they tightened up on the subcontracting and helper systems. They built up their own staffs of foremen, record keepers, 'speed and feed' men, and production engineers. They introduced new piecework and bonus systems intended to circumvent craft controls and to rationalize work systems. Above all, they wished to retain the initiative in production in order to respond effectively to the vagaries of the market. For example, faced with acute labour shortages, building employers steadfastly resisted trade union limitations on apprentices, which they declared in 1898 would 'trench upon the just and inalienable rights of the employer and would be a national calamity'.[20]

Repression was not, however, the only means of exerting control over labour or of securing the initiative in industrial relations. Towards the end of the nineteenth century far more considered and deliberate attention was devoted by employers to new methods of organization and control, and to the more efficient utilization of labour and materials than had prevailed hitherto. In addition, a significant proportion of employers in 'new' and 'old' industries alike welcomed extended welfare provision within the firm and a more positive approach to social reform in general believing that both would help to counter growing domestic and foreign competition by lowering costs through increased labour efficiency.[21] Although co-partnership and profit-sharing schemes might have been introduced with a measure of idealism on the part of some employers, they were on the whole aimed more at preserving managerial prerogatives through incorporative provisions directed especially at binding skilled labour to the firm, containing industrial conflict, and undermining the power and influence of established trade unions. Profit-sharing schemes were introduced in industries as diverse as gas, transport, printing, brewing, building, soap, woollen textiles and ship building, often with anti-union and no-strike clauses.[22] George Livesey, Chairman of the South Metropolitan Gas Company, openly admitted that its profit-sharing scheme was adopted 'to retain or obtain the allegiance of the workmen, which was in fact passing away in the Autumn of 1889 under the influence of the Gas Workers' Union'.[23]

By the turn of the century the employers' immediate situation was strengthened by legal decisions against the trade unions (e.g., Temperton v. Russell 1893; Taff Vale 1901).[24] These decisions coupled with the more hostile aspects of employers' reaction to the 'new unions', appeared to pose a threat to the entire labour movement and thereby inflamed relations between opposing sides in industries relatively untouched by the counter-attack of the 1890s.[25] In the circumstances many employers, anxious to retain their authority, but keenly aware that successful adaptation to market pressures against a background of inferior technology and inadequate re-equipment of industry required the skill, effort and co-operation of trade unionists, encouraged further extensions of formal collective bargaining and disputes procedures. Granting concessions by negotiation in return for adjustments in working practices and the guarantee of stability of production clearly had some advantages over risky attempts to weaken the unions and to replace union by non-union labour.

The problems posed by craft controls and the growth of wage

demands based not on custom but on preconceived ideas of what the market could bear conflicted directly with employers' efforts to reduce unit costs of output and to alter working methods and techniques to their advantage. A lock-out in the cotton industry was settled in 1892 only after employers secured the ability to enforce unilateral changes in working conditions and to impose a maximum limit on the frequency and scale of wage adjustments. The position of union officials as mediators of conflict was enhanced through an elaborate grievance procedure as the employers' authority over production, prices and wages was simultaneously strengthened.[26] Intense foreign competition from Germany and the USA convinced engineering employers of the need to expand the employment of cheaper, less skilled labour to improve technology and, above all, to retain overall control over the management of their affairs. The $6\frac{1}{2}$ months' engineering lock-out of 1897–8 was over what the employers called 'the principle of freedom to employers in the management of their works'.[27] The terms on which the dispute was settled assisted the exercise of managerial authority. They formally established the liberty of employers to man machines as they thought fit, to determine work arrangements, to work virtually unrestricted overtime, and to introduce piecework. The unions, in addition, agreed to accept negotiating machinery which, by strengthening the influence of the unions' national leadership over district committees, seriously weakened the power of local work groups.[28]

Industrial depression and strict legal control over the affairs of trade unions strengthened the employers' position between 1902 and 1906. But there was no recurrence of a major offensive against employees. Disputes in the printing, textile, iron and building trades were quickly settled on terms generally favourable to the employer as depressed market conditions robbed workers of any effective counter-attack. Wage adjustments in the coal, engineering and shipbuilding industries were determined in the main according to prevailing constitutionalism with its emphasis on moderation and the avoidance of open conflict. Some of the unions in turn became increasingly conciliatory as they realized that their survival and growth in key industries and large works depended upon continuing employer recognition.[29] In railways, however, a marked rise from the turn of the century in the ratio of working expenses to gross receipts reinforced further the employers' long-standing resistance to collective bargaining with organized trade unions which they felt could only increase costs against fairly rigid revenues.[30]

Although 1906 witnessed important legal concessions in favour of the trade unions it also ushered in a period of marked disenchantment among the rank and file with the existing methods and achievements of collective bargaining. Employers until then had been particularly successful in restraining workers from exploiting their market situation by encouraging union representatives to agree to fractional changes in money wage rates in line with what employers felt was fair and reasonable in the prevailing economic circumstances. According to Porter, the terms and methods of operation of conciliation boards and agreements effectively limited the bargaining power of employees in the hosiery and lace, iron, footwear, cotton spinning and coal industries. 'A more militant policy would have secured even greater gains,' he writes, 'had the unions not been restricted . . . and had they been able to take full advantage of periods of prosperity.'[31] The failure of money wages in general to keep pace with rising prices during the first decade of the twentieth century marked the first serious halt to rising real wages for at least a quarter of a century. Rapid growth of trade unionism, moreover, had done little to check an unfavourable shift in the share of wages in total income in Edwardian Britain.[32]

1908 saw the outbreak of major disputes in engineering, cotton and shipbuilding. The ship building employers, anxious to meet the demand of a national market for ships but without sufficient scope in a craft-dominated industry to improve efficiency through greater mechanization, turned local disputes into national lock-outs by a series of reprisals during 1907–08 aimed at forcing men to abide by agreements won by their leaders. They demanded the acceptance of a central disputes procedure and agreement that limitations in activity should be reflected in nationally-determined wage adjustments.[33] It was important for employers to contain any growing dissatisfaction within industry which might hinder their competitive position. Trade union growth and activity had encouraged organization among employers, but it was the employers' federations which ultimately wrested the initiative from work groups and unions. According to Clegg they 'forced the unions into industry-wide conflicts in place of the favourite union strategy of picking off one group of employers at a time, and they used their victories to redesign the system of industrial relations to a pattern of their own choice – the central procedure agreement'.[34]

Railway employers finally conceded union recognition in 1907, but only after agreement that disputes over wages and hours should first be handled company by company through the 'usual channels' before recourse to a central board of arbitration, a procedural agreement which provided ample scope for obstruction and delay, without obliging employers to accept industry-wide bargaining.

Mounting industrial unrest during 1911–12 robbed employers in key industries of the power to dictate peace terms to the unions. From the government's point of view, the disputes on the railways and mines posed an intolerable threat to the entire nation forcing the government to intervene directly, in preference to relying on the established conciliation service. The establishment in 1911 of the Industrial Council, equally representative of employers and labour, was a further reflection of the idea that the two sides of industry should seek mutual co-operation through new procedural mechanisms. But fundamental changes were occurring in the climate of industrial relations. Trade union membership increased rapidly during 1911–13 against a background of low unemployment, heightened class consciousness, and a persistent call for a living wage as a first charge on industry. Labour's offensive, moreover, was seen by trade unionists as more likely to succeed if it was deployed on a broad front, and especially if it incorporated the threat of an industry-wide strike in a basic sector. The formation of the Triple Industrial Alliance in 1913 among the miners, railwaymen and transport workers in defence of each other's industrial demands signalled a parallel development, but one whose potential effects on employer strategy were curtailed by the outbreak of war. By then few employers could afford or wished to pursue an exclusively antagonistic or repressive policy towards labour as a matter of principle. But many had resolved also to approach labour in the immediate future with an even greater determination to preserve their power and control and to retain the initiative in industrial relations.[35] As one contemporary observer noted, 'The position just before the outbreak of war was that . . . inroads on the power of management in the shops had become so serious that, had the war not intervened, the Autumn of 1914 would probably have seen an industrial disturbance of the first magnitude'.[36]

The aim of this essay has been to show that an adequate treatment of industrial relations history requires a consideration of the role of employers and managers. It has indicated how employers developed organizational structures and strategies in response to the problems they encountered in the product and labour markets and in the workplace where they were concerned to extract effort from their labour force. Formal trade unionism was, thus, only part of the problem which they faced. At first many tried to exclude unions altogether from their workplaces. But by the end of this period, many employers had concluded that unions could not be permanently ignored. Moreover to defeat unions was becoming increasingly expensive, and a growing number of employers had realized that there might even be advantages in recognizing unions and dealing with them, especially if they could do this on a collective basis through their employers' organizations. There thus developed, in large part on managerial initiative, district and national systems of procedural and substantive rules which added to the more informal framework of internal workplace rules. In this way was laid down the formal system of industrial relations which was to survive into the second half of the twentieth century.

If employers and managers played as formative a role as is suggested here, then there is certainly ample scope for further research. In particular more work needs to be done on the development of organizational structures, especially those internal to the firm, about which we know precious little. In addition, there is also a pressing need for more detailed case studies of a number of industries to discover the extent to which industrial relations did in fact develop on the employers' terms, and to examine the factors which determined the particular strategy employers adopted when faced with advancing technology, a growth in the level and intensity of national and international competition, and changes in the patterns of worker organization.

References

1   See, for example, A. Chandler, *The Visible Hand*, (1977); and L. Hannah, *The Rise of the Corporate Economy*, (1976).
2   J. Woodward, *Industrial Organisation: Behaviour and Control*, (1970).
3   H. Braverman, *Labor and Monopoly Capital*, (1974).
4   R. Edwards, *Contested Terrain: The Transformation of the Workplace in the Twentieth Century*, (1979).
5   A. Friedman, *Industry and Labour*, (1977).
6   D. F. Schloss, *Methods of Industrial Renumeration*, (1892), p. 120.

7   For more information on subcontracting and other forms of labour management, see H. F. Gospel, 'The Development of Management Organisation in Industrial Relations,' in (ed.) K. Thurley & S. Wood, *Management in Industrial Relations*, (1981).

8   *Ibid*. See also J. Melling, 'Non-Commissioned Officers: British Employers and their Supervisory Workers, 1880–1920,' *Social History*, 5, (1980).

9   M. M. Niven, *Personnel Management 1913–63*, (1967) pp. 21–9.

10 A. Smith, *An Inquiry into the Nature and Causes of the Wealth of Nations*, (1976), Book I, ch. 8, pp. 81–2.

11 Public Record Office/Lab.2/427/259/1918.

12 A. Yarmie, 'Employers' Organizations in Mid-Victorian England,' *International Review of Social History*, 25, (1980).

13 E. J. Hobsbawm, *Labour's Turning Point 1880–1900*, (1974), pp. 10–11.

14 For details of these agreements see Board of Trade, *Report on Collective Agreements*, Cd.5366, London 1910. For engineering see below p. 114, refs. 27 and 28.

15 See H.F. Gospel, 'Employers' Organisations: Their Growth and Function in the British System of Industrial Relations in the Period 1918–1939,' London, Ph.D., 1974.

16 During 1873–96 only nine of the sixty-one wage arbitration awards gave advances while thirty-five gave reductions. J. H. Porter, 'Wage Bargaining under Conciliation Agreements, 1860–1914,' *Economic History Review*, 23, 1970.

17 K. Burgess, *The Origins of British Industrial Relations. The Nineteenth-Century Experience*, (1975), pp. 248–9.

18 J. Saville, 'Trade Unions and Free Labour: The Background to the Taff Vale Decision,' in (ed.) A. Briggs & J. Saville, *Essays in Labour History*, (1967). Employers in the Liverpool shipping industry organized themselves independently of other national shipping bodies. Those with otherwise opposing interests joined in an Employers' Labour Association to counteract the aggressive unionism of seamen and dockers. See R. Bean, 'Employers' Associations in the Port of Liverpool, 1890–1914,' *International Review of Social History*, 21, (1976).

19 G. Aldermen, 'The National Free Labour Association. A Case Study of Organized Strike-Breaking in the Late Nineteenth and Early Twentieth Centuries,' *International Review of Social History*, 21, (1976). For details of other 'free labour' organizations, see E. Phelps Brown, *The Growth of British Industrial Relations*, (1959), pp. 164–8.

20 National Association of Master Builders, *Minutes*, 25 January 1898. Cited in H.A. Clegg, A. Fox & A.F. Thompson, *A History of British Trade Unions since 1898, Vol. 1, 1889–1910*, (1964), p. 157.

21 R. Hay, 'Employers and Social Policy in Britain: the Evolution of Welfare Legislation, 1905–14,' *Social History*, 4, (1977); R. Hay, 'Employers' Attitudes to Social Policy and the Concept of 'Social Control, 1900–1920,' in (ed.) P. Thane, *The Origins of British Social Policy*, (1978).

22 See E. Bristow, 'Profit-Sharing, Socialism and Labour Unrest,' in (ed.) K.D. Brown, *Essays in Anti-Labour History*, (1974); S. Pollard & R. Turner, 'Profit-Sharing and Autocracy: The Case of J. T. and J. Taylor of Batley, Woollen Manufacturers, 1892–1966,' *Business History*, 18, (January 1976); R. Church, 'Profit-Sharing and Labour Relations in the Nineteenth Century,' *International Review of Social History*, (1971); J. Melling, 'Industrial Strife and Business Welfare Philosophy: The Case of the South Metropolitan Gas Company from the 1880s to the War,' *Business History*, 21, (July 1979).

23 Melling, *loc.cit.*, p. 169.

24 See ch. 6 of this volume.

25 E. J. Hobsbawm, 'Trends in the British Labour Movement since 1850,' in *Labouring Men*, (1964), p. 336.

26 J. H. Porter, 'Industrial Peace in the Cotton Trade, 1875–1913,' *Yorkshire Bulletin of Economic and Social Research*, 19, (1967).

27 Federated Engineering and Shipbuilding Employers, *Examples of Restriction of Output and Interference with the Working Machines, with Overtime, and the Management of Shops*, (1897).

28 Burgess, *op.cit.*, pp. 60–73. E. L. Wigham, *The Power to Manager: A History of the Engineering Employers' Federation*, (1973).

29 Though in the case of the gasworkers certain groups of skilled men still retained sufficient power within the existing productive process to counteract employers. See E. J. Hobsbawm, 'British Gas-Workers 1873–1914,' in *Labouring Men*, *op.cit.*, Ch. 9.

30 Before 1907 there were no significant developments in collective bargaining within railways as employers steadfastly refused to recognize the unions. The one notable exception was that of the North Eastern Railway Company. G. Alderman, 'The Railway Companies and the Growth of Trade Unionism in the late Nineteenth and early Twentieth Centuries,' *Historical Journal*, (1971).

31 Porter, 'Wage Bargaining under Conciliation Agreements,' *loc.cit.*, p. 475.

32 T. Gourvish, 'The Standard of Living,' in A. O'Day, *The Edwardian Age, Conflict and Stability 1900–1914*, (1979); S. Pollard, 'Trade Unions and the Labour Market 1870–1914,' *Yorkshire Bulletin of Economic and Social Research*, 17, (1965).

33 S. Pollard & P. Robertson, *The British Shipbuilding Industry 1870–1914*, (1979), pp. 162–6.

34 H.A. Clegg, *The Changing System of Industrial Relations in Great Britain*, (1979), p. 66.

35 For details of some aspects of employers' labour activity after the First World War see W. R. Garside, 'Management and Men. Aspects of British Industrial Relations in the Inter-War Period,' in (ed.) B. Supple, *Essays in British Business History*, (1977); G. W. McDonald & H. G. Gospel, 'The Mond-Turner Talks, 1927–1933: A Study in Industrial Co-operation,' *Historical Journal*, 16, (1973); G. W. McDonald, 'Insights into Industrial Politics: the Federation of British Industries Papers, 1925,' *Business Archives*, 38, (1973); H. F. Gospel 'Employers'

Labour Policy: A Study of the Mond-Turner Talks 1927–33,' *Business*)
History*, 21, (1979).

36   J. R. Richmond, *Some Aspects of Labour in the Engineering Industries*,
(1917), quoted in Melling, *loc.cit.*, (1980).

6

Trade Unions and the Law

Kenneth D. Brown

'The old, old story,' grumbled the editor of the *Bee-Hive* in 1867 when the composition of the recently announced Royal Commission on trade unions was made public, 'the wolves sitting on a commission inquiring into the benefits and promotion of the sheep interests.'[1] Yet both the London Trades Council (at this time dominated by the big amalgamated societies) and the London Working Men's Association had urged just such an inquiry on the government. By so doing they hoped to be able to offset the public outcry occasioned by recent revelations of trade union violence and intimidation in Sheffield.

More generally, it was hoped to focus attention on the many inequities and uncertainties still persisting in the unions' legal position. Trade unionists had for some years been agitating against the unfair working of the Master and Servant Laws which deemed that breaking an employment contract was a criminal offence if committed by an employee, but only a civil offence if perpetrated by an employer. Again, the failure of the Combination Laws Repeal Amendment Act of 1825 to offer precise definitions of terms such as 'threat', 'molestation', 'intimidation' and 'obstruction' had left the unions very much at the mercy of judicial whim. The net result of R. v. Duffield (1851) and R. v. Rowlands (1851) appeared to be that while combinations to raise wages were not illegal, virtually all means of exerting pressure on employers were denied. Even the Molestation of Workmen Act in 1859 brought little relief. While peaceful persuasion to quit work was excluded from criminal liability, picketing still remained a perilous business, as London tailors found to their cost in 1867. In R. v. Druitt (1867) Baron Bramwell judged that the tailors, who had organized a thorough but peaceful picket of their masters' shops, were guilty of conspiracy to molest. Finally, in Hornby v. Close (1867) it was ruled that trade union funds were not protected by the Friendly Societies Act of 1859, even if they had registered under it. When the Queen's Bench considered the case, in which the Bradford branch of the Boilermakers' Union was attempting to recover £24 from its absconded treasurer, it agreed that as unions operated in restraint of trade they had no right to the protection of the courts at all. This decision, said William Allan of the Amalgamated Society of Engineers, placed the unions in 'a very different position from what we expected we occupied'.[2] The *Bee-Hive* agreed, saying that it put 'all societies at the mercy of any of their officers or members who may rob them of their funds'.[3]

Despite the paper's doubts about the impartiality of the commissioners, the outcome of their investigations was in fact quite favourable, a tribute to the skilful way in which the dominant union figures had organized their case in conjunction with sympathetic commissioners, such as Thomas Hughes and Fredric Harrison.[4] The Trade Union Act of 1871, which followed the publication of the commission's various reports, laid down that trade unions could no longer be prosecuted for conspiracy in restraint of trade; consequently their funds could not be denied legal protection on the ground that they were illegal. Secondly, section 4 of the Act declared that no court could directly enforce certain named internal union agreements, such as those relating to a member's rights to benefit. Finally, the unions were permitted, if they so wished, to register with the Registrar of Friendly Societies. The government's original intention was to include in the Act a list of defined and proscribed offences. Since these included almost all of the usual techniques by which pressure could be brought to bear on employers and blacklegs, the union response was naturally very hostile. An intensive campaign organized by the fledgling Trades Union Congress persuaded the government to incorporate these recommendations in a second, separate measure, the Criminal Law Amendment Act of 1871. There were many who found in the evidence collected by the commission ample support for the widely held view that trade unions were 'lawless and overbearing' despotisms, and it is not surprising, therefore, that the House of Lords amended this Bill, making it much more stringent.[5] 'Persistently following' and 'watching and besetting' were added to the list of proscriptions, and the offences were to be illegal if done by one or more persons, as opposed to the two or more stipulated in the original measure. The Commons was not inclined to oppose these amendments, since their own discussions took place against the background of the Communard rising in Paris and, according to A. J.

Mundella, society at large was already tending to equate trade union legislation with 'Red Republicanism, Communism and Atheism'.[6] It may be, as a contemporary TUC circular claimed, that the Trade Union Act of 1871 was 'a complete charter legalising trade unions', but the decision to restrict union activity so rigidly by the Criminal Law Amendment Act generated considerable resentment.[7] In the *Bee-Hive's* view the government's action had forfeited any claim it had either to 'merit or gratitude' for the Trade Union Act.[8] Several prosecutions were brought under the Criminal Law Amendment Act and though some were withdrawn and others dismissed, a few resulted in stiff prison sentences. Two months after the Bill became law, the wives of striking colliers each received a week in prison for shouting and banging kettles at a strike-breaker leaving the Navigation Colliery at Mountain Ash in Wales. Farm labourers' wives at Chipping Norton were similarly treated and for an almost identical offence, hooting at – and thus it was ruled intimidating – blacklegs.

Even more disturbing from the unions' point of view was the decision in R. v. Bunn (1872) which neatly side-stepped the protection given by the Trade Union Act. Gasworkers in London had blacked out a considerable part of the capital during a strike. Mr Justice Brett acknowledged that union activity was no longer punishable as a conspiracy in restraint of trade but decided that the gasmen were guilty under common law of conspiracy to coerce. Since the sentences he proceeded to impose were four times the maximum permitted under the Criminal Law Amendment Act there was a justifiable outcry at what the London Trades Council was moved to describe as this new and 'critical legal position'.[9] A number of eminent lawyers, among them such future judges as Henry James, R. Wright and C. H. Hopwood, also questioned the correctness of Brett's judgment, much to the embarrassment of the government. The Attorney General admitted in the House of Commons that Brett's had been a novel interpretation of the law of conspiracy. The Solicitor General went even further, dismissing it out of hand, while the Home Secretary intervened to reduce the sentences to four months. After an amending Bill was shelved by the government in 1872, union resolve to amend the Criminal Law legislation hardened. A second Royal Commission which the government set up in the hope of defusing union hostility was largely ignored by the unions who feared that it was designed to provide a platform for the National Federation of Associated Employers of Labour, a body set up to secure annulment of the 1871 Trade Union Act. Instead, the unions continued to lobby MPs, and when a general election came round in 1874 they gave selective support on a cross party basis to those candidates whose views on the state of labour law were deemed satisfactory. Aspiring members of parliament were doubtless mindful of the fact that the union movement was currently enjoying something of a boom in 1874 with membership reaching 1,200,000, a figure not surpassed until the 1890s. Nor could they have been unmindful of the implications of the wider franchise prevailing since 1867, and which was to help return the first ever working men to parliament in 1874. The conservatives won the election and the new Prime Minister, Disraeli, ignored the recommendations of the Royal Commission. Instead, his government produced the Conspiracy and Protection of Property Act (1875) giving the unions immunity from prosecution for the crime of simple conspiracy so long as a strike was in contemplation or furtherance of a trade dispute. It also provided for the first time some limited protection for peaceful picketing, though it did list a number of specific crimes in connection with it. In the same year the Employers and Workmen Act was also passed, ending workers' criminal liability for breach of employment contracts and making them liable only in civil law.

Here substantially the position remained for several years, the TUC publicly affirming that the 'work of emancipation' was 'full and complete'.[10] Certainly it was now the case that while a trade union's actions might be challenged, its very right to exist was now beyond question. Yet the fact that the next few years saw relatively little legal argument concerning the unions was not so much because the legislation of 1871 and 1875 was foolproof, but rather because union strength and combativity diminished in the face of economic depression after 1874. Legal controversy re-emerged with the resurgence of militancy in the late 1880s.

The match girls' strike in 1888 and the London dock strike the following year triggered an astonishing response. While most attention was focused, naturally enough, on the spread of organization among groups where unionization had so far made little permanent progress, such as gasworkers, dockers, seamen and municipal employees, the older established unions were also expanding. Everywhere it seemed labour was on the offensive, taking advantage of high labour demand to press for better wages, an eight-hour day, and in many cases the very right to organize a union. In these circumstances employers tended at first to give way, but resistance gradually hardened and it was to the courts that they looked to restrict union activity. Thus *The Times* was able to comment in 1895 that 'questions as to labour have of late . . . been more heard of in our Courts than used to be the case'.[11] Although J. Havelock Wilson, the seamen's leader, was successfully prosecuted, the employers met with little initial success, a reflection perhaps of Dicey's maxim that the law tends to follow public opinion, for the first stages of the New Unionism created considerable public sympathy. When the Recorder of Plymouth judged as guilty of intimidation some local trade unionists who had threatened to strike if their employer did not dismiss non-union labour, his decision was overruled by the Queen's Bench. In Curran v. Treleaven (1891), the Bench decided that intimidation must involve actual violence or damange. Another case which was generally held to have implications for the unions was Mogul v. McGregor, Gow and Co. (1892). The defendants were a group of shipowners who set out to destroy competition in the China tea-carrying trade. To this end they reduced freight charges and threatened to boycott those shipping agents who refused to deal exclusively with the group. This, it was ruled, was in order as a lawful activity in pursuit of trade. Applied to trade unions it seemed to imply that even if he suffered economic injury, an employer had no right of action against a union whose members struck against him for taking on non-union labour (so long as no violence or breach of contract was involved). This at least was the view of Sir Frederick Pollock when he appended a memorandum on combination law to the final report of the Royal Commission on Labour (1894). There was, he suggested, no difference in principle between the activities of combinations of employers and combinations of workmen.[12]

Even so, union leaders themselves were worried about certain ambiguities in the law – those relating to picketing. They had first come to prominence during the expansionist phase of the New Unionism since much of the movement's success had hinged very largely on the ability of organized workers to keep out strike breakers. Resolutions demanding changes in the Criminal Law Amendment Act appeared almost annually at TUC conferences after 1891, and William Inskip was voicing a widely held trade union opinion when he claimed at the 1894 conference that the Act was 'so lax that it was construed in almost every case according to the wish, whim, or desire of the judge, who might be interested or prejudicial'.[13] These fears were reinforced when in Lyons v. Wilkins (1897) Mr Justice Byrne argued that picketing was only lawful if it was confined to communicating information. Picketing to persuade to strike, he said, was actionable, a decision upheld in 1899 by the Court of Appeal. In the same year picketing was still further constrained when, in Charnock v. Court, two joiners were found guilty of watching and besetting Irish workers. All they had in fact done was to meet the Irishmen off the boat at Fleetwood and ask them not to break the joiners' strike at Halifax. But the decision effectively appeared to limit the communication of information to letter.

The impact of this verdict was as nothing, however, compared with the next major legal case involving the unions, for Taff Vale was to become a byword in union folklore. The case concerned an action for damages brought by the Taff Vale Railway Company against the Amalgamated Society of Railway Servants. With coal prices high and the local labour market under some pressure due to the call-up of army reservists for the Boer War, the South Wales railwaymen decided to strike in the hope of forcing the company to offer formal recognition to the union. As the Taff Vale line was the critical link between the ports and the steam coal on which both the fleet and the merchant navy depended, the men were in a particularly advantageous position. Their determination was strengthened by encouragement from the militant socialist western area organizer for the ASRS, James Holmes. The company manager, Ammon Beasley, was, however, an equally resolute and tough-minded individual, and he brought an action for damages incurred as a result of the strike. This was rejected by the Court of Appeal on the grounds that unions were not corporations, had no legal personality and could not, therefore, be sued. To everyone's astonishment the House of Lords upheld the Taff Vale Company's claim. Two week later in Quinn v. Leatham (1901) the Lords ruled that the efforts of the Belfast Butchers' Union to prevent meat being purchased from an employer who had taken on non-unionists, constituted a civil conspiracy to injure. Lord Lindley's verdict distinguished between a *warning* or *intimation* to an employer that his men would be asked to strike, and a *threat* that they would be ordered to do so. The latter he argued, was illegal as a civil conspiracy. The doctrine of civil conspiracy had been developed in Temperton v. Russell (1893), a case involving building unions in Hull. They had tried to force a building firm to comply with certain building regulations and the plaintiff, who supplied materials to the firm, was threatened with a strike unless he stopped the supplies. He brought an action against the union officials both as representatives of the union and as individuals. The Appeal Court upheld his action against the officials as individuals both in respect of existing and future contracts which he had been compelled to break because of the union's action. Lord Macnaghten argued that the principles involved in Quinn v. Leatham were identical with those of Temperton v. Russell. The difference, however, lay in the implications of the verdict. As a result of the Taff Vale ruling that unions could themselves be sued, it was the unions' funds, rather than those of individual members or officers, which now lay open to legal claims.

Prior to Taff Vale the assumption had been that because unions were not corporations they could not be sued. The 1871 Trade Union Act had permitted unions to register if they wished, but had not declared, as had been done in the Companies Act of 1862. that on registration a union became a separate legal entity or 'person'. On the contrary, in stipulating that trustees be nominated to hold union funds, the Act seemed to imply that unions were not corporations, since it was usual for trustees to be appointed for unincorporated groups. One member of the Court of Appeal which had overthrown the original injunction granted to Ammon Beasley had argued on precisely this point. 'If a trade union can be sued in its registered name,' he said, 'what is the good of this section expressly enabling the trustees or other officer of the union to sue or be sued in respect of property?'[14] The Royal Commission on Labour had discussed whether unions which did register should be given corporate status, obviously assuming that the 1871 Act had not conferred it. The trade union members of that inquiry had decisively rejected the idea, realizing that it would expose their funds to legal action.

> To expose the large amalgamated societies of the country . . . to be sued for damages by any employer . . . or by any discontented member or non-unionist . . . would be a great injustice. If every trade union were liable to be perpetually harassed by actions at law . . . if trade union funds were to be depleted by lawyers' fees and costs, if not even by damages or fines, it would go far to make trade unionism impossible for any but the most prosperous and experienced artisans.[15]

It is true that civil proceedings had been instigated in Trollope v. London Building Trades Federation (1892) and Pink v. Federation of Trade and Labour Unions (1892) but neither case had been fully defended or taken to the House of Lords. The unions' immunity had apparently been confirmed in Temperton v. Russell in that the plaintiff's action had been brought under the terms of a General Order of 1883 which tried to circumvent the problem of enforcing liability on unincorporated institutions composed of a large number of individuals. The order facilitated use of the device known as the representative action, whereby one or more persons could be sued as representing the whole. But in Temperton v. Russell the Appeal Court had ruled that this did not apply to trade unions and the plaintiff's action was upheld against the unionists only in their capacity as individuals. There was little likelihood of this encouraging other similar actions since even if favourable verdicts were handed down, plaintiffs often found it almost impossible to get any money. Eight months after a firm of plate glass bevellers was awarded £1217 damages against some members of the National Plate Glass Bevellers Union, for example, only £5.00 had actually been recovered. Taff Vale challenged this fundamental assumption that in the exercise of their characteristic functions trade unions were to be treated as a collection of individuals, none of whom was responsible for the actions of any other. Now Lord Macnaghten argued that it was illogical for a union to use its collective resources in a strike and then, when sued, to claim to be only a number of individuals. Further, he added, it was not in the public interest that such powerful institutions as trade unions should be not liable for their actions, and it had not been in parliament's mind in 1871 to create bodies 'capable of owning great wealth and of acting by agents with absolutely no responsibility for the wrong they may do to other persons by the use of that wealth and the employment of those agents'.[16] Lord Lindley concurred:

> I entirely repudiate the notion that the effect of the Trade Union Act, 1871, is to legalize trade unions and confer on them the right to acquire and hold property, and at the same time to protect the union from legal proceedings if their managers or agents acting for the whole body violate the rights of other people.[17]

For some, Quinn v. Leatham and Taff Vale merely confirmed what they had always thought – that the courts were intrinsically biased against working men. Thus, Ben Tillett had claimed in 1895 that British courts were 'centres of corruption and our judges are class creatures and instruments for the maladministration of the law'.[18] W. Mosses of the Patternmakers affirmed at the 1900 TUC conference that he would not 'trust the judges of this country to give a fair and impartial verdict on any question as to the conditions of labour which might be remitted to them'.[19] It would be easy to dismiss such comments as sour grapes, but working men generally were able to play very little part in any legal process and the law therefore remained as a subject of some suspicion.[20] Certainly, there appeared to be a double standard in operation. The decision in Trollope v. London Building Trades Federation (1895) was that for a union to publish the names of firms blacklisted for employing non-union labour represented conspiracy, though the Mogul case referred to above appeared to permit shippers to publish similar blacklists of proscribed firms. Furthermore, the Quinn v. Leatham and Taff Vale verdicts did come at a time when public anti-union feeling was running high. After the initial successes of the New Unionism, many employers had themselves become more resolute in their bargaining, determined above all to reassert their absolute right to hire and fire labour. Something of a counter-offensive developed, particularly in the docks and shipping industries. Well supported by groups such as the Shipping Federation and the Liberty and Property Defence League, this campaign reached its industrial climax in the long engineers' strike of 1897. Thereafter, it was mainly the press and the courts which kept the pot boiling. *The Times* produced its famous series on ca' canny in 1902, and E. A. Pratt kept up the onslaught in *Trade Unionism and British Industry* (1904), in which he maintained that British industry was losing its competitive edge because of the restrictive practices used by the unions.

Yet if there were trade union voices raised to demand that the unions be granted total immunity from all civil actions, not everyone was hostile to the Taff Vale verdict. James Sexton of the dockers reckoned it was a 'blessing in disguise' since it would strengthen central control over 'irresponsible action in localities'.[21] Richard Bell of the ASRS suggested that their previous immunity had been in the nature of a 'privilege' which had been 'taken away from us . . . for abusing it'.[22] He took a strong and consistent line at the 1903 TUC conference.

> He failed to see how they could meet their opponents in the House with an argument for being placed in a position different and apart from all others under the civil law. Having argued that employers should be responsible for all accidents to workmen, no matter by whom or how they were caused, they were now, on the other hand, asking that what-

ever act might be committed, intentionally or deliberately under the rules of an organization by its executive government . . . they should not be responsible for any action thus committed. He thought that illogical.[23]

Thomas Burt, MP had already argued in a similar way, reckoning that unions ought to 'accept responsibility for the action of their agents when their agents were acting by the authority of executive councils'.[24] Clem Edwards, another of the older generation of miners' MPs, recognized that public opinion was against total immunity and advocated a scheme whereby unions would be able to opt for the status of voluntary associations or that of a corporation.[25] The positive advantage to be gained from incorporation was that unions would be able to enter into legally enforceable contracts, including wage settlements with employers, but there was little prospect of Edwards' scheme being accepted since trade unionists in Britain had always preferred to keep the law out of industrial relations as much as possible. Even a socialist like George Barnes of the ASE admitted in private that the unions should be more closely monitored by the law, but he argued for total immunity on the grounds that it made for better propaganda.[26]

Initially at least, it was the moderate view that prevailed within the TUC, partly because it was realized that the conservative majority in the House of Commons would never accept any measure conferring total immunity. Indeed, the appointment of a Royal Commission in 1903 seemed to indicate that the government wished to shelve the matter, certainly for the foreseeable future. Thus the draft Bill drawn up jointly by the TUC, GFTU and Labour Representation Committee, was designed to confer immunity only in those cases where actions had not been expressly authorized by executive officers. When David Shackleton, a member of the Weavers' Union and MP for Clitheroe, introduced this measure, however, he was told by the Speaker that he must drop the clause referring to union liability as it fell outside the scope of the Bill's title, 'A Bill to legalize the peaceful conduct of trades disputes'. This saved the TUC considerable embarrassment when, in 1903, it was decided to press instead for the more radical measure giving the unions immunity against all actions for damages. What changed the TUC's mind was the size of the final Taff Vale settlement – £23,000 – announced in January 1903, and the prospects of even heavier awards being made in a number of other cases where legal action had been initiated by employers. For example, the Glamorgan Coal Company was in the process of suing the South Wales Miners' Federation, and a similar action was pending in another mining dispute at the Denaby and Cadeby Main collieries. Fearful for their funds, the unions moved now to support more strongly the Labour Representation Committee, for it was evident that a more vocal presence at Westminster could greatly assist the campaign for reform of the law. By early 1903 trade union affiliation to the Party had risen to almost 850,000 as against some 350,000 in 1900. As L. T. Hobhouse put it, 'that which no socialist writer or platform orator could achieve was effected by the judges'.[27] Furthermore, the emergence of tariff reform as a major issue in 1903 appeared to threaten the government's unity, and some trade union leaders decided that this was an advantageous situation in which to press for the more radical measure. The resulting Bill, however, was defeated in 1905.

In January 1906, the Liberals were swept to a massive electoral victory which left them with an overall majority of 132 over the Conservatives, Irish nationalists and the LRC. They thus had complete freedom in drawing up their legislative programme. The background to the cabinet's deliberations on a suitable parliamentary measure was provided by the report of the Royal Commission which Balfour had appointed in 1903. It confirmed what most legal experts had been saying since the Taff Vale verdict had first been delivered – that it raised no new issue of principle and was quite consistent with existing trade union law. It pointed out that the immunity which the unions had hitherto enjoyed did not derive from any statute but merely from the impracticability of enforcing liability on a host of defendants; an obstacle now overcome by the device of the representative action. 'No assurance of such immunity has ever been held out, no public Commission as a body has represented that they ought to be exempt; no Government has promised that they would be exempt by forthcoming legislation; and no judge has pronounced that they are exempt.'[28] Accordingly, the Bill which the Liberals proceeded to introduce provided only for a limited protection of union funds. It ran immediately into a storm of protest from the thirty or so Labour members who had been elected to the Commons. At this, Campbell-Bannerman, the Prime Minister, in a speech described by a contemporary as one of 'amazing levity and recklessness', performed a *volte face* and announced that the legislation would, after all, be amended to grant the unions the total immunity which they had been seeking.[29]

It was an extraordinary change of tack and one which was to have a profound effect on the subsequent development of industrial relations in Britain. In one short speech the Prime Minister had thrown over the views of most legal experts, a Royal Commission, and his most senior cabinet colleagues, such as Asquith and Haldane who had favoured the limited immunity proposed originally. Campbell-Bannerman also thoroughly exposed his Attorney General, Sir J. Lawson Walton, who, in introducing the first government Bill, had attacked the Labour demand as a plea for class privilege. 'Do not,' he had said, 'let us create a privilege for the proletariat and give a sort of benefit of clergy to trade unions.'[30] Yet this was precisely what was now proposed, in total contradiction, be it said, of Campbell-Bannerman's own pre-election promises. Opening the Liberal campaign at the Albert Hall in December, he had proclaimed that the purpose of all Liberal legislation, including a Bill to change the law with regard to trade unions, would be to 'promote the welfare and happiness and interest not of any particular class or section of the community but of the nation at large'.[31] The reasons for Campbell-Bannerman's decision to adopt the core of the Labour Bill have remained largely unexplored by historians, perhaps because the lack of direct evidence reduces explanation to the level of speculation in which few have been willing to indulge.

The Times suggested that trade union law was now in such a state of uncertainty that the Prime Minister's concession represented a clean cut and quick way out of the morass. 'There is a desire, widespread and deep, to have done with the state of confusion, the hair-splitting and uncertainty, the unedifying litigation which has been going on for years.'[32] An anonymous writer in the *Quarterly Review* agreed. 'The feeling with which we rise from a consideration of the various legal points on which issue is joined on the controversy between trade unionists . . . and the law of the land, is one of despair.'[33] But why did Campbell-Bannerman opt for this particular solution? The alternative as contained in his own government's original measure would have been equally clear cut and incisive. Perhaps the Prime Minister was sensitive to Labour charges that anything less than total immunity would cause many Liberal MPs to violate their election pledges? This was certainly the view of Campbell-Bannerman's private parliamentary secretary, Arthur Ponsonby. In his personal diary Ponsonby wrote that:

The great error so far was the Trades Disputes Bill, the Asquith-Haldane opinion (it being a legal point) prevailed in the Cabinet. The Lord Chancellor gave in and so did C.B.... The consequence was they inserted a clause which was in direct opposition to the pledges given by three-quarters of the party.... I hope there will be no doubt that the clause as to the immunity of Union funds will be amended in the direction shown by the Labour Bill.[34]

But there must exist some doubt as to whether support for the original government Bill would in fact have involved Liberal members in breaking election promises. Certainly, most of those who had been opposed at the polls by LRC or socialist candidates had affirmed their commitment to granting total immunity. But most Liberals, of course, had *not* faced LRC or socialist opposition and most of these had simply suggested a return to the *status quo*. This was highly ambivalent, however, since the *status quo* was exactly what was in dispute. As one barrister had said, the law was so confused that in the Taff Vale case 'a judge of first instance and the House of Lords ... came to the conclusion that union funds were liable in tort [while] the Court of Appeal came to the diametrically opposite conclusion'.[35] Analysis of election manifestos suggests strongly that most Liberal candidates had in mind a moderate Bill of the sort first introduced by David Shackleton in 1903.[36]

Perhaps Campbell-Bannerman's action sprang from the fact that neither he nor his followers regarded the matter as one of prime importance. It had certainly not been a major Liberal concern during the election campaign. It is noticeable too that the Trade Disputes Act occupies relatively little space in either *Hansard* or the *Annual Register*, certainly when compared with the Education Bill which was the government's primary measure in its first year of office. This is perhaps indicative of how lightly Liberals regarded the matter. Campbell-Bannerman had even referred privately to his own Bill as one of 'two sops for Labour' and in announcing that he was going to accept the principle of total immunity he confessed quite openly that he was not 'very intimately acquainted with the technicalities of the question, or with the legal points involved in it'.[37] It seems that in these matters he was content to be guided by John Burns rather than his own legal officers for whom he had little time, or senior colleagues like Asquith and Haldane. He still had every reason to be wary of the latter; after all it was only a matter of weeks since they had been involved in attempts to manoeuvre him into the House of Lords as a figurehead prime minister. Burns, on the other hand, had been included in the cabinet as the authentic voice of labour. His stock was still high in trade union circles, and it would have seemed strange to ignore his opinion so soon after his appointment. Moreover, Burns had acted for several years as a sort of unofficial adviser to Campbell-Bannerman on trade union and labour affairs, and he was fully conversant with the legal situation since it was he who had organized and led the campaign for the TUC Bill in 1905.[38] In cabinet, Burns' voice was probably loudest of those in favour of conferring total immunity. When the decision was first taken to adopt a limited scheme he wrote in high dudgeon to the Prime Minister: 'I am compelled after what I hear tonight to remind you of what a serious step the Cabinet took when it adopted alternative No. 2. The bold course is to take No. 1 to Lords and then let them throw it out.'[39] Burns, of course, was quite genuine in his desire to secure total immunity for the unions. Campbell-Bannerman, whose career had been marked by a certain sympathy for labour, may well have been equally genuine. If, however, he did calculate that adopting the Labour measure would gain trade union plaudits for the government, but be perfectly harmless because the Lords would throw it out, thereby precipitating the inter-House clash for which many Liberals were hoping, then he came sadly unstuck. Lord Lansdowne, Unionist leader in the upper chamber, certainly had no liking for the Bill, but his party's morale was so low that he had no wish to add to its problems by antagonizing the unions. 'I regard it,' he said, 'as conferring excessive privileges upon one class and on one class only . . . but I also hold that it is useless for us, situated as we are, to oppose this measure.'[40] In the end, too, opposition within the cabinet was overcome. Asquith agreed to support the Prime Minister so long as the immunity being conferred on unions was extended as well to employers' groups. Haldane seems to have kept quiet for reasons of political expediency, for some years later he was to be found putting an interpretation on the 1906 Trade Disputes Act which it was never intended to support.[41]

Thus it was that by Act of Parliament in 1906 peaceful picketing was legalized, and concerted acts adjudged not actionable unless actionable if done by an individual. No trade union activity could be illegal if it induced a breach of contract. Section 4 of the Trade Disputes Act laid down that 'an action against a trade union, whether of workmen or masters, or against any members of officials thereof on behalf of themselves and all other members of the trade union in respect of any tortious act alleged to have been committed by or on behalf of the trade union, shall not be entertained by any Court'.[42] Legal opinion was outraged at the creation of this special class above the ordinary civil law. The most prominent constitutionalist of the day, A. V. Dicey, warned that the Irish nationalists would be able to claim the protection of the Act for their boycotting activities. This was perhaps not altogether unfounded since in negotiating for John Redmond's support for the TUC's Bill in 1905 Burns had offered this possibility as an inducement.[43] Neither Dicey nor Burns, it seems, put much store on the Attorney General's argument that this was impossible as the 1876 definition of a trade union excluded agrarian combinations. Other leading legal figures who attacked the Bill included Lord Lindley and John Westlake, Professor of International Law at Cambridge since 1888.[44]

It could be argued, as Professor Phelps Brown has done, that the Liberal Act merely recognized what had been the *de facto* if not the *de iure* situation since 1871.[45] That it was not the *de iure* situation seems indisputable. Certainly, the framers of the 1871 Act had deliberately refrained from bestowing corporate status on the unions, but they had never considered the possibility that a union might be sued by anyone other than its own members, and it is certain that they had no intention of placing unions above the law. If union immunity was the *de facto* situation this had arisen not so much because of any general understanding to this effect, but because the question had not really risen until the climate of industrial relations deteriorated in the later years of the nineteenth century. When the question did arise in the Taff Vale case the decision represented a logical application of the law of representative action which had really developed *after* the passage of the 1871 Trade Union Act.

It is tempting to see the pattern of industrial relations in Britain at this time as a reflection of the unions' legal position, with a diminution of strikes following the Taff Vale verdict and a rise in unrest when the Trades Disputes Bill came into effect after 1906. But this is something of an oversimplification since the number of strikes had begun to fall even before Taff Vale and the tempo did not really pick up again until 1910. Besides, the Belfast dock strike of 1907 showed that there were still difficulties in interpreting those parts of the Trade Disputes Act which dealt with picketing. When Jim Larkin addressed a strike meeting on the quayside he contravened a harbour bylaw which banned all unauthorized meetings in the harbour area. In his defence he cited the picketing provisions of the 1906 Act but Lord O'Brien (Larkin v. Belfast Harbour Commissioners (1908)) ruled that it 'was never intended to authorize as a matter of right . . .[46] entry against the will of the owner into a place of business'.[46] Nor is there much evidence that the unions actively sought to capitalize on their recently won statutory freedom. Despite claims to the contrary, they had sought – and received – not a charter to facilitate all out offensive industrial action, but rather a safeguard against employers who wished, for whatever reason, to circumvent or ignore the normal processes of unfettered collective bargaining. The unions had always preferred to keep the law out of their affairs, but the Trades Dispute Act of 1906 was the only means by which their ultimate sanction in such bargaining, the right to strike, could be protected. Hardly any union would have dared strike at all if legal action could be taken against it. It may not have been a good or very equitable law but it did ensure that collective bargaining could be meaningful, and conducted between parties of more or less equal standing.

That legal opinion was far from happy at the implications of the legislation is seen in the way that the judges and House of Lords attempted to use the other notorious Edwardian trade union case, ASRS v. Osborne (1910), to impose some form of quasi-corporate status on the unions. The case involved the attempt made by W. V. Osborne to prevent his union (once again the hapless ASRS) from raising a capital levy on members in order to support Labour members of parliament. While several different arguments were used by members of the various courts through which the case passed on its way to the House of Lords, the main one was that political activity was *ultra vires* for a trade union. This was the thrust of the Lords' final decision. Under existing law a company established by statute had its powers and functions defined by Act of Parliament. A registered company, on the other hand, defined its own objectives in its constitution. In 1905 the House of Lords had applied *ultra vires* doctrine to the case of the Yorkshire Miners' Association v. Howden. Howden's claim that the union should not provide strike pay was upheld on the ground that a union was like a registered company, and the payment of strike pay was not specifically mentioned in its constitution. But the same tribunal now found for Osborne by arguing that political activity lay outside the purposes of a trade union *as defined by statute* in 1871 and 1876, though Lord Halsbury, among others, specifically argued that those measures had constituted 'as it were a charter of incorporation'.[47] This failure to pursue the analogy of the registered company as used in YMA v. Howden was doubly anomolous in that the Registrar General had already accepted the legitimacy of trade union political activity as a result of Steele v. South Wales Miners Federation (1907). The practical implications of the Osborne verdict were two: benefit funds came under threat since these were not mentioned in the defining statutes of 1871 and 1876: sixteen Labour MPs lost their salaries and few trade unionists were enthusiastic enough to provide much voluntary support. Of the Engineers' 117,000 members, for example, only 5000 were willing to pay a voluntary levy of a shilling per head to support the union's MPs. Eventually, in return for Labour's support of the controversial National Insurance Bill, Asquith (who had replaced the ailing Campbell-Bannerman in 1908) introduced a measure for the payment of MPs. In 1913 the government also steered through a Trade Union Bill which permitted unions to use their funds for political purposes if a majority of the members agreed, and dissenters' rights to contract out were guaranteed.

It is true, as Philip Snowden remarked in his memoirs, that the Osborne case did not excite trade unionists to anything like the same extent that Taff Vale had done.[48] This was hardly surprising as the earlier case had threatened the very existence of trade unionism whereas Osborne threatened only the financial security of the Labour Party which a majority of trade unionists probably did not support anyway. Yet the peers' ruling did feed the suspicions of those who had always maintained that the British legal system was inherently prejudiced against the interests of the working classes. Undoubtedly there were biased judges but it is difficult to sustain the view that generally in the years 1875 to 1914 the vagaries of the unions' legal position was the outcome of fluctuating fortunes in the class struggle in which the law was an instrument of capitalism. Rather, those vagaries reflected the difficulties of a judicial and political framework striving to adjust to the demands of institutions potentially as powerful as parliament itself. The real problem, as one contemporary observed, was that trade unionism 'as a distinct and fundamental conception, has never found its true place in our political and juridicial systems'.[49]

References

1 *Bee-Hive*, 6 April 1867.
2 *First report of the Commissioners appointed to inquire into the organisation and rules of trades unions and other organisations together with minutes of evidence, British Parliamentary Papers*, 32, (1867), p. 42.
3 *Bee-Hive*, 19 January 1867.
4 Harrison later wrote that the opposition 'was well supplied with facts and figures by the masters' agents, but not nearly so well supplied as we were by Applegarth, Howell and Allan, the Union Secretaries'. F. Harrison, *Autobiographic Memoirs* (1911), I. p. 322.
5 Anon., "First second and third reports of the Commissioners appointed to inquire into the organisation and rules of trades' unions and other associations together with the minutes of evidence', *Edinburgh Review*, 126, (1867), p. 457.
6 Quoted in W. H. Fraser, *Trade Unions and Society*, (1974), p. 191
7 G. Howell, *Labour Legislation, Labour Movements and Labour Leaders*, (1902), p. 188.
8 *Bee-Hive*, 22 April 1871.
9 Quoted in K. Wedderburn, *The Worker and the Law* (Penguin ed., 1971), p. 311.
10 Quoted in H. McCready, 'British Labour's Lobby, 1867–75,' *Canadian Journal of Economics and Political Science*, 22, (1956), p. 160.
11 *The Times*, 29 July 1895.
12 See J. Saville, 'Unions and Free Labour: the background to the Taff Vale Decision', in (ed.) A. Briggs & J. Saville, *Essays in Labour History*, (1967), pp. 340–3.
13 Quoted in H. Clegg, A. Fox & A. Thompson, *A History of British Trade Unions since 1889*, (1964), p. 307.
14 N. A. Citrine, *Trade Union Law*, (1970 ed.), p. 149, n. 73.
15 Quoted in E. H. Phelps Brown, *The Growth of British Industrial Relations* (1965), p. 194.
16 K. Wedderburn, *Cases and Materials on Labour Law*, (1967), p. 542.
17 *Ibid.*, p. 544.
18 Dock, Wharf, Riverside and General Workers Union, *Annual Report for 1895* (1896), p. 11.
19 TUC, *Annual Report* (1900), p. 77.
20 See generally on this theme H. Pelling, 'Trade Unions, Workers and the Law', in H. Pelling, *Popular Politics and Society in late Victorian Britain* (2nd ed., 1979).
21 Quoted in Clegg, Fox & Thompson, *op. cit.*, p. 319.
22 Quoted in F. Bealey & H. Pelling, *Labour and Politics, 1900–1906* (1958), pp. 74–5.
23 *The Times*, 10 September 1903.
24 *Ibid.*, 6 February 1903.
25 C. Edwards, 'Should Trade Unions be Incorporated?', *Nineteenth Century*, 51, (1902), pp. 233–51.

26 See his letter to S. Webb quoted in Pelling, *op. cit.*, p. 81.
27 Quoted in P. Clarke, *Liberals and Social Democrats*, (1978), p. 139.
28 Quoted in D. F. MacDonald, *The State and the Trade Unions*, (1976 ed.), pp. 55–56.
29 Anon., 'Trade Unions and the Law,' *Quarterly Review*, 204 (1906), p. 498.
30 *Hansard*, 4th series, CLIV, 28 March 1906.
31 *The Times*, 22 December 1905.
32 *Ibid.*, 30 March 1906.
33 Anon., *Quarterly Review*, 204, pp. 488–9.
34 A. Ponsonby, Diary, 16 April 1906, *Ponsonby Papers*, Bodleian Library MS Eng. hist. c. 653, f. 11.
35 H. Cohen, 'Total Immunity of Trade Union Funds,' *Fortnightly Review*, 80, (1906), p. 929.
36 For this analysis, see A. K. Russell, *Liberal Landslide*, (1973), pp. 71–2.
37 For his private reference, see H. Campbell-Bannerman to H.H. Asquith, 21 January 1906, Bodleian Library, Asquith MSS Vol. 10, f. 200. For his public statement, see J. Wilson, *A Life of Sir Henry Campbell-Bannerman*, (1973), p. 505.
38 Thus Burns' Diary, 16 February 1903, Burns Papers, BL Add MSS 46321. 'Called on C-B and advised him as to speech on Unemployed, Taff Vale, etc.' See also *ibid.*, 24 February 1905. BL Add MSS 46323.
39 J. Burns to H. Campbell-Bannerman, 26 March 1906, *ibid.*, Add MSS 46282, f. 30.
40 Quoted in Clegg, Fox & Thompson, *op. cit.*, pp 60–1.
41 As Lord Chancellor in 1913 he argued that Section 4 of the Trade Disputes Act drew a distinction between a union and its trustees, and rendered the property of a union liable, as suggested in Taff Vale, for tortious acts committed on its behalf. Actions, he suggested, could be brought against the trustees. This has been described by Citrine as 'an absurdity which the legislature could never have intended'. Citrine, *op. cit.*, p. 493.
42 MacDonald, *op. cit.*, p. 61.
43 Burn's Diary, 24 February, 27 February and 10 March 1905, Burns Papers, BL Add MSS 46323. See also a note in Burns' writing, dated 6 March 1905 describing the changes demanded by Redmond as the price of his support. *Ibid.*, BL Add MSS 46308, f. 73.
44 See Westlake's speech reported in *The Times*, 19 November 1906; and Lindley's article in *ibid.*, 10 December 1906.
45 Phelps Brown, *op. cit.*, pp. 297–98.
46 Citrine, *op. cit.*, p. 457.
47 C. Drake, *Labour law* (1969), p. 238.
48 P. Snowden, *An Autobiography* (1934), I. p. 223.
49 J. H. Greenwood, "Trade Unions and the Law,' *Westminster Review*, 176, (1911), p. 613.

7

The Government and Industrial Relations

Chris Wrigley

Lord Penrhyn . . . said: 'This is my private affair; it is my business.' The Board of Trade said that it was not his business alone, where the rights of three thousand men were concerned. It was not his business when there was nothing between ten thousand people and famine but the charity of their sympathetic countrymen (cheers). 'My property', 'my affairs!' Lord Penrhyn's economic and political creed seemed to be an exhaltation of the possessive pronoun. 'My property', 'my private affairs', 'my men'. No they were not (cheers) . . . it was time that they taught those Lords that there was not a man in the country who suffered from wrong or injustice, but that it was the affair of every man in the country to right it (cheers). That theory of 'private affairs' was an old one but, in the present age of enlightenment, civilization and humanity, it was exploded (applause). (Lloyd George, 1897)[1]

By the late nineteenth century the idea that major strikes and lock-outs were a purely private matter was one which was being seriously challenged in governing circles. Whilst Penrhyn's views were shared by many employers at the end of the century, they were not the orthodoxy that they had been earlier in the century; and, indeed, amongst some employers they were a source of embarrassment when put so bluntly.

Earlier in the century ministers had deplored the thought of government interference in industrial disputes in much the way Penrhyn did at the end. Thus in 1829, Sir Robert Peel refused to allow government involvement in a textile dispute on the grounds that even an expression of government opinion would be 'the commencement of an interference in matters of private concern to be greatly depre-cated'.[2]

In the 1820s and 1830s Tory and Whig ministers had vied with each other to be the most vigorous denouncer of trade unionism. In 1825 Peel had proclaimed the trade union system of delegation to be 'an excessive and infamous tyranny' and to be 'in complete contrad-iction of any notion of free trade'. Lord Melbourne in 1831 recalled that when he succeeded Peel as Home Secretary he was warned by Peel, when they discussed the state of the country, that the national and general unions were 'the most formidable difficulty and danger with which we had to contend; and it struck me as well as the rest of His Majesty's servants in the same light'.[3] In office, as Home Secretary and then Prime Minister, Melbourne was much taken to fulminating against the 'gross injustice and blind tyranny' carried out by the trade unions[4]; yet by his own savage actions in 1834 he transformed seven Dorset labourers into 'the Tolpuddle Martyrs' for their trade union activity.

By the last quarter of the nineteenth century attitudes to the trades unions had mellowed amongst most leading political figures. The trade unionism of the quarter century after Chartism was dominated by craft unions in trades which were relatively thriving (unlike the trade unionism of the 1820s and 1830s which at times was dominated by embattled declining trades) and its aspirations could be accommodated in the political system of the period. This trade unionism did not directly threaten the personal interests of the predominantly landed political establishment; whereas in the 1830s the upswing in trade unionism had spread as far as agriculture and at the time of the trial of the Tolpuddle Martyrs it was frequently asserted by landowners that tough sentences were needed to stop trade unionism snowballing amongst farm labourers (indeed the judge told the Martyrs that their actions were 'calculated to shake the foundations of society').

Craft trade union leaders, George Odger and George Potter alike, were willing to work within the framework of the mid-Victorian political system. Their trade unionism became one interest amongst the many interest groups which operated on the Liberal side of politics, even though they received repeated rebuffs and humiliations from those middle-class men who dominated local Liberal organizations. The way that some trade unions, like non-conformist bodies, put their organizations at the disposal of the Liberal Party at election time aroused the envy of Conservative politicians.[5] Naturally the attitude to trade unionism of Liberal leaders, nationally and locally, changed. It was difficult for them to welcome trade union support at popular demonstrations for Reform, Italian unification or for whatever was the popular cause of the time, yet condemn the unions' aims out of hand.

Also, as the nineteenth century went on, an increasing number of employers, especially those running large enterprises, found that trade unionism could bring a certain amount of stability into labour relations and into their own and their rivals' labour costs. By the time of the 1868 Royal Commission on Trades Unions thirty-one of forty-seven trade societies and branches which submitted answers to it claimed to have some measure of recognition from their employers.[6] In some industries employers were happy to work with the unions on joint boards and committees to adjust wage rates without conflict; a practice which could have benefits for both sides, but frequently appears to have reduced the gains the workers would have made in good times if they had resorted to strikes or threats of strikes.[7] So by the final quarter of the century trade unions were a fact of life in some sectors of the economy.

Also governments in their role as employers were made aware of trade union attitudes. From the 1860s the trade unions had some success in pressing governments to respect trade union standards. When, in 1861, the building of the Chelsea barracks was disrupted by the London building strike, trade unionists were successful in getting stopped the use of sappers of the Royal Engineers to continue the work. Similarly the use of troops for harvesting during agricultural disputes was ended in 1873. In the Royal Dockyards in 1882 demarcation lines between shipwrights and fitters were disregarded until the trade unionist MP, Henry Broadhurst, managed to get dockyard policy changed.[8] The last two decades of the century were marked by trade union successes in getting the London County Council, other county and local authorities, and various government departments to adopt 'fair wages' policies.

However, for all this, politicians in office remained disinclined to get involved in settling industrial disputes. The stronger side in disputes resented compromise which it felt robbed it of outright victory. In the nineteenth century this was usually the employers. Employers when faced with strong trade unions joined together to deal with the unions, using 'the document' (a form pledging the worker to renounce trade unionism and which had to be signed before work was given), concerted lock-outs and 'free labour'. If they went to others, they turned to the courts not the government.

However industrial disputes could always lead to violence. Here governments continued to play their traditional role as the providers of law and order. Law and order involved protecting employers, property and 'free labour' – so in practice police and troops were always used against discontented workers and their families. Thus in 1893 troops were sent to Hull to protect blackleg labour brought in by the employers to break a strike in the port, and later in that year to quell unrest amongst locked-out miners at Featherstone, Yorkshire, an occasion when three miners were shot dead. In the second half of the nineteenth century, whilst there could be local violence during disputes, turbulent industrial relations did not threaten the whole social order.

Nevertheless, bitterness in industrial relations, of course, spread bitterness in the wider community. As Britain industrialized, and as the numbers of persons affected by disputes grew, politicians found major strikes and lock-outs worrying. Autocratic behaviour by some employers could be seen as undermining acceptance of authority at the workplace – and likely to lead to an undermining of social discipline generally. Hence arbitrary actions by major employers seemed less and less defensible as purely private matters. With the extensions of the franchise in 1868 and 1884 there was a greater likelihood that more Members of Parliament would be aware of the sufferings of the families of men involved in industrial disputes.

Governments had to take more notice of industrial disputes when they affected the economy. Trials of strength in industries required organization on both sides. It is estimated that as late as 1910 only one-fifth of the labour force was affected by collective bargaining; but as British trade unionism was heavily concentrated in certain industries (notably mining, textiles, metals, engineering and building) these were areas where major clashes could take place. By the second half of the nineteenth century with the spread of industrialization, the widespread use of steam power and the coming of the railways, the British economy was becoming increasingly interdependent: a national mining strike or a national rail strike would have widespread economic repercussions. Hence two of the earliest disputes to cause governments major concern for the economy were the 1893 coal lock-out and the threatened 1907 national rail strike.

The 1896 Conciliation (Trade Disputes) Act was a permissive piece of legislation whereby the Labour Department of the Board of Trade could offer conciliation if one party to a dispute asked it to intervene and arbitration if both parties asked.[9] Whilst that which it empowered to be done was hardly revolutionary, it nevertheless was symbolically significant. It was a much clearer recognition than anything that had gone before that the state had a duty to be concerned about industrial relations and not to view such matters as being private affairs. Previous Acts which had dealt with conciliation and arbitration (notably those in 1824, 1867 and 1872) had been ineffective.[10]

The 1896 Act was passed by Lord Salisbury's Conservative and Unionist government and aroused no real controversy at the time. After $3\frac{1}{2}$ decades' experience of *ad hoc* arbitrations and of local boards of arbitration and conciliation in various industries, many employers and politicians were ready to accept the Board of Trade being endowed with powers to act in this way. So frequently had eminent men been called upon to act on an *ad hoc* basis in the 1860s and 1870s that one editor in 1875 had referred to there being an 'arbitration craze'.[11] Arbitration and conciliation boards had attractions to many employers. They removed much of the unpredictability out of labour relations. At the boards industrialists were often successful in pressing the case for moderating wage claims on such grounds as the lower labour costs of foreign competitors. As with sliding-scales the net effect may well have been to lessen labour's gains in times of economic prosperity. Overall, the result may have been, as Vic Allen has argued, that 'trade unionism was contained and disarmed at a significant stage of its growth'.[12] Such considerations in favour of the 1896 Act were reinforced by the majority report of the 1891–4 Royal Commission on Labour which favoured the Board of Trade offering conciliation and arbitration,[13] and the actual practice of the Board of Trade in intervening before it was given statutory powers for such action.

Hence it is not surprising that there was no uproar at the time of the 1896 Act's passage. Such opposition as there was to its operation, that is to government activity in trying to settle disputes, was more often than not expressed in Parliament from the Conservative benches; whereas those calling for government activity in industrial relations were more likely to be found amongst part of the Radical wing, or from the Imperialist wing of the Liberal Party. In the 1890s many Liberals were coming to see a liberal-capitalist society requiring state intervention to mitigate class war and industrial strife and thereby help to stabilize it.[14]

The 1896 Act was similar to proposals put forward in 1893 by A. J. Mundella, the then Liberal President of the Board of Trade. Mundella himself had been a major figure, perhaps the major figure in initiating and popularizing arbitration boards, starting with a famous success in a dispute in the hosiery trade in Nottingham in 1860. Mundella represented a very different strand of radicalism from that of men such as John Bright or Henry Fawcett; the latter not only was hostile to trade unions but deplored state intervention in industry and society generally.[15] Mundella, a self-made wealthy hosiery manufacturer, was associated with trade union and labour causes throughout his parliamentary career. He consistently tried to bring both sides of industry together, arguing that there should be an identity of interest between masters and men; he sought to substitute a balance between capital and labour within a prospering capitalist economy for class conflict.[16] During his first spell as President of the Board of Trade, Mundella had set up a statistical bureau to collect and publish labour statistics for labour as well as trade statistics for industrialists. In his second period as President (1892–4) the statistical bureau was transformed into a separate Labour Department, with special staff at the centre and thirty local correspondents and the funds to publish the *Labour Gazette* in order to publicize the information. The Labour Department was to be the administrative body most involved in government interventions in industrial relations before the First World War.[17]

Mundella was also involved in settling the great coal lock-out of 1893, which was notable for being the first time a government intervened to end an industrial dispute. Gladstone intervened when the coal lock-out had lasted from July to November and was seriously threatening to cause major disruption to other industries and to put domestic coal supplies for the winter in jeopardy. There had been various attempts at conciliation, involving distinguished people including mayors and Mundella himself. Gladstone, however, formally invited both sides to a conference 'under the chairmanship of a member of the government', suggesting Lord Rosebery, then Foreign Secretary and soon to succeed Gladstone as Prime Minister. The conference took place on the 17 November and a settlement was reached that day. This success was another factor in preparing the way for the 1896 Conciliation Act.[18]

Some writers have expressed surprise or found it paradoxical that such an intervention should have taken place first under Gladstone. Obviously the exigencies of the situation largely determined the matter. However Gladstone was generally pragmatic in such matters. He himself had acted as an arbitrator in industry – in a railway demarcation dispute on routes in the Sheffield area in 1857. He had

had previous experience of the problems arising from a dislocation of coal supplies. In the winter of 1872–3 a shortage of coal had also brought factories to a standstill and caused serious problems for domestic users. Then, in February 1873, Gladstone had at first refused an inquiry, but a fortnight later his government reversed the decision and a Select Committee had been appointed.[19]

Moreover in the latter part of his career Gladstone showed some measure of sympathy for trade unionists. In contrast to John Bright, whose attitude to the role of trade unions remained dismissive, Gladstone's view did moderate somewhat with time. Gladstone was impressed by the 'respectable' craft trade unionists of the 1860s, who embodied self-help and thrift. His meeting in 1864 with a deputation from the Amalgamated Society of Engineers which wanted him to modify the rules of Post Office Savings Banks so that they could deposit union funds in the safe-keeping of the government has been seen as one event helping to convert him to a further major extension of the franchise. Whilst in 1875 he could still rebuke a deputation of striking miners for committing an offence against liberty in demanding a closed shop, by the late 1880s he was shocking many Liberals by his attitude to the New Unionism. Thus, speaking of industrial relations to his constituents in 1890, he asserted, 'where it has gone to sharp issues, where there have been strikes on one side and lock-outs on the other, I believe that in the main and as a general rule, the labouring man has been in the right'.[20] With regard to industrial relations, as in many other areas, Gladstone's attitudes were complex; but here, as in other matters such as Ireland and railway legislation, there was a shift in his concern from simply aligning himself with the views of the propertied interests directly concerned.

Under the 1896 Act government intervention in industrial disputes depended on the agreement of both sides to accept its mediation. Such mediation was accepted quite often in the late 1890s; indeed in the case of the 1895 lock-out by boot manufacturers such action by the Board of Trade (in the form of Sir Courtenay Boyle, the Permanent Secretary) helped to resolve a major dispute ahead of the legislation.[21] However, many employers were fearful of what might be conceded during such mediations. In spite of Lord Rosebery's success in November 1893, apparently the coal owners were unwilling to have him further involved as he had been willing to bring into the discussions the issue of minimum wages in the mines.[22]

The fact that governments could easily be rebuffed in their efforts to settle disputes under the 1896 Act was highlighted by the controversies concerning Lord Penrhyn's tyrannical treatment of his quarrymen. In 1879 the Conservative President of the Board of Trade, C. T. Ritchie, was humiliatingly rebuffed when, having been approached by the quarrymen's union, he wrote to Lord Penrhyn offering to arrange a joint conference. Lord Penrhyn informed Ritchie that 'my acceptance of it would establish a precedent for outside interference with the management of my private affairs'. The Permanent Secretary of the Board of Trade could do no more than reply,

> I am to state that there is no desire to press the matter against your wishes, but I am to point out that in view of the provisions of the Conciliation Act, the Board cannot admit that the settlement of a prolonged dispute affecting some thousands of men and their families, can be rightly regarded as a matter of private interest only.[23]

Trade unionists and Radicals were enraged by Penrhyn's intransigence both during the 1896–7 and the further 1899–1903 strikes of his quarrymen. They felt frustrated by the fact that under the existing legislation the state could not coerce him. This was well expressed by Lloyd George at a meeting of the Festiniog quarrymen in 1897. He complained,

> Both political parties in the country had admitted the injustice and necessity of the Conciliation Act of 1896. When the Act had been brought before the House of Commons there was not a voice raised against it. Even when it went to the Lords, of whose House Lord Penrhyn was a member, no one expressed dissent from it, not even Lord Penrhyn. The principle of the Act was admitted upon all sides. Very recently that huge corporation, the London and North Western Railway, took steps which the men resisted and, though that Company employed considerably more thousands of men than Lord Penrhyn ever did, its directors preferred to submit the matter to the Board of Trade rather than risk a strike. The consequence was that peace was restored in a day.[24]

Lord Penrhyn's rebuff made Presidents of the Board of Trade exceedingly wary of political interventions in industrial disputes for nearly a decade. The Conservative Presidents anyway were very receptive to the views of management, and in particular to the view that labour relations should be left to management. Under Gerald Balfour, Ritchie's successor, the Board of Trade was markedly more notable for its concern for the interests of big business.[25] The scale of Board of Trade interventions in industrial relations did not increase markedly until Lloyd George and his Liberal successors took over.

The Liberal Government, which took office in December 1905, was faced with the threat of a national rail strike in 1907 and a wave of industrial unrest after 1910. In this period the number of interventions by the Board of Trade increased and it made a substantial contribution to the settlement of industrial disputes.[26]

David Lloyd George, President of the Board of Trade from 1905–08, achieved a major political success in 1907 when he personally intervened to avert a national rail strike.[27] Such a strike would have threatened large sectors of British industry. As a result there was widespread support for the government intervening. Thus *The Economist* in October 1907 propounded the rule, 'Railway strikes and railway lock-outs cannot be permitted. They are contrary to public policy', and the journal called for Board of Trade intervention and, if this failed, Parliament should arrange compulsory arbitration.[28]

In intervening, Lloyd George was careful to guard himself against a political humiliation such as Ritchie had suffered in dealing with Lord Penrhyn. Having arranged an informal meeting with some of the railway directors, Lloyd George wrote to Campbell-Bannerman, the Prime Minister, advising him,

> It is too early to put the Conciliation Act into operation but there is a real danger of a strike being rushed owing to the ill-advised insolence of the directors – witness their dismissal of union officials – unless something is done at once to get into contact with them. Before I meet them I want your sanction as to the general line of action which I should suggest should be pursued . . . in the event of my being met with a blank refusal to negotiate.

Lloyd George argued that if the directors refused conciliation then, 'We must, when Parliament meets, at once introduce a measure making arbitration in railway disputes compulsory in all cases where the Board of Trade consider the nature and magnitude of the dispute warrants such a course being adopted.' Lloyd George concluded by commenting,

> Bell [the Secretary of the Amalgamated Society of Railway Servants] cannot hold back his men unless I can assure him that the government mean to take a strong line on the distinct condition that there is no strike before Parliament meets. The Conciliation Act is a poor thing. It broke down hopelessly in the Penrhyn case. It is only the knowledge that there is something behind it that will induce the directors to pay any attention to it.[29]

He received the Prime Minister's support. Lloyd George further strengthened his hand during the negotiations by getting *The Daily Mail*, on the 29 October, to publish an article demanding compulsory arbitration for railway disputes.

Whilst the resulting Railway Conciliation Scheme went further than the tougher directors wanted, it did not give direct union recognition and it appears to have been very close to proposals put forward by the management side. The scheme had major advantages for the railway companies, as Lloyd George pointed out in a speech when he received the Freedom of Cardiff in January 1908:

> From the point of view of the railways, the important thing is that for seven years, at any rate, you are guaranteed that you will have no great labour trouble. It gives what is above all important to capital, and through capital to industry – a sense of security. It is insecurity that disturbs a market and, when you have that sense of security railway companies will be able to make their plans and appeal to the markets to back them up with the development of their plans. From that point of view, it has undoubtedly been a great settlement.[30]

Lloyd George certainly reaped a rich political harvest from it; this success probably being the major factor in ensuring he succeeded Asquith as Chancellor of the Exchequer. For once he even received regal approval. Lord Knollys informed Campbell-Bannerman, 'Mr Lloyd George appears to have done admirably in connection with the railways' dispute. I believe the Railway Boards think so, and Sir William Lewis told me the other day that he [Mr. L. G.] was acting absolutely impartially and with no bias towards the men'.[31]

Whilst the railway dispute was his great success, Lloyd George also intervened in other disputes during his time at the Board of Trade. In early 1907 Lloyd George had been tempted to make 'a sensational appointment' in the London music hall strike which was attracting major press coverage. However, when T. P. O'Connor declined, the Board of Trade appointed George Askwith, who had frequently acted for it since 1897 and later in the year was to join it as a civil servant.[32] After the railway dispute Lloyd George successfully intervened in a dispute concerning the cotton spinning unions in Oldham and less successfully in an engineering strike on the Tyne.[33] Such interventions had none of the political drama of the rail dispute, but they nevertheless helped to consolidate acceptance of government intervention in industrial disputes.

Lloyd George put great store on conciliation to promote social harmony. In March 1908 he said in a speech, 'in my judgment, the era of strikes and lock-outs is – or, at any rate, ought to be – over. They really do not settle the justice or injustice of any point in dispute'. He observed:

> There is no trade in which, if you get a dispute, you will not find a whole link of other industries involved, which suffer in consequence. I was amazed, when I went to try to settle the cotton dispute . . . to find the innumerable trades, great and small, which would suffer. In a dispute of this kind, who suffers? Unskilled labour, very often unorganized, with no great funds, where a week out of work means poverty and privation.[34]

Winston Churchill, his successor at the Board of Trade, at that time was also a warm advocate of conciliation to avoid industrial strife. Both he and Lloyd George were in favour of state control of major services, including the railways. Electioneering in Dundee in May 1908, Churchill declared his view of the role of Liberalism to be 'grand, beneficent and ameliorating':

> It is in the nice adjustment of the respective ideas of collectivism and individualism that the problem of the world and the solution of that problem lie in the years to come. But I have no hesitation in saying that I am on the side of those who think that a greater collective element should be introduced into the state and municipalities. I should like to see the state undertaking new functions, stepping forward into new spheres of activity, particularly in services which are in the nature of monopolies. There I see a wide field for state enterprise.

Within this framework he expressed the hope that this form of liberalism would be able to win working-class support. He told his audience, 'Labour in Britain is not socialism' even if socialists received trade union funds.

> But trade unions are not socialistic. They are undoubtedly individualistic organizations, more in the character of the old guilds, and lean much more in the direction of the culture of the individual than in that of the smooth and bloodless uniformity of the mass. Now, the trade unions are the most respectable and the most powerful element in the labour world. They are the social bulwark of our industrial system. They are the necessary guard-rails of a highly competitive machine.[35]

Like Lloyd George, Churchill was concerned at the lack of teeth in the 1896 Conciliation Act. Soon after entering office, he instructed his officials to draw up possible legislation which would give the government stronger powers to intervene in disputes which were deemed to threaten the public interest. The proposals put forward by Llewellyn Smith, involving the appointment of a court of inquiry and a cooling-off period whilst recommendations were made and considered, resembled a piece of Canadian legislation, the Lemieux Act. This idea was abandoned after consultations with both sides of industry.[36]

Churchill instead had to satisfy himself by developing the existing conciliation procedure. On September 1908, he prepared a memorandum for Chambers of Commerce, employers' associations and trade unions which explained the proposed workings of a Standing Court of Arbitration which he was setting up. Churchill carefully explained that,

> It is not proposed to curtail or replace any of the existing functions or practices under the Conciliation Act, nor in any respect to depart from its voluntary and permissive character ... But the time has now arrived when the scale of these operations deserves, and indeed requires, the creation of some more formal and permanent machinery.

His Court of Arbitration was to be made up of people drawn from three panels – one of 'persons of eminence and impartiality', one of employers, and one of 'workmen and trade unionists'. Churchill argued that this would be a means of 'consolidating, expanding and popularizing the working of the Conciliation Act'.[37] Before the First World War a few courts were established under this system, but widespread use of this method only took place in the latter part of the war.[38]

However, Churchill's interventions in disputes, like Lloyd George's, strengthened the moves towards the establishment of boards of conciliation in industry. Between Lloyd George's success in the 1907 rail dispute and the end of 1909 sixty-seven new boards were set up.[39] In the case of the cotton industry, Churchill made considerable efforts to get both sides to agree to a new sliding-scale agreement. In March 1909 at a Board of Trade conference called to discuss 'the advisability of the adoption of some equitable scheme for the future automatic regulation of wages', he deplored the 'succession of crises' of the previous five years and urged that they arrive 'at some scientific basis for avoiding these periodical crises'.[40] However, in this case nothing came of his moves for the employers were unwilling to concede anything of substance.[41]

Churchill was succeeded at the Board of Trade by Sidney Buxton in February 1910. Buxton was no heavyweight in national politics. The fact that he did not intervene boldly in disputes as Lloyd George and Churchill had done was partly a reflection of his personality and partly his views. When he addressed the 1911 Industrial Council, a body which he hoped would become a national conciliation board, he said:

> One disadvantage of the existing system is undoubtedly that it brings into action and prominence the Parliamentary Head of the Board of Trade, who is necessarily a politician . . . and a member of the government, in disputes and conciliations which ought to be purely industrial. It has been my policy, and, I hope my action, during my two years at the Board of Trade to efface as far as possible my personality as a political President, and I believe my department has won the confidence of the public and of the two industrial sides to a remarkable degree. At the same time I realize that, if the action of the department in these matters could be still further removed from the sphere of politics or the suspicion of politics, it would give even greater confidence, and there would be greater willingness by the parties to a dispute to seek the assistance of the Board of Trade. The President cannot, of course, dissociate himself from all responsibility, and in certain circumstances the Government may have to intervene as a last resort.[42]

In expressing these views Buxton was in line with the views of his senior civil servants. Under Buxton, the Board of Trade continued to be successful in solving increasing numbers of disputes without political interventions. Askwith, backed from 1911 by his own separate department devoted to dealing with labour unrest, intervened successfully himself in several major disputes before the First World War. Interventions by non-political figures did avoid political embarrassment for the Liberal Government and did lessen the dangers of one or other, or both, sides of disputes taking political offence.

However, the pressures which had forced government intervention in past disputes were very much present in the 1910–14 labour unrest. Several of the disputes threatened the economy, many of them threatened public order, and in some cases they even appeared to endanger the stability of society.

The severity of the pre-war industrial unrest ensured that many disputes were discussed by the whole cabinet. In March 1910 Buxton reported to it that there was a serious danger of strikes in the South Wales and the Northumberland and Durham areas over the working of the recent Eight-Hours' Act. He informed them:

> The Board of Trade are doing their utmost to promote the ascendancy on both sides of conciliation counsels, but the men show a disposition to repudiate the pacific advice of their own leaders. If an arrangement

becomes impossible, there is a real danger of a general strike throughout the coal fields of the country, which would be a national calamity.

A week later he could report that 'through his own intervention and that of his staff the parties to the coal dispute had been brought into conference' and that a settlement was expected.[43] Later in the year the strike of miners working for the Cambrian Combine in South Wales erupted into violence, involving police action in Tonypandy and later the sending in of troops to the area. This strike was settled in 1911 with the assistance of George Askwith.[44]

However, whilst the Cambrian Combine dispute still dragged on, industrial militancy broke out amongst seamen and dockers.[45] As strikes spread amongst transport workers in the summer of 1911, ministers became restive at leaving disputes to the Board of Trade. In July in the cabinet, Churchill called for 'a careful inquiry, perhaps presided over by the Prime Minister, into the causes of and remedies for these menacing developments of industrial unrest'. Three weeks later the main question before the cabinet was 'the formidable industrial situation which has arisen in London. It was agreed that the government must assume responsibility in the last resort for the food supply of London'. In resolving the London dock strike, Sidney Buxton was aided by John Burns.[46]

However, when the unrest spread naturally from the ports to the railways, Asquith and then Lloyd George intervened. The threat of a national rail strike led to Asquith, accompanied by Buxton, offering the railway union executives a Royal Commission to investigate the working of the 1907 conciliation agreement. Asquith was brusque – and the trade union leaders rejected his offer and called the strike. The strike had an immediate major impact – and Lloyd George convinced his colleagues that the government needed to be more conciliatory. Lloyd George was successful in bringing pressure to bear on the employers to make concessions and in settling the dispute.[47]

The national coal strike of 1912 was the most serious dispute that the Liberal Government had to face.[48] With the strike called for 1 March 1912, Asquith, Lloyd George, Sir Edward Grey (the Foreign Secretary) and Buxton had separate conferences with masters and men at the Foreign Office on 20 February. These and subsequent meetings were of no avail and the strike took place. After a fortnight the cabinet agreed that if talks failed to produce a solution then it would have to take legislative action. Later in the month the government was forced to bring in legislation whereby a minimum wage could be fixed. This led to the ending of a strike which revealed clearly the power of organized labour in putting pressure on a government. It also revealed the growing gulf between it and the Liberal Party. Moreover, as Lloyd George observed during the strike: 'Asquith's declaration for a minimum wage sounded the death-knell of the Liberal Party in its old form.'[49]

In April 1912, after the coal strike was settled, Asquith set up a cabinet committee on industrial unrest under Lloyd George. At a cabinet meeting on 16 April he urged,

> the desirability in view of the existing unrest in the industrial world, and of the possibility of serious trouble in the near future in the transport and distributive trades, of at once appointing a small cabinet committee, which would see and discuss matters with representative men among both employers and employed, with the object, if possible, of preventing the stoppage of work, and of taking in advance such precautionary measures as the situation, actual or prospective, may seem to require. Their work would be a useful preliminary to the more general and comprehensive investigation of the whole problem which the cabinet must shortly undertake.[50]

The record of this committee's attempts to intervene in disputes was a poor one. It became involved in the transport strike of 1912, which was centred on the Port of London. Lloyd George, Haldane, McKenna, Buxton, Simon, Burns and Elibank were all involved in trying to settle the dispute. At one stage, to George Askwith's scorn, 'five ministers began interviewing both sides, or, rather, different sections of both sides, but without the slightest effect'.[51] Lloyd George accompanied by other ministers, got a deputation from the Transport Workers' Federation to accept a joint conciliation board on 31 May, but the employers refused to accept it and a national strike was called. Lloyd George and Haldane wanted to settle the strike by legislation dealing with wages in the Port of London. Asquith and the cabinet refused to do this, and the settling of the strike was passed on to the Industrial Council. This the cabinet could do with safety as the strike was doomed to failure. According to Askwith, after this ministerial failure, 'The Prime Minister was so annoyed that he gave strict orders that ministers, even the President of the Board of Trade who, if any minister should intervene, was the proper minister to intervene, were to leave industrial disputes alone and not mix themselves up with them'.[52]

This may well be true. However, the impetus for such interventions diminished after 1912. There were no major disputes to threaten the economy in the way that the 1907 and 1911 rail disputes and the great 1912 coal strike had done. In 1911, when industrial unrest had been especially menacing, the government had set up the Industrial Council which was intended to bring together all those on both sides of industry who shared the ideal of 'the substitution in the industrial sphere of co-operation for antagonism in the relations between employers and employed.'[53] This was to be the first of several such bodies established in time of acute industrial unrest which brought together centre opinion; the Whitley Committee and the National Industrial Conference of 1919 were similar responses and, as with the Industrial Council, the government's interest in them evaporated as the pressure on the existing social structure lessened.

Overall however, under Campbell-Bannerman and Asquith, government intervention in major industrial disputes became accepted and, indeed, expected. In 1911 Buxton observed, 'It is generally recognized now that industrial disputes are not merely the concern of the parties who are immediately involved, and the question is not whether the state should interfere more in trade disputes but what form should their [sic] interference take'.[54] That this should be the case was a measure of the growing power of organized labour and its determination to see that profit levels should no longer be the major criterion for fixing wage rates and working conditions.

Government legislation other than the 1896 Conciliation Act, of course, also had an impact on industrial relations. The most notable was the 1906 Trade Disputes Act which undid the harm done to the legal position of the trade unions by the Taff Vale and other court decisions.

In the House of Commons Campbell-Bannerman conceded more than his cabinet had wished, must to the chagrin of the lawyers who had wanted to provide limited exemption of trade union funds.[55] There was also opposition to the legalization of peaceful picketing. Indeed, before the Bill was introduced the King informed Campbell-Bannerman that 'he trusts sincerely it will not include a clause allowing what he thinks is rather absurdly called "peaceful picketing", as if it could be ensured that any form of picketing could be free from occasional acts of violence, and at any rate of constant intimidation'.[56] Whilst the Act was criticized at the time, substantial opposition to it was only mobilized during the wave of strikes of

1910–14, when there was much pressure for counter legislation.

The Liberal Government, especially in its early days, made many small concessions to labour. Herbert Gladstone, commenting on the Home Office's activities in these years, recalled, 'The presence for the first time in the 1906 Parliament of men directly representing labour, including Lib-Lab members, numbering nearly seventy, was a valuable stimulus to inquiry and effort'.[57] After taking office, the Liberal Government was quick to recognize the Post Office Trade Union, something which the Balfour government had refused to do. It also conceded a wider coverage in its Workmen's Compensation Act than it had first intended, including domestic servants amongst the six million persons added to the 1897 Act.

Much of the legislation affecting working conditions received vehement opposition from at least some employers. Thus, in the case of Joseph Chamberlain's 1897 Workmen's Compensation Act, there was strong criticism from Liberal as well as Conservative spokesmen in Parliament. One Liberal coal owner commented, 'There was more socialism pure and simple in the Bill than in any Bill which had been submitted for the last half century'.[58] In operation the provision proved to be far from revolutionary, indeed many workmen had to resort to litigation to get their rightful compensation.

Yet the effect of such measures and of the Liberal Government's social reforms was to make for a more efficient, more contented labourforce. The government and employers wanted to stabilize society and industrial relations – and the removal of gross injustices at work and at home was a major way to do this. The Liberal social reforms were in line with a strand of management thought of increasing influence. Some employers were themselves bringing in various welfare provisions in order to hold scarce labour or to enhance its efficiency. Similarly one element in the Liberal reforms was a desire to make the labour market less anarchic and make British labour more efficient. In matters such as old age pensions and national insurance, benefits could be withheld if the working person could be deemed to have behaved unworthily. Moreover, at work the amelioration of working conditions helped to lessen the tendency to support militant trade unionism or to resort to violence. Moderate trade unionism was encouraged by joint boards and by co-partnership schemes.[59]

Thus Churchill's Trades Board Act of 1909 was aimed at preventing sweating in the tailoring, paperbox making, lace and chainmaking trades. However, trade boards were also seen as a means of preventing violence in the trades concerned. Thus the Balfour Committee's Report in 1926 commented, 'while strikes on a large scale are beyond the capacity of such workers, sporadic outbursts, which in the aggregate may not be negligible, are likely to occur among them, and the existence of Trade Boards tends to reduce or even extinguish the likelihood of such outbursts'. Moreover, the fixing of minimum wages, which in employers' eyes became standard wages, made it very hard to unionize the workforce.[60]

However, some of the increased state activity, intentionally, or unintentionally, helped the spread of trade unionism. There is not just the controversial involvement of the trade unions in operating the 1911 National Insurance Act, which, whatever else, certainly helped greatly to expand trade unionism amongst such groups as shopworkers. Government decisions helped white-collar unions in the Post Office and the civil service. Other government regulations had effects in various industries. Thus the Mines Regulation Act of 1887 had safety clauses concerning length of work experience for faceworkers which could be used to exclude blackleg labour.

Government legislation resulted from a wide variety of pressures. Within capitalism there is a wide division of interests; divisions between the interests of money and of industry, and divisions within industry. In some areas vested interests combined against others – most notably in the case of the railways. Here other employers pressed the government to regulate railway rates – and increasingly after 1870 the government came to intervene in regulating not only rates but working conditions[61] The subject of general government legislation and its effect on industrial relations deserves a book to itself to explore the nature of the legislation and the conflicts of interest behind such legislation.

Historians have a strong tendency to see things evolve, for things to develop in a similar way to that in which Parliament was seen to evolve by the Whig historians of the past. Anyone searching for a clear line of developing cabinet policy towards strikes before 1914 is likely to have a hard task. Government intervention, especially from 1910–14, was very much on an improvised basis. Little was learnt from previous experiences.

The manner of government intervention owed much to the character and political stature of the President of the Board of Trade. Men such as Lloyd George and Churchill were keen to display themselves as men of action and were not slow to publicize their actions. Their basic outlook was in line with that of Mundella. They were eager advocates of conciliation and firm believers in bringing both sides of industry together. Both Lloyd George and Churchill believed in efficient, competitive, capitalist enterprise and felt that the bulk of trade unionists could be won to their point of view.

In periods of major labour unrest government action was in part motivated by a desire to be seen to be doing something. The Salisbury Government, faced with the successes of the New Unionism in 1889–90, set up the Royal Commission on Labour, which completed its activities in 1894 after that challenge of labour had faded. Similarly, the Asquith Government's motivation in setting up the National Industrial Council was in part, as Buxton observed at the time, to reassure those alarmed by the strikes of 1910–11 that something was being done; once the threat of these strikes diminished the Council was increasingly disregarded by the government.

Government involvement in industrial disputes was a profoundly costly matter for Liberals. On the whole Liberals looked for a balance between labour and capital and saw rights and duties on both sides; whilst the more advanced Liberals went further, being keen to attack landlords and unearned wealth generally. Many Liberals in the early years of the twentieth century saw their party as a national not a class party and as one which was concerned with efficiency in industry. Class conflict was inimical to the Liberals and would polarize their support away from them. Sir Lewis Harcourt in 1902 warned against the 'principle of Government interference in strikes' as it involved the government in taking one side or the other.[62]

This became a very serious problem for the Liberals in the 1910–14 period. George Dangerfield in his *The Strange Death of Liberal England*[63] was right in respect of seeing the industrial unrest of this period being damaging to the Liberals to an extent well beyond anything that had happened before. Askwith in a cabinet paper of July 1911 observed:

> It looks as though we are in the presence of one, of those periodic upheavals in the labour world such as occurred in 1833–4, and from time to time since that date, each succeeding occurrence showing a marked advance in organization on the part of the workers and the necessity for a corresponding change in tactics on the part of employers.[64]

The militancy of labour in 1910–14 greatly alarmed many employers.[65] They demanded tough action, including the repeal of the
1906 Trades Disputes Act. At the time of the 1906 Act's enactment
lawyers not employers had been most vocal in opposition to it – and
there had been no employers' campaign to prevent its passage.
Though the Liberal Government rescued the employers from trouble
in the 1912 coal strike, they were not grateful. Thus one coal owner,
who had wanted to fight the matter out with his men, wrote to his
friend Walter Runciman, 'If you were not our MP I would not vote
Liberal at the next election'.[66]

Liberal interventions in strikes did not please the strikers either.
Government action in sending in troops to strike areas usually
caused widespread resentment. Thus in 1893, when troops were sent
into the colliery districts of South Wales at the time of the coal
hauliers' strike, local indignation was made known to the Liberal
MPs and to Keir Hardie. Tom Ellis, then junior government whip,
was informed:

> A mass meeting of the inhabitants of Pentre was held today to protest
> against the importation of the military into the district. All classes were
> present and it was felt as an insult to our humanity, loyalty and Christian-
> ity. There is *no disturbance — perfect order* is maintained. The police
> inspector was very much surprised to see the military.
>
> The meeting strongly urged you to take steps to have the military
> *recalled*. They are not wanted in the Rhondda. They always create
> disturbance and the experience in Wales ought to convince the
> Authorities that we require them not.[67]

This was nothing compared with the bitterness engendered by
police action and, later, the sending in of troops in the Rhondda in
1910. As Kenneth Morgan has observed, 'Tonypandy joined Peter-
loo, Tolpuddle and Featherstone in the people's martyrology'.[68]

In 1910–14 when labour was in a strong position, governmnt
intervention was frequent and it was aimed at moderating labour's
gains.[69] The strikers' enemies increasingly became not just the employers but also the government. In this context socialist and syndicalist arguments were likely to make many converts. Government intervention in this period, as in the post-war unrest and the General
Strike, raised many questions about the role of the state; especially
whether or not, as Liberals liked to see it, it was above classes and
was in some strange way a neutral unbiased body that would dispense justice to all impartially.

References

1   *Rhyl Recorder and Advertiser*, 9 January 1897.
2   N. Gash, *Mr. Secretary Peel*, (1961), p. 602.
3   *Ibid.*, p. 350. Sidney & Beatrice Webb, *The History of Trade Unionism*, (revised ed., extended to 1920), (1920), pp. 138–9.
4   P. Ziegler, *Melbourne*, (1976), pp. 155–62.
5   For example Lord Salisbury in the 1880s; see P. Marsh, *The Discipline of Popular Government*, (1978), p. 185.
6   W. H. Fraser, *Trade Unions and Society*, (1974), pp. 99–103 & 223.
7   J. H. Porter, 'Wage Bargaining under Conciliation Agreements 1860–1914,' *Economic History Review*, (1970) pp. 460–75.
8   S. & B. Webb, *op.cit.*, pp. 247, 332–4, & 353.
9   On this measure and its working see ch. 8; and R. Davidson, 'Social Conflict and Social Administration: The Conciliation Act in British Industrial Relations,' in *The Search for Wealth and Stability*, (ed.) T.C. Smout (1979), pp. 175–97.
10 On these see Lord Amulree, *Industrial Arbitration in Great Britain*, (1929), pp. 46–88; and I.G. Sharp, *Industrial Conciliation and Arbitration in Great Britain*, (1950), pp. 280–9.
11 Quoted from *Capital and Labour*, 27 October 1875 by V. L. Allen, 'The Origins of Industrial Conciliation and Arbitration,' in *The Sociology of Industrial Relations*, (1971), p. 69.
12 *Ibid.*, p. 82.
13 For brief surveys of the Royal Commission see E. H. Phelps Brown, *The Growth of British Industrial Relations*, (1959), pp. 181–5; and P. S. Bagwell, *Industrial Relations*, (1974), pp. 95–99.
14 D. A. Hamer, *Liberal Politics in the Age of Gladstone and Rosebery*, (1972), p. 231.
15 Leslie Stephen, *Life of Henry Fawcett*, (1886), pp. 156–60, 403 & 405.
16 W. H. G. Armytage, *A.J. Mundella 1825–1897: The Liberal Background to the Labour Movement*, (1951); R. Harrison, *Before The Socialists*, (1965), pp. 34–9; Hamer, *op.cit.*, pp. 13–18.
17 V. L. Allen, *Trade Unions and the Government*, (1960), pp. 47–56; and R. Davidson, 'Llewellyn Smith, the Labour Department and Government Growth 1886–1909,' in *Studies in Nineteenth-Century Government*, (ed.) G. Sutherland, (1972), pp. 227–62.
18 Lord Askwith, *Industrial Problems and Disputes*, (1920), p. 76. For further details of the coal lock-out see ch. 9, pp. 200–02; and H.A. Clegg, A. Fox & A. F. Thompson, *A History of British Trade Unions Since 1889: Volume 1 1889—1910*, (1964), pp. 106–08.
19 H. C. G. Matthew (ed.), *The Gladstone Diaries*, vol. 5 (1978), pp. 187, 216, 237 & 266. A. J. Taylor, 'An Earlier Coal Crisis: High Prices and Absenteeism in 1873,' *Manchester Guardian*, 1 February 1951, p. 4.
20 K. Robbins, *John Bright*, (1979), pp. 18 & 221; P. Magnus, *Gladstone*, (1954), pp. 161 & 232; M. Barker *Gladstone and Radicalism*, (1975), pp. 92–4.
21 On this intervention and the background to the dispute, see A. Fox, *A*

History of the National Union of Boot and Shoe Operatives 1874–1957, (1958), pp. 217–37.

22   J. E. Williams, 'The Miners' Lock-out of 1893', in Society for the Study of Labour History's *Bulletin*, 24, (1972), pp. 15–16.

23   *House of Commons Debates*, 4th series, Vol. 45, 1897, col. 694.

24   *Merioneth News*, 7 January 1897.

25   R. Davidson, 'The Board of Trade and Industrial Relations 1896–1914', *Histoical Journal*, 21, 3, (1978), pp. 577–8.

26   See ch. 8 on this.

27   On the background and the resulting settlement, see P. Bagwell, *The Railwaymen*, (1963), ch. 10; G. R. Askwith, *op.cit.*, ch. 13; C. Wrigley, *David Lloyd George and the British Labour Movement*, (1976), pp. 50–8; and also ch. 11 of this book.

28   19 October 1907, pp. 1754–5.

29   Lloyd George to Campbell-Bannerman, 19 October 1907; Campbell-Bannerman Papers, British Library Add. Ms. 41,240, ff. 105–8.

30   *South Wales Daily News*, 25 January 1908.

31   Knollys to Campbell-Bannerman, 7 November 1907; Campbell-Bannerman Papers, British Library Add. Ms. 41,208, ff. 105–6. Sir W. T. Lewis, a prominent Cardiff colliery owner, had been involved in the negotiations. Lloyd George praised his advice in his Cardiff speech.

32   On this see Lord Askwith, *op.cit.*, ch. 11; and E. Halévy, *The Rule of Democracy 1905–14*, (1934), pp. 106–7.

33   On these see C. J. Wrigley, *op.cit.*, pp. 58–9.

34   *Ibid.*, pp. 59–60.

35   14 May 1908, in W. S. Churchill, *Liberalism and the Social Problem*, (1909), pp. 156–7.

36   E. Wigham, *Strikes and the Government 1893–1974*, (1976), p. 22.

37   R. S. Churchill, *Winston S. Churchill*, Vol. 2, Companion Part 2, (1969), pp. 836–8.

38   Askwith, *op.cit.*, p. 127.

39   Phelps Brown, *op.cit.*, pp. 311–15.

40   R. Rhodes James (ed.) *Winston S. Churchill: His Complete Speeches*, Vol. 2, (1974), pp. 1181–3.

41   J. L. White, *The Limits of Trade Union Militancy*, (1978), pp. 82–4; and ch. 10 of this book.

42   Cited in Askwith, *op.cit.*, p. 183.

43   Asquith's Cabinet Reports to the King, 23 and 30 March 1910; Asquith Papers, Bodleian Library, Vol. 5, ff. 202–4.

44   On Askwith's role in the South Wales strike see Askwith, *op.cit.*, pp. 143–5; and in more detail D. Evans, *Labour Strife in the South Wales Coalfield 1910–11*, (1911), chs. 7 & 8.

45   For an analysis of the causes of the wave of strikes of the period see J. E. Cronin, *Industrial Conflict in Modern Britain*, (1979), pp. 99–109; and also ch. 4 of this book.

46   Asquith's Cabinet Reports to the King, 21 July and 11 August 1911; Asquith Papers, *op.cit.*, Vol. 6, ff. 58 & 66; K.D. Brown, *John Burns*, (1977), pp. 163–5.

47 For the details see P. Bagwell, *Railwaymen*, ch. 12; and C. J. Wrigley, *op.cit.*, pp. 62–5.
48 For the details see ch. 9 of this book; R. P. Arnot, *the Miners: Years of Struggle*, (1953), pp. 57–86; and C. J. Wrigley, *op.cit.*, pp. 67–73.
49 To Riddell, 2 March 1912; Lord Riddell, *More Pages from My Diary, 1908–1914*, (1934), p. 42.
50 Asquith's Cabinet Report to the King, 16 April 1912; Asquith Papers, *op.cit.*, Vol. 6, ff.131–2.
51 Askwith, *op.cit.*, pp. 223–4. Askwith's comments on ministerial interventions, especially those by Lloyd George, are usually unduly vitriolic. This is partly because of his own outlook as a successful conciliator, and partly due to bitterness arising from being ousted from his government position at the end of the First World War. When his book was published in 1920 he was leader of the Middle-Class Union. However with regard to the efforts of this committee in 1912 there is more justification for his scorn than on some other incidents.
52 *Ibid.*, p. 230.
53 On the Industrial Council, see R. Charles, *The Development of Industrial Relations in Britain 1911–1939*, (1973), Part 1.
54 In a memorandum, 'Conciliation and the Board of Trade', 9 August 1911, CAB 37/107.
55 On this, see ch. 6 of this book; J. A. Spender, *The Life of the Right Hon. Sir Henry Campbell-Bannerman*, Vol. 2, (1923), pp. 277–80; and G.W. Keeton, *A Liberal Attorney-General*, (1949), ch. 10.
56 Lord Knollys to Campbell-Bannerman, 13 February 1906; Campbell-Bannerman Papers, *op.cit.*, Add. Ms. 41,207, ff. 48–9.
57 In his typescript memoirs; Herbert Gladstone Papers, British Library, Add. Ms. 46,118, f. 133.
58 J. L. Garvin, *The Life of Joseph Chamberlain*, Vol. 3, (1934), pp. 155–9.
59 On this see, J. R. Hay, *the Origins of the Liberal Welfare Reforms 1906–14*, (1975); and his 'Employers' Attitudes to Social Policy and the Concept of Social Control 1900–1920,' in *The Origins of British Social Policy*, (ed.) P. Thane (1978); and J. Melling's work in this area, stemming from his University of Glasgow Ph.D. Thesis, 'Employers and Industrial Welfare in Britain,' (1980).
60 D. Sells, *The British Trade Boards System*, (1923); and K. G. J. Knowles, *Strikes: A Study in Industrial Conflict*, (1952), pp. 92–3.
61 See G. Alderman, *The Railway Interest,* (1973); and T. R. Gourvish, *Railways and the British Economy, 1830–1914*, (1980), ch. 7.
62 Hamer, *op.cit.*, p. 230.
63 Published New York, 1935; London, 1936.
64 'The Present Unrest in the Labour World,' 25 July 1911; CAB 37/107, and widely cited.
65 H. V. Emy, *Liberals, Radicals and Social Politics 1892–1914*, (1973), pp. 265 & 273–4.
66 Crawshaw to Runciman, 2 April 1912; Runciman Papers, Newcastle University Library, WR 63.

67   Richard Morris to Tom Ellis, 19 August 1893; Tom Ellis Papers, National Library of Wales, 1524. The matter was discussed at meetings of the Welsh Liberal MPs on 21 and 23 August 1893; J. H. Lewis Papers (1963), National Library of Wales, Vol. 2, f. 15.
68   K. O. Morgan, *Rebirth of a Nation: Wales 1880–1980*, (1981), pp. 147–8.
69   I do not find convincing the argument that many of the strikes of this period were aimed at bringing in government intervention (and thereby greater gains) in view of the spontaneous nature of many of the strikes and the nature of government mediation. The 1912 miners' strike is an exception – a point made long ago by the Webbs; see *op.cit.*, p. 665. So also was the purpose of the Triple Industrial Alliance of 1914.

8

Government Administration

Roger Davidson

Any effective survey of late Victorian and Edwardian industrial relations must incorporate an analysis of the role of Whitehall. While the relationship between administration and the development of policy was 'extremely complex, with the initiative passing back and forward between administrators, experts and social groups or classes',[1] it is evident that government measures relating to industrial relations were largely determined by departmental ministers in conjunction with their permanent officials.[2] Labour unrest was rarely discussed in a systematic fashion at cabinet level and the frequent lack of consensus among the political and managerial élite as to the correct strategy to adopt in the face of industrial strife ensured that the initiative in framing labour policy normally resided in Whitehall.[3] Furthermore, the fact that much of the regulation of British industrial relations before the First World War was defined by broad permissive legislation rather than a detailed mandatory code, and that this period witnessed a marked trend within the British constitution towards delegated legislation, created the optimum environment for the exercise and effect of administrative discretion.[4] As a result, while popular, class, or interest group pressure played a significant part in originating legislation, its impact could be substantially modified by the economic and social ideology of civil servants. Even where they failed to fulfil a genuinely innovative role, they remained highly influential. It is also clear that industrialists and labour leaders regarded the social and economic objectives of the Board of Trade and Home Office as prime determinants of the government's industrial relations policy, and that these objectives often provided the focus for contemporary debate upon the role of the state in the labour market.[5]

The administration of late nineteenth and early twentieth-century industrial relations is best viewed in three chronological phases. The period 1875–90 was one of bureaucratic quiescence in which statutory powers of intervention in collective bargaining remained largely inoperative. From 1890–6, the role of government in the labour market was the focus of political debate during which new powers relating to the containment of industrial unrest were formulated, with the onus of responsibility shifting from the Home Office to the Board of Trade. Thereafter, by means of innovative administration, these powers were slowly transformed into an effective means of state intervention in labour relations with, after 1906, a significant impact upon the incidence and repercussions of industrial disputes. Meanwhile, throughout the period 1875–1914, the Home Office administered a wide range of industrial regulations affecting the material conditions of production in the workplace and, indirectly, the social relations through which it was organized.

The Councils of Conciliation Act of 1867 and the Arbitration (Masters and Workmen) Act of 1872 empowered the Home Office to co-ordinate the formation and functions of voluntary collective bargaining machinery, and to strengthen its status and efficiency by licensing Equitable Councils of Conciliation, modelled upon the *Conseils de Prud'hommes* operating in France and Belgium, to issue legally enforceable awards in industrial disputes arising out of existing working agreements. However, during the period 1875–96, such powers remained wholly inoperative. No licences were either applied for or granted.[6] Indeed, as in the 1878 Lancashire cotton dispute, or the Staffordshire chain-makers dispute of 1887, the Home Office explicitly disclaimed any right to mediate in strikes and lock-outs.[7] Its declared role in industrial relations was solely to preserve law and order (in particular, to enforce the Conspiracy and Protection of Property Act) and to ensure that statutory regulations relating to industrial health and safety were properly enforced.[8] While the latter might involve the appointment of assessors and arbitrators by judges of the county courts, such procedures did not relate to the determination of general industrial disputes.

Several explanations for the apparent negativism of the Home Office can be advanced. First, existing trends in the structure of British industrial relations rendered a policy of positive state intervention superfluous. The reform of trade union legislation in 1871 and 1875 'inauguarated a period of growing institutionalism designed to resolve conflict between employers and employed' with the proliferation of voluntary conciliation and arbitration machinery.[9] Secondly, industrial opinion was unreceptive to state intervention in labour relations. Employers were hypersensitive to bureaucratic interference in the prerogatives of management. There had been a steady decline in friction between the Home Office and industrialists generated by the administration of the Factory and Workshop Acts. Nonetheless, employers were determined that labour renumeration should be subject to market and not 'social' or 'statutory' criteria.[10] Moreover, while the TUC recommended the provision of Councils of Conciliation and Arbitration in the chief industrial centres of the United Kingdom, it was equally concerned to retain the 'autonomy' of collective bargaining procedures.[11] The desire to introduce statutory agencies appears to have been confined to certain poorly unionized workers in London, such as building operatives. It was not shared by the labour force of the staple industries.

Indeed, there was considerable opposition in labour circles to any extension of Home Office powers in the labour market. The existing role of the Home Office was viewed as repressive; identified with the use of troops to crush unrest, the legal harassment and intimidation of trade unionists, and the protection of capital and 'scab' labour.[12] The reports of the Factory Inspectorate served to reinforce this impression. Their annual survey of the labour market revealed an overriding concern with productivity, profit margins and factor costs, and a basic antipathy to trade unionism. The latter was accused of undermining the productivity of capital and labour, of retarding technical innovation and depressing the level of domestic investment.[13] Furthermore, the magistracy, so vital to the enforcement of Home Office industrial policy in the localities, was deeply distrusted by the labour movement for its social bias and commitment to the economic objectives of employers. Any involvement of voluntary collective bargaining with Home Office administration would, it was argued, merely extend the hegemony of the bench over questions of wage determination.[14]

Finally, neither the inspectorate nor the central secretariat of the Home Office favoured an interventionist industrial relations policy. In the period 1875–90, the Department tended to adhere to a conservative policy towards its industrial duties. The first heroic wave of inspectors had given way to a cautious, less innovative second generation.[15] They favoured the extension of private arbitration operating according to commercial criteria but were unreceptive to the extension of state intervention, on the grounds that it might distort labour costs and compromise the viability of private enterprise. 'Labour,' as one inspector observed, 'like any other commodity [had] to be bought and sold in a free competitive market' uninhibited by 'collectivism'.[16] The secretariat shared these views. Despite his former association with positivism and trade union reform, Godfrey Lushington, as legal adviser and Permanent Under-Secretary, held a traditional view of Home Office responsibilities, wishing them to be confined as much as possible to law, justice, and criminal administration.[17] Under his régime, industrial issues within the remit of the Domestic Department were accorded low status within the Office and relatively neglected. The Mines and Factory Inspectorates were given strict instructions to avoid involvement in industrial stoppages, while pressure from public opinion for the Home Office to mediate in the larger and more protracted disputes of the period was firmly resisted.[18]

However, the emergence of a new and more militant trade unionism in the 1880s generated mounting public and political pressure for a reappraisal of the role of government in industrial relations. Not only did industrial unrest endanger social stability, it was also regarded in government circles as a major obstacle to British economic growth. In an attempt to stabilize labour relations, a range of policy options were considered. Schemes involving compulsory arbitration with a statutory cooling-off period and/or compulsory arbitration with legally binding awards were widely canvassed in the press, in Parliament, and before the Royal Commission on Labour. However, the consensus of expert opinion, endorsed by leading labour administrators within Whitehall, favoured permissive legislation.[19] Any attempt to impose legal coercion upon collective bargaining would, it was argued, be resisted by industrialists and be certain to produce a confrontation between labour and the state. The only realistic course of action was for government to rely upon the extension of existing conciliation and arbitration machinery and the 'moral sanction' of public opinion. Administrative intervention in industrial relations should be confined to the provision of voluntary state dispute procedures which might serve to co-ordinate and to supplement private systems of collective bargaining operating within British industry.

Accordingly, in redefining the role of Whitehall in industrial relations, the 1896 Conciliation (Trades Disputes) Act endorsed a volun-

tarist strategy. When an industrial stoppage occurred or was anticipated, the Board of Trade was empowered to inquire into its causes
and circumstances and to facilitate negotiations between the parties
concerned. It might also appoint a conciliator or arbitrator at the
request of the disputants. There was no provision in the Act for a
compulsory cooling-off period, and state arbitration could only be
initiated by the voluntary submission of a dispute by both the parties
involved. Moreover, arbitration awards were not legally binding.

At first sight, the fact that the enforcement of the Conciliation Act
was entrusted to the Board of Trade appears surprising. Within the
Home Office, the factory inspectorate possessed extensive information on local labour markets. It frequently collected information on
working-class income and expenditure patterns. It had a detailed
knowledge of working conditions and procedures of payment
(which occasioned about 20 per cent of all industrial stoppages), of
the more exploitative trades and practices within British industry, of
the impact of technical innovation on wage differentials and the level
of employment, and of the economic determinants of industrial
unrest. Not only was it familiar with collective bargaining procedures but, under the Factory and Workshop Acts, involved in arbitration proceedings designed to regulate working conditions in
dangerous trades. In contrast, before 1886, the Board of Trade had
little formal contact with industrial relations. In administering mercantile marine and railway regulations, the Board was involved in
issues relating to remuneration and conditions of employment, such
as the transmission of seamen's wages, the prosecution of crimping,
and the efficiency of railway employees, but it was powerless to
intervene in actual disputes.[20] Furthermore, as advocates of free
market liberal individualism, the Board's most influential permanent
officials, Sir Thomas Farrer and Robert Giffen, were opposed in
principle to such intervention.[21]

Nonetheless, the problem of industrial unrest was increasingly
viewed by late Victorian administrators as primarily one of
economic dislocation rather than law and order. It was therefore
more logical that the Board of Trade should assume responsibility
for dealing with it. The adoption of a voluntarist rather than coercive
strategy towards collective bargaining in the Conciliation Act also
rendered the Board the more appropriate body for implementing the
measure. Another decisive factor was the ability of the Labour
Department of the Board of Trade, established in 1893, to supply

relevant data and expertise. The importance of labour statistics for the furtherance of industrial peace had been a central argument in the debate over the 'Labour Problem'.[22] The overriding need as defined by policy-makers was for the clarification of the issues involved in order to dispel the 'militancy of ignorance' and mobilize the moral suasion of 'enlightened' public opinion. The Labour Department appeared uniquely qualified to satisfy such a need. It was the recognized information bureau on all that pertained to industrial conflicts, possessing *systematic* data on strikes and lock-outs, trade combinations, employment and wage rates, easy access to more general economic data, and an establishment which included several experienced industrial negotiators.

In contrast, the industrial statistics of the Home Office were the target of extensive criticism in press and Parliament.[23] The reports of its inspectorate were often highly subjective, and their reliance upon Poor Law Guardians and manufacturers for evaluating 'the social conditions of the workforce' seriously impaired the credibility of their observations.[24] More seriously, the Domestic Department lacked the expertise and commitment to collate and present industrial data in a constructive fashion so as to isolate significant trends within the labour market, to delineate policy options, and to monitor the impact of existing industrial legislation.[25] It is significant that it was administrators within the Board of Trade who had identified the key issues upon which the Royal Commission on Labour should focus its investigations and who had provided the data base for the subsequent debate over industrial relations policy, culminating in the Conciliation Act.[26]

The problems that confronted the Board of Trade in extending the role of the state in industrial relations were formidable. Third-party arbitration and conciliation had never figured prominently in either the prevention or settlement of British disputes, the overwhelming majority of strikes and lock-outs having traditionally been settled by direct arrangement between the parties.[27] Furthermore, despite the absence of compulsion from the Conciliation Act, many industrialists and trade unionists were initially opposed to its widespread application. In general, the Labour Movement did not regard the Act as a progressive measure, viewing it as an evasion of the fundamental problems of income inequality.[28] This distrust was reinforced by disillusionment in labour circles with the system of wage arbitration already operating in many sectors of British industry. As the majority of umpires made their awards according to fluctuations in the level of economic activity or commodity prices, with little regard to working-class living standards, the bulk of arbitration awards during the depression in industrial prices after 1873 had imposed wage reductions.[29] The Board of Trade's unofficial handling of industrial disputes prior to the Conciliation Act had given trade unionists little confidence that state arbitration would prove more favourable. The two major industrial settlements in which the Board had been involved – the coal settlement of 1893 and the boot and shoe settlement of 1895 – had both represented major setbacks to labour.[30] In 1896, with a trade revival, fuller employment and rising prices, the more militant leaders and rank and file of the trade union movement not unnaturally gave a cool reception to legislation that threatened to restrict the power of organized labour to gain wage advances and protect its standard of living.

Many employers were equally apprehensive. They viewed state intervention in industrial relations as an unjustified invasion of private enterprise. Moreover, in 1896 industrialists were not in a conciliatory mood. Confronted by growing demands from labour militants for industrial power as well as wage advances, and the need to reduce unit costs of production to counter foreign competition in home and export markets, the employers' associations were preparing for a major counter-attack on the trade union movement. The extension of government conciliation machinery was therefore regarded as highly inappropriate, especially as its administration was to be entrusted to the Labour Department of the Board of Trade staffed by former trade unionists and middle-class radicals.[31]

The Labour Department sought to overcome this consumer resistance to the Conciliation Act by developing a vigorous and persuasive marketing strategy based upon a liberal and innovative interpretation of its powers.[32] Thus, the Department exploited its right to investigate the causes and circumstances of industrial unrest so as to induce employers and trade union leaders to submit their differences for settlement under the Act.[33] Furthermore, when disputes were exceptionally bitter and prolonged, the Department interpreted its powers of enquiry as a mandate to exert public pressure upon Capital and Labour to modify their demands. For example, in 1898, the progress reports of the Board's conciliator in the South Wales Coal Strike were published to discredit the claims of the more militant miners for a minimum living wage and to rally support for an amended sliding-scale as recommended by the union executive.[34]

The right of the Board of Trade under the Conciliation Act to facilitate industrial negotiations was exercised in an equally forceful fashion. It was primarily designed to encourage recourse to state *conciliation* when local negotiating procedures proved ineffectual. In contrast, the Labour Department used it to promote state *arbitration* which presented a higher probability of securing a definite settlement. Its industrial diplomacy was therefore focused upon obtaining the joint submission of disputes to arbitration. When only one party to a dispute was amenable to state intervention, instead of appointing a conciliator, the Department frequently delayed formal proceedings until either social hardship, declining profits or further negotiations induced the intransigent party to submit to arbitration.[35] Even when it received a *joint* application for the appointment of a conciliator, the Department seized every opportunity to extend his terms of reference to arbitration.[36]

Such tactics were particularly suited to three categories of industrial dispute. First, there were disputes, such as the 1901 compositors' strike, in which the levels of management concession and union expectation were so divergent that only informal negotiations by the Board of Trade to reduce the magnitude of disagreement between the parties, followed by the authoritative award of an independent umpire, could avert a protracted stoppage.[37] Secondly, there were disputes in which industrialists or union leaders entrenched themselves in unrealistic bargaining positions from which they were unwilling to retreat for fear of 'losing face'. At the same time, the prospect of social distress, depleted benefit funds, and reduced profit margins rendered them equally anxious to secure a settlement. In such instances, as for example in the Welsh tinplate stoppage of 1903–04, Labour Department officials had little difficulty in persuading local negotiators of the desirability of state arbitration as a means of breaking the deadlock.[38] Thirdly, there were disputes in which collective bargaining procedures failed to resolve essentially qualitative issues, such as conditions of work and labour discipline. On such occasions, the Board of Trade might persuade the parties to translate their demands into more tangible financial claims better suited to arbitration.

In its efforts to promote state conciliation and arbitration, the Labour Department left nothing to chance. In each labour dispute, its strategy was based upon a detailed assessment of factors likely to determine industrial response to state intervention, from economic variables such as the cost structure and profit margins of the firm and the financial resources of the union involved, to social and bureaucratic determinants such as the previous history of labour relations and bargaining procedures within the trade and the structure of authority within management and union hierarchies.

Just how successful was the Board of Trade in reducing industrial unrest after 1896?[39] Before 1906, its achievements were modest. It was involved in only 3.5 per cent of industrial disputes, and settled only 2.5 per cent, affecting a mere 5 per cent of the workforce involved in strikes and lock-outs. It resolved only one-quarter of the 'major industrial stoppages'[40] in which it intervened. After 1896, the majority of industrial stoppages continued to be settled by direct arrangement between the parties. Although the success rate of proceedings under the Conciliation Act for the period 1896–1905 was high, averaging 71 per cent, and arbitration awards were normally adhered to, this performance was far less impressive than it appears, for after 1900 the Board of Trade was increasingly selective in its choice of disputes in which it was prepared to intervene. It carefully avoided the growing number of stoppages involving controversial issues of social justice and industrial power and concentrated instead upon simple wage disputes in which both sides were receptive to state arbitration. Most strikes and lock-outs settled under the Conciliation Act before 1906 were small, both in terms of days lost and workmen involved. Moreover, the Board's efforts to reduce industrial unrest were heavily overcomitted to the building sector, where the unions were weak and disorganized, and it made relatively little headway in staple industries such as mining and textiles where stoppages were more protracted and damaging to the economy.

The preventive work of the Board of Trade up to 1906 is also unimpressive. Although the Conciliation Act had empowered the Board to establish conciliation machinery in any trade where its provision was deemed inadequate, and generally to co-ordinate the private system of collective bargaining, such powers remained largely inoperative. The growing resort to conciliatory agencies in many leading industrial sectors stemmed from the disillusionment in labour circles with arbitration boards and with the automatic dependence of wages on sliding-scales, rather than from any influ-

ence of the Conciliation Act. At most, about 2 per cent of conciliation boards operating in 1905 can be said to have owed their existence directly to the efforts of the Labour Department.

It was only after 1906 that the Board of Trade began to make any
real impact upon industrial relations. In the period 1906–14 it
settled nearly 10 per cent of all industrial stoppages, affecting 25 per
cent of the workforce involved in strikes and lock-outs. Compared
with the preceding decade, this represented a dramatic increase in the
role of state conciliation and arbitration. The Board of Trade intervened in over 85 per cent of the 'major industrial disputes' between
1906 and the outbreak of the First World War, and resolved nearly
75 per cent of them. While only 15 per cent of disputes settled under
the Conciliation Act up to 1906 involved over 1000 employees,
thereafter, some 34 per cent were of similar magnitude. Furthermore, despite its involvement in larger and more intractable disputes
after 1905, the Labour Department's mean annual success rate
remained above 80 per cent, and the growing prominence of third-
party intervention in collective bargaining was primarily a reflection
of this success. The trade distribution of disputes resolved under the
Conciliation Act continued to be skewed away from staple industries, but the Labour Department secured far greater influence in the
two industries traditionally most resistant to state intervention –
coalmining and cotton textiles. Moreover, notwithstanding the
deterioration in industrial relations after 1909, and the absence of
legal sanctions, arbitration awards were generally observed and
suffered no consistent fall in life expectancy.

The preventive work of the Labour Department also had a significant effect upon British industrial relations after 1905. By 1914,
labour policy in many sectors of the economy was regulated by
arbitration and conciliation schemes inspired by its industrial
negotiators, and often providing for appeal to the Board of Trade in
the event of deadlock. Even in the coalmining, engineering and
textile industries, many employers and trade union leaders had been
persuaded either to establish or reconstruct collective bargaining
machinery with which they might resolve their differences. At a
conservative estimate, some 17 per cent of the joint boards of conciliation and arbitration operating in 1914 had originated as a
by-product of industrial settlements negotiated by the Board of
Trade, and they affected some 27 per cent of the organized labourforce. The significance of this achievement was very clearly reflected

in the concern of socialist commentators. According to *Justice* and the *Socialist Review*, in reducing the incidence of strikes and lock-outs the Board had proved itself 'to be a subtle enemy of the pro-letariat', while the Independent Labour Party viewed the Conciliation Act as 'the most effective device by which the trade union movement [had] been humbugged by the dominant class'.[41]

Although this conspiracy theory of government labour administration lacks credibility, the Labour Movement had ample reason to distrust the Board of Trade's role in late Victorian and Edwardian industrial relations. Its leading negotiators rejected the wage-fund theory, but still considered that economic viability and investment in capital assets should remain the prime determinants of wage levels. In their view, industrial remuneration had to conform to the profits-fund whose security was crucial. Only an increase in profit-margins, improved productivity, and shifts in labour supply, could justify wage advances. Although they were prepared to expound upon the diseconomies of 'sweated' labour, demands for a national, statutory, minimum 'living wage', fixed according to social rather than economic criteria, were resisted by the Labour Department as 'inde-fensible and self-defeating'. By reducing profit-margins and invest-ment incentives, it would, in the long run, merely create unemploy-ment and lower wage levels. Board of Trade officials therefore considered that trade union wage policy should be confined firmly within the limiting factors of the state of trade, fluctuations in the labour market, and the return on capital.[42] Such views were rein-forced by the fact that senior labour officials also administered the commercial functions of the Board and shared the growing concern in government circles at the effects of trade union militancy upon industrial productivity and British cost competitiveness in world markets.[43]

Their economic philosophy was clearly reflected in the operation of the Conciliation Act. The overwhelming majority of arbitrators and conciliators appointed by the Board of Trade were from the professional and upper classes.[44] While the Board never imposed any formal wages policy upon its umpires, the type of arbitrator selected inevitably conditioned the criteria adopted in their determination of wage awards. Generally, they adhered to the traditional criteria of the state of trade, the competitive needs of a district, or changes in the selling price of the product involved. The underlying assumption of all wage awards was that wage rates should fluctuate with the market. Umpires refused to countenance any demand from labour negotiators for a 'socialistic minimum' or 'living wage'. They argued that it constituted a violation of the laws of political economy that would undermine the cost competitiveness of British industry. Umpires were also aware that if they based their awards on considerations other than strictly commercial criteria, employers would refuse to submit to state arbitration. Changes in the costs of living and the minimum level of subsistence were rarely taken into consideration, and little allowance was made for the marked decline in the real wages of the working classes after 1900. After the Board's costs of living inquiry of 1906, a few umpires did pay more attention to local variations in rents and commodity prices, but even their awards accorded such criteria very little importance as compared with the needs of the market economy.

As a result, throughout the period 1896–1914, wage awards under the Conciliation Act strongly reflected the trend of average industrial prices and short-run variations in the level of economic activity. Under both the Conservative and Liberal administrations, over 70 per cent of awards giving wage advances occurred in the upswing of the trade cycle, while over 75 per cent of wage reductions occurred in the downswing. In contrast, any correspondence between awards under the Conciliation Act and the level of industrial profits was purely incidental. Umpires rejected labour demands that wage awards should be based upon profit margins. They appreciated that the level of profits was the most accurate indicator of the ability of industry to pay a certain level of wages and the most accurate guide to trade union leaders as to whether there was sufficient surplus for the possibility of successful wage claims, but they were equally aware that industrialists would refuse to accept the profit criterion as the determinant of wage awards. The Conciliation Act did not require employers to produce detailed accounts in arbitration proceedings, and in most disputes arbitrators were content to rely on evidence of selling prices or of comparative labour costs and working conditions. When, in the course of negotiations, businessmen pleaded low profit margins or actual losses they rarely submitted their balance sheets for the umpire's perusal. Labour negotiators were therefore placed at a distinct disadvantage. While they were starved of vital information on production costs and industrial profits, the labour statistics published by the Board of Trade provided employers with data on comparative wage rates and the financial reserves of trade unions.

Trade union bargaining power was also impaired by the duration of many agreements negotiated under the Conciliation Act. While long-term wage agreements helped employers to stabilize labour costs and maximize profit margins during the upward price trend after 1896, such agreements not only restricted general wage advances being gained by the trade union movement, but also frustrated the attempts of rank-and-file militants to gain local advances.[45] The opportunity costs in wages and working conditions incurred by trade unionism in adhering to long-term settlements under the Conciliation Act were considerable, especially during the upswing of the business cycle from 1909–14.[46]

It is not, therefore, surprising that in the period 1896–1914, labour fully achieved its objectives in only 21 per cent of disputes settled under the Conciliation Act as compared with 27 per cent of all industrial stoppages. What has also to be remembered is that the overwhelming majority of disputes handled by the Board – some 84 per cent – stemmed from trade union demands for wage advances and improved working conditions in a period when the rising cost of living and cyclical unemployment were eroding the real earnings of the British workman. Therefore, the very high percentage of compromise settlements under the Conciliation Act represented a serious failure on the part of labour to achieve its aims. Clearly, state arbitration was no more help than private arbitration in securing for the labour movement a larger share for wages of the national income.[47] It is arguable that had trade union leaders opted more frequently for direct negotiation, they would have gained more wage advances in the upswing of the trade cycle, conceded less cuts in the downswing and, at the same time, promoted greater labour solidarity by appeasing their rank-and-file militants.

Why, therefore, did trade unionists continue to participate in state conciliation and arbitration? Several explanations can be advanced. Although the Conciliation Act was widely criticized in the left-wing press, the majority of trade union negotiators did not perceive it as exploitative. While the more militant union leaders remained committed to the attainment of a minimum living wage defined by 'social need', most labour negotiators were prepared to bargain within the bounds of existing wage relativities and orthodox market criteria.[48] Indeed, awards which *did* incorporate more 'progressive' criteria such as regional variations in the cost of living often received an unfavourable reception from labour.

Secondly, while the Board of Trade's choice of umpires and conciliators was socially exclusive, it also favoured expertise and accorded a minimal role to employers; a recruitment pattern which did much to gain trade union confidence. The role of occupational groups with least industrial experience, such as lawyers, national politicians and ecclesiastics, was significantly less in state arbitration than in domestic dispute procedures. Equally marked was the very much higher representation of specialists such as architects and surveyors, and the extensive use made by the Labour Department of scientific and industrial expertise from within the civil service inspectorates.

Thirdly, although vilified in the socialist press, the labour officials of the Board of Trade and its leading negotiator, George Askwith, were highly regarded in trade union circles. They were widely viewed as 'progressive' administrators with a genuine commitment to social reform and to the elimination of the more serious imperfections of the labour market.[49] Their efforts to erode the most dictatorial forms of industrial management, such as those prevailing in the railway and shipping industries, were duly appreciated, as was their campaign for the reform of trade union law.[50]

Finally, despite increasing disenchantment in labour circles with Lib-Lab consensus tactics and growing concern amongst left-wing ideologists at the apparent 'incorporation' of trade unionism within the 'Servile State', the industrial strategy of the labour movement after 1906 involved *increasing* recourse to state arbitration and conciliation. The insistence by labour negotiators upon national wage settlements revealed the inability of private collective bargaining to effect industry-wide agreements on substantive issues.[51] Furthermore, state intervention was an integral part of the tactics of even the most militant unions. Thus, the Triple Industrial Alliance proceeded upon the assumption that even if the threat of massive strike measures failed to induce employers to concede improved pay and working conditions, by activating the Board of Trade's arbitration and conciliation machinery, it would, in effect, impel the government to impose a settlement upon management.[52]

The increased significance of government administration in British industrial relations after 1906 was determined by a variety of other social, political and institutional factors. The shift in the political context of labour administration was clearly vital. Liberal policy proved increasingly receptive to government intervention in labour relations. In their concern with social utility, radicals urged that the state adopt a more active role in the determination of factor costs, and even Liberal leaders of more orthodox persuasion were prepared to sanction intervention to protect the 'community interest' as the scale of industrial confrontation escalated.[53] The shift of public opinion in favour of state involvement in industrial relations was equally marked. The effects of nation-wide stoppages in the mining and transport sectors upon the supply of essential goods and services and on the level of employment in related trades provoked a growing demand for more stringent action to preserve industrial peace.[54] Furthermore, a growing number of industrialists were receptive to an extension of government conciliation and arbitration. An increasing proportion of the business community shared the view of the Board of Trade that state intervention in wage determination was compatible with productive efficiency and that consensus strategies rather than confrontation constituted the most effective antidote to labour unrest.[55]

The increasing impact of the Board upon industrial relations also reflected its more forceful administration of the labour market. After 1906, it was prepared to intervene in every major trade dispute, even where the concern of management and unions to preserve industrial self-government, the polarity of their respective bargaining positions, or the intractability of the issues involved were such as to exclude the possibility of arbitration.[56] To discredit the confrontation tactics of both right- and left-wing extremists, the Board also instituted a series of public enquiries into labour relations in trades worst affected by industrial unrest. For example, its investigations into the 1912 London dock strikes and Dublin transport workers stoppage aimed to discredit the victimization of union officials and the provocative use of free labour by employers, and by revealing the adverse income and employment effects of the disputes, to expose the anti-social aspects of syndicalist tactics such as sympathetic strike action.[57]

The ability of the Board of Trade to adopt a more vigorous role was greatly enhanced by the establishment in 1911 of a separate industrial relations department staffed by full-time negotiators under the direction of George Askwith as Chief Industrial Commissioner. This injected fresh expertise at a critical juncture. As, after 1905, senior labour officials had become preoccupied with a massive programme of commercial and welfare legislation, the strategy of the Board towards labour unrest had become administered increasingly by 'generalists' who lacked both the termperament and specialist skills necessary for successful industrial diplomacy.[58] Askwith and his assistant commissioners were less inhibited by bureaucratic imperatives. They were more conversant with recent shifts in the ideology and tactics of management and labour, and therefore better equipped to modify state dispute procedures accordingly. Moreover, at a time when labour unrest was becoming a highly sensitive political issue, and when the personal involvement of Lloyd George and Churchill in disputes had created the suspicion that the Board of Trade's peace formulas and arbitration awards were purely motivated by political expediency, the greater autonomy vested in the administration of the Conciliation Act was a significant factor in conserving industrial confidence in state conciliation and arbitration.[59]

Meanwhile, quite apart from its involvement in the legal implications of industrial combination and confrontation, the industrial duties of the Home Office had a significant bearing on late Victorian and Edwardian industrial relations. Its regulation of working conditions, including hours of work, the provision of adequate ventilation, sanitation and lighting, of safety precautions, and of equitable payment procedures, must clearly have influenced the social relationships of production. Such regulations could have a substantial impact upon status and motivation within the workplace which were perhaps as vital as broader cultural and community factors in defining the occupational and class attitudes of labour. Moreover, the industrial administration of the Home Office could modify the effect of technology on the organisation of production and the general structure of the labour market.[60] Such effects were reinforced by the extension in 1891, 1895 and 1901 of the Factory and Workshop Acts, designed to encompass a broader range of industries and processes as well as additional aspects of the working environment.[61]

There is insufficient data to measure the impact of Home Office administration upon working conditions. Other variables such as shifts in relative factor costs, market environment and profit-margins, or in the ideology and relative bargaining strengths of management and labour, as well as trends in social expectations with respect to work environment and leisure, were also relevant in determining working conditions and hours in British industry.[62] However, what can be argued with a fair degree of certainty is that there was a significant shortfall between the objectives and effect of factory and working legislation.

This can be attributed to a number of factors. Even after the establishment of an Industrial Department and the overhaul of its industrial statistics between 1893 and 1896, the Home Office still lacked an innovative response to labour administration.[63] The appointment of university educated generalists by open competition after 1870 meant that by the 1890s, the majority of the senior establishment had little specialist knowledge of the needs of industry and the realities of the labour market. Such officials were career rather than problem-orientated and viewed social administration primarily as a source of income and professional status. Moreover, the increasing power of generalists within the Home Office sec-retariat drastically reduced the access of the inspectorates to the policy-making process with a consequent erosion of their morale.[64] The response of the Industrial Department to specialist advice was aptly compared in 1907 to the reaction of a 'Jesuit establishment to heresy'.[65] As a result, the innovative role of expertise that had charac-terized Home Office industrial administration in the mid-Victorian period was markedly absent after 1890.

The administration of the Factory and Workshop Acts was also constrained by the economic philosophy of senior Home Office officials and their political chiefs. In so far as any sustained depart-mental 'view' can be identified, it was that, while the more overt forms of industrial exploitation should be eradicated, it was equally imperative that the government should avoid welfare measures which might trench upon the profits fund, erode managerial incen-tives, and reduce the level of capital accumulation.[66] Wherever poss-ible, labour costs should be freely exposed to market forces and the ultimate responsibility of employers for the safety and well-being of their workforce preserved.[67]

It was a defensive ideology which seriously weakened the ability of the Department to resist Treasury control upon Home Office expen-diture. As a result, its inspectorates were inadequately funded and staffed. Admittedly, the Factory Inspectorate expanded from an establishment of fifty-six in 1878 to one of 223 in 1913. Nonetheless, the enlargement of the Factory Inspectorate failed to keep pace with the increasing range and complexity of its duties after 1890, and with the continual growth in the number of premises and processes under inspection. Routine inspection was increasingly disrupted by the pressure of other commitments such as involvement in 'dangerous trade' arbitrations, accident inquests, and proceedings under the Workmen's Compensation Acts, or in liaison work with medical, sanitary and educational authorities.[68] The consequent loss of rigour and uniformity in standards of inspection was reinforced by the failure of the Home Office secretariat to collate factory and workshop statistics so as to provide the inspectorate with an overview of the existing incidence and impact of inspection and of the optimum deployment for its resources.[69]

The ability of the inspectorate to sustain an innovative response to social and industrial problems was also inhibited by the recruitment and promotion procedures of the Home Office. Recruits to the Factory Inspectorate were not required to demonstrate practical experience of factory work and conditions, merely 'broad culture' and 'the ability to deal with manufacturers on equal terms'.[70] They were recruited predominantly from the middle and professional classes and generally adhered to conventional economic views with respect to the labour market and industrial remuneration.[71] In contrast, the Inspectors' assistants who *were* recruited from workmen with direct experience of industrial employment, were confined to workshop inspection and barred from promotion to the higher eschelons of the Factory Inspectorate. This social bias in Home Office administration seriously eroded the co-operation of the workforce in the enforcement of the Factory and Workshop Acts. It was the considered view of many TUC delegates that 'from their social standing' the factory inspectorate 'were naturally the friends – of the employing class' and that inspection was 'invariably from the employers point of view'.[72]

The efficient and uniform enforcement of industrial welfare measures was further impeded by the inertia or hostility of local authorities and magistrates. The Factory and Workshop Amendment Acts of 1891, 1895 and 1901 devolved increasing responsibility for workshop regulation upon local authorities. While some authorities remodelled their health and sanitary departments accordingly, many others, especially in small urban centres and rural areas, either remained apathetic towards workshop regulation or retained a vested interest in its evasion. As a result, co-ordination between the work of Medical Officers of Health and the Home Office Inspectorate, upon which any effective regulation of the local working environment rested, was often seriously impaired.[73] The attitude of the lay magistracy constituted an additional handicap. Only nominal fines were imposed on employers for contravention of factory and workshop legislation. The average penalty imposed in any one year for the period 1890–1914 never exceeded 19s 8½d, and in real terms the annual average fine actually decreased during the greater part of the period.[74] As the Chief Inspector of Factories observed with heavy irony in 1899, 'the level of penalties [was] such as to tend in some cases towards the scandalous imputation of the sympathy on the part of magistrates with evasion of the law'.[75]

The deficiencies of factory and workshop inspection in this period cannot be measured in any systematic fashion. However, the evidence clearly indicates that a significant proportion of the British working environment was visited with insufficient regularity to secure the most elementary standards of industrial welfare.[76] During 1900, only 42 per cent of factories and 40 per cent of workshops in the United Kingdom were inspected. Thereafter, while on trend the percentage of industrial premises visited annually increased substantially, there were significant fluctuations and regional variations in the efficiency of divisional inspectorates.[77] While the ratio of inspectors to registered factories and workshops had halved between 1875 and 1913, on the eve of the First World War it was still of the order of 1:1332.[78] Furthermore, variations in the incidence and stringency of inspection actively generated fresh problems in the labour market. Until the mid-1890s, the more rigorous remit and application of factory as compared with workshop regulations contributed in London and possibly other industrial centres to the movement of labour in certain trades such as clothing away from centralized factory production. Similarly, after 1900, while the gap between factory and workshop conditions diminished, the increasing divergence between the regulation of workshop and outwork production caused a rise in homework with the attendant evils of 'sweating'. Thus, legislation designed to bring standardization to the labour market and working conditions could, within the local economy, actually foster 'the growth of the least-regulated and least desirable modes of industrial organization'.[79]

The impact of factory and workshop legislation on late Victorian and Edwardian industrial relations appears to have been highly ambivalent. While it removed potential areas of industrial friction, it also generated higher levels of welfare expectations. Similarly, while such expectations were often articulated in the form of labour unrest, and, indeed, constituted an important rallying point for unionization,[80] they also served to contain industrial confrontation; to focus militancy upon the procedure rather than the equity of industrial remuneration, the safety rather than the ownership of capital assets. Finally, while variations in the rigour of Home Office industrial administration tended in some sectors to encourage the growth of modes of production such as homework which inhibited unionization and class consciousness, the failure of factory and workshop regulation to eliminate the threat of 'sweated' outwork labour to the wages, solidarity, and work status of factory labour, unified and radicalized specific working class groups, especially in London.[81]

There is no apparent trend in the causes of industrial disputes for the period 1896–1914 which can be firmly attributed to Home Office administration. Marginal shifts in the proportion of stoppages relating to working conditions and payment procedures are clearly attributable to a range of social and economic factors unrelated to Home Office intervention in the labour market,[82] and the incorporation of a 'dummy' variable within existing econometric models of strike activity to 'capture' its impact would be a dubious exercise.

The historian has, *faux de mieux*, to rely on inference and evidence of a non-quantifiable kind. Given that the Home Office administered industrial issues which precipitated some 20 per cent of strikes and lock-outs in the period 1896–1914, it is likely that, on balance, it performed a positive preventive role. The annual reports, diaries and autobiographies of the Factory Inspectorate confirm this. In the course of their formal duties, they fulfilled an informal but extensive conciliatory function, mediating between management and workforce on a range of contentious issues affecting the conditions of production in the workplace.[83] It is probable that such efforts averted a considerable number of industrial stoppages. Indeed, further research may reveal that, as with the conciliation and arbitration work of the Board of Trade, it was the advisory and liaison function of Home Office officials rather than their administration of a mandatory code *per se* which had the more profound effect upon pre-war industrial relations.

References

I should like to express my gratitude to the Social Science Research Council whose financial assistance (Grant HR 7262) made possible much of the original research upon which this essay is based.

1 J. R. Hay, *The Development of the British Welfare State 1880–1975*, (1978), p. 107.
2 R. Davidson, 'The Board of Trade and Industrial Relations 1896–1914,' *Historical Journal*, 21, (1978), pp. 571–2.
3 H. V. Emy, *Liberals, Radicals and Social Politics 1892–1914*, (1973), p. 270.
4 *Report of Committee on Ministers' Powers*, PP 1931–32, C. 4060, 12, p. 22.
5 Davidson, *op.cit.*, p. 572.
6 I. G. Sharp, *Industrial Conciliation and Arbitration in Great Britain*, (1950), pp. 280–9.
7 *Hansard*, 3rd series, CCXL, 34–5, 16 May 1878; CCCXVI, 407, 17 June 1887.
8 *Hansard*, 3rd series, CCXLIII, 949, 27 February 1879; CCCXLVI, 686, 3 July 1890.
9 For an explanation of this development, see K. Burgess, *The Origins of British Industrial Relations*, (1975), pp. viii–xi.
10 See, e.g. *ibid.*, p. ix; *Economist*, 33, (1875), pp. 175 & 309; 36, (1878), p. 455.
11 *TUC Report*, (1875), pp. 25–6; (1878), p. 14; (1880), p. 38.
12 H. Pelling, *Popular Politics and Society in Late Victorian Britain*, (1968), pp. 69–70; J. Stevenson & R. Quinault (ed.), *Popular Protest and Public Order*, (1974), pp. 160–1 & 206–7.
13 See e.g., *Report of the Chief Inspector of Factories* (hereinafter cited as *RCIF*), PP 1876, C. 1434, 16, p. 25; 1879 C. 2489 14, pp. 19 & 29; 1888 C. 5328, 26, p. 63; 1890, C. 6060, 20, pp. 17–18.
14 *TUC Report*, (1876), p. 13; (1881), pp. 16–17; Pelling, *op.cit.*, pp. 5, 71.
15 J. H. Pellew, 'Administrative Change in the Home Office 1870–96,' (unpublished PH.D. Thesis, University of London, 1976), pp. 158–202.
16 *RCIF*, PP 1879, C. 2489, 14, p. 36; 1888, C. 5328, 26, p. 67; 1889, C. 5679, 18, p. 141.
17 See PRO HO45/9769/B1067/1, minute by Lushington, 8 March 1887.
18 See e.g., *RCIF*, PP 1890, C. 6060, 20, p. 31; *Hansard*, 3rd series CCCXXXV, 752–3, 29 April 1889.
19 See especially the memoranda contained in PRO BT 13/26/E 12293/1896.
20 PRO MT 9/263/M 19241/1885; MT 9/365/M 1544/1890; *Hansard*,

3rd series, CCXXX, 336; CCCXXXVII, 424; CCCXLII, 504.

21 P. Smith, *Disraelian Conservatism and Social Reform*, (1967), pp. 53–7 & 231–2; *Journal of the Royal Statistical Society*, LXIII, (1910), p. 532.

22 G. Sutherland (ed.), *Studies in the Growth of Nineteenth-Century Government*, (1972), p. 252.

23 See e.g., PRO HO45/9862/B 13323/1.

24 *TUC Report*, (1879), p. 9; *RECIF*, PP 1888, C. 5328, 26, p. 52.

25 Pellew, *op.cit.*, p. 181.

26 See, Hicks-Beach Papers, County Record Office, Gloucester, PC/PP/60, memoranda on the proposed terms of reference of the Labour Commission.

27 PP *Reports on Strikes and Lock-outs; Reports on Changes in the Rate of Wages and the Hours of Labour*.

28 Davidson, *op.cit.*, p. 592. There *were* exceptions to this view. Some workers, such as the dockers and railwaymen, viewed state intervention as a means of gaining union recognition. The Fabian view that the Conciliation Act might constitute a step towards a state regulated minimum living wage also appealed to several of the more prominent leaders of New Unionism: see, E. H. Phelps Brown, *The Growth of British Industrial Relations*, (1959), pp. 187–8.

29 J. H. Porter, 'Wage Bargaining under Conciliation Agreements 1860–1914,' *Economic History Review*, 23, (1970), p. 472.

30 J. E. Williams, 'Labour in the Coalfields,' *Labour History Bulletin*, 4, (1962), p. 26; *The Times*, 25 April 1895.

31 H.A. Clegg, A. Fox & A.F. Thompson, *A History of British Trade Unions since 1889: Vol I 1889–1910*, (1964), p. 177.

32 For a more extended analysis of this strategy, see R. Davidson, 'Social Conflict and Social Administration: the Conciliation Act in British Industrial Relations,' in (ed.) T. C. Smout, *The search for Wealth and Stability*, (1979), pp. 175–97.

33 See e.g. PRO Lab 2/75/L1094/1898; Lab 2/9/L908/1899; Lab 2/75/L776/1902.

34 PP 1898, C.9031, 72, pp. 7–9; PRO Lab 2/101/L1312/1901. In fact, during the committee stage of the Conciliation Bill, the Board of Trade had been specifically denied the right to report upon the merits of industrial disputes for the guidance of public opinion. (*Hansard*, 4th series, LX, 75, 24 June 1898.)

35 See e.g. PRO Lab 2/75/L776/1902.

36 See e.g. PRO Lab 2/75/L1094/1898. As a result, although state arbitration had been conceived of in 1896 as 'a last resort', it subsequently accounted for 72 per cent of industrial settlements achieved under the Conciliation Act prior to the First World War.

37 PRO Lab 2/102/L247/1901.

38 PRO Lab 2/141/L1483/1904.

39 Analysis in this section is based upon material contained in PP *Annual Reports of Proceedings under the Conciliation Act; Annual Reports on Strikes and Lock-outs*.

40 Officially defined as those stoppages involving not less than 5000 employees and/or the loss of more than 100,000 working days.

41 *Justice*, 6 November 1913; *Socialist Review*, 7, (1911), p. 248; *Labour Leader*, 24 September 1909.

42 Davidson, *op.cit.*, pp. 584–5.

43 See e.g. PRO Lab 2/480/L555/1900, papers relating to the effect of strikes and lock-outs upon the performance of British exports.

44 Unless otherwise stated, the following analysis is based upon material contained in PP *Annual Reports of Proceedings under the Conciliation Act; Annual Reports on Strikes and Lockouts; Abstracts of labour statistics*; PRO Lab 2, Labour Department correspondence.

45 Porter, *op.cit.*, p. 472.

46 See e.g. the adverse effects of the awards in the 1909 Swansea and Scottish coal mines disputes, and the South Wales Sliding-Scale Agreement of 1910; Porter, *op.cit.*, p. 474; R. Page Arnot, *A History of the Scottish Miners*, (1955), p. 111; N. Edwards, *History of the South Wales Miners Federation*, (1938), pp. 29–31.

47 For the economic effects of private arbitration, see Porter, *op.cit.*, pp. 460–75.

48 See especially, the minutes of arbitration proceedings under the Conciliation Act contained in PRO Lab 2 archives.

49 Wilson Fox Papers, Bwlch, Breconshire, 'In Memoriam,' pp. 10, 13 & 23.

50 For details, see Davidson, *op.cit.*, pp. 573–7.

51 H. A. Clegg, *The System of Industrial Relations in Great Britain*, (1970), p. 203.

52 G. A. Phillips, 'The Triple Industrial Alliance in 1914,' *Economic History Review*, 24, (1971), p. 65. For a quantitative approach to the relationship between government intervention and strike activity in this period, see James E. Cronin, *Industrial Conflict in Modern Britain* (1979), pp. 101–05.

53 H. V. Emy, *op.cit.*, pp. 264, 269–70 & 275.

54 PRO Cab 37/107/98, 9 August 1911.

55 R. Charles, *The Development of Industrial Relations in Britain 1911–1939*, (1973), pp. 24, 39 & 51.

56 Whereas in the period 1896–1905 conciliation accounted for only 7 per cent of settlements under the Conciliation Act, in the period 1906–1914, it accounted for 19 per cent.

57 PP 1912–13, C. 6229, 47; PRO Lab 2/100/IC4614/1913.

58 PRO BT 13/134, H. Fountain to Llewellyn Smith, 13 March 1909.

59 PRO Cab 37/107/98, 9 August 1911.

60 See, J. A. Schmiechen, 'State Reform and the Local Economy: An Aspect of Industrialisation in late Victorian and Edwardian London,' *Economic History Review*, 28, (1975), pp. 413–28.

61 For example, additional regulations to ensure that pieceworkers were fully conversant with the 'particulars' upon which their remuneration was calculated, and to protect the health and safety of the workforce at a time when new forms of power, especially electricity, were transform-

ing industrial processes and plant layout.

62 See especially, M. A. Bienefeld, *Working Hours in British Industry*, (1972), ch. 7. Even statistics such as the annual returns of factory accidents, which might at first sight appear to provide a rough indicator of the welfare effects of industrial regulations, prove on closer inspection to be highly ambiguous; See PP 1911, C. 5535, 23, pp. 9–13.

63 R. Davidson & R. Lowe, 'Bureaucracy and Innovation in British Welfare Policy 1870–1945,' in (ed.) W. J. Mommsen *The Emergence of the Welfare State in Great Britain and Germany 1850–1950*, (1981).

64 *Ibid.*, p. 11; R. A. S. Redmayne, *Men, Mines and Memories*, (1942), p. 142.

65 H. Cunynghame to H. H. Asquith, 19 December 1907; British Library Add MSS 45989, fos 172–3.

66 See e.g. C. E. Troup, *The Future Work of Free Trade in English Legislation*, (1884), pp. 38–40; PRO HO45/9726/A 52571/6; HO45/B 10296A/9837.

67 See e.g. PRO HO45/9770/B1137/49.

68 See e.g. *RCIF*, PP 1901, C. 668, 10, p. 154; 1904, C. 2139, 10, p. 99.

69 See e.g. *RCIF*, PP 1900, C. 223, 11, p. 146.

70 *Royal Commission on the Civil Service, Mins. of Ev* PP 1912–13, C. 6210, 15, p. 5253; *Departmental Committee on Accidents in Factories, Mins of Ev* PP 1911, C. 5540, 23, pp. 35–46.

71 See e.g. *RCIF* PP 1894, C. 7368, 21, p. 22; 1895, C. 7745, 19, p. 208; 1900, C. 223, 11, p. 145.

72 *TUC Reports*, (1879), p. 9; (1880), p. 29; (1884), p. 24; (1891), p. 68; PP 1911, C. 5540, 23, p. 540.

73 *RCIF*, PP 1898, C.8965, 14, pp. 41 & 99; 1900, C. 223, 11, p. 157; 1902, C. 1112, 12, p. x; 1908, C. 4166, 12, p. x; 1910, C. 5191, 28, pp. 43 & 118; 1912–13, C. 6239, 25, p. 38.

74 *RCIF*, PP 1898, C. 8965, 14, pp. 86 & 119; 1900, C. 223, 11, p. 80; 1906, C. 2848, 15, p. 328; 1911, C. 5693, 22, p. xxvi. Significantly, the average fine imposed by stipendary magistrates was eight times that imposed by lay magistrates (PP 1904, C. 2139, 10, p. 97).

75 PP 1900, C. 223, 11, p. 223.

76 See especially, PP 1911, C. 5535, 23, p. 63; in the opinion of one MP, inspections were 'like angels' visits – occurrences which happen very seldom' – *Hansard*, 5th Series, 27, 264, 26 June 1911.

77 *RCIF*, PP 1901, C. 668, 10, p. 154; 1902, C. 112, 12, p. 1; PRO HO45/10553/164207, *Report of Departmental Committee on the Factory Inspectorate*, 23 December 1907.

78 PP 1911, C. 5540, 23, q.979.

79 Schmiechen, *op.cit.*, p. 427.

80 Bienefeld, *op.cit.*, pp. 143 & 214.

81 J. A. Schmiechen, 'Sweated Industries and Sweated Labour: A Study of Industrial Disorganization and Worker Attitudes,' (unpublished Ph.D. Thesis, University of Illinois, 1975), pp. 262 & 269.

82 See, Cronin, *op.cit.*, chs. 3–4.

83 See e.g. H. Martindale, *From One Generation to Another 1839–1944*

(1944), pp. 86–7; R. Squire, *Thirty Years in the Public Service: An Industrial Retrospect*, (1927), p. 46.

Industrial Relations Case Studies

9

Coalmining

John Benson

The coal industry has always been notorious for the bitterness of its industrial relations.[1] As a result it has invariably received the close scrutiny of contemporaries and historians alike: thus a new and wide-ranging, though by no means exhaustive, bibliography of the industry lists over 2500 secondary works, a fifth of which deal primarily with industrial relations.[2] Unfortunately, however, many of these studies have served merely to duplicate or amplify what is already known. It is only comparatively recently that historians have turned from the study of central bargaining procedures and official disputes to examine the effect of the industry's economic structure and performance, the influence of working and social conditions and the attitudes and procedures which were adopted at the local level. These are factors which, for all their complexity, must find a place in any serious study of industrial relations in the coalmining industry between 1875 and 1914.

The notoriety of coalmining's industrial relations was not without foundation. Indeed, many of the features which distinguished mining from other industries served also to encourage the labour difficulties for which the industry was so well known. The economic structure and performance of the industry exercised a profound effect upon industrial relations. With output rising from 133 million tons to 287 million tons between 1875 and 1913 and the labourforce expanding from 536,000 to 1,128,000, the industry came to assume a commanding role in the economic and political life of the nation. By the end of the period the typical colliery employed well over 300 people and the industry as a whole was dominated by firms and companies owning several collieries and employing large numbers of men: in 1911, for example, the Fife Coal Company and the Powell Duffryn Steam Coal Company of Aberdare each had a labourforce of over 10,000, and an annual output of more than two million tons. Large undertakings such as these tended to widen the gulf between employer and employed, their long channels of communication encouraging misunderstandings to arise, grievances to multiply, and trade unionism to develop.[3]

It would be a mistake to assume, however, that the period between 1875 and 1914 was one of uninterrupted growth and expansion. Coalmining, like other extractive industries, was subject to the law of diminishing returns. As the thickest and most accessible seams began to be exhausted, so labour productivity started to decline. Output per man fell from 319 tons a year in 1879–83 to 257 tons in 1909–13 and it is not difficult to imagine how employers' efforts to reverse this decline might lead to resentment and discontent.[4] Even more likely to generate conflict were the economic fluctuations to which coalmining, like textiles and shipbuilding, was so vulnerable. Both the vagaries of the weather and the rhythms of the trade cycle affected prices, profits, wages and employment and thus engendered a sense of insecurity within the industry. Mild winters like those of 1881 and 1884 hit collieries producing for domestic consumption, while a severe winter, like that of 1900, could close canals and create serious bottlenecks on the railways. The trade cycle was particularly serious. Good years, like 1884, 1890, 1900, 1907 and 1913, alternated with bad, 1879, 1886, 1895–6, 1905 and 1909. Thus between 1896 and 1900 the average pithead price of coal – the most reliable indicator of the industry's general prosperity – rose by 85 per cent, only to fall again by more than 35 per cent over the next five years.

While economic fluctuation, declining productivity and increasing concentration of production were all important determinants of industrial relations, it should not be imagined that their effect was uniform over every coalfield: nothing could be further from the truth. The economic development of the Lancashire and Cheshire coalfields was not the same as that of Northumberland and Durham; the experience of East Scotland was far removed from that of the East Midlands; the history of the Black Country could scarcely have been more different than that of South Wales. In fact regional variation has always been one of the most conspicious features of the British coalmining industry.

There is space here to compare only two coalfields: South Wales and the Black Country. The latter suffered a catastrophic decline after 1875. The ease with which the famous Thick Coal could be worked had made South Staffordshire the hunting ground of any number of small capitalists. Although their pits were small (never employing an average of more than a hundred men each) and often under-capitalized, for the first three-quarters of the century they enjoyed a ready market among local domestic and industrial consumers, especially in the iron trade. Thus the decline of the regional iron industry during the last quarter of the century contributed to the complete stagnation of coalmining. Black Country production plummetted from 9 million tons in 1877, to 6 million in 1886 and barely 3 million in 1913.[5]

In South Wales, on the other hand, the persistently buoyant demand for high quality steam coal, particularly for export, enabled the industry to grow prodigiously. Production increased from 21 to 57 million tons between 1880 and 1913, and employment leapt from 69,000 to 233,000. The large amounts of capital needed to work the deep, difficult steam coal seams of the Aberdare and Rhondda valleys meant that already in 1875 nearly half of South Wales production was controlled by limited liability companies. By the end of the period the labourforce at the typical South Wales colliery stood at 376, 10 per cent above the national average, and nearly four times larger than in the depressed Black Country. There were growing economic difficulties however, and labour productivity in South Wales fell from 314 tons per man in 1883 to 228 tons in 1911.[6]

The development of the coal industry, then, was far from uniform. Industrial relations in the Black Country, for example, were conducted in an economic environment unlike that found in the country as a whole, and strikingly different from that pertaining in South Wales. Yet there can be no doubt that in every coalfield the economic structure and performance of the industry did affect employer–employee relationships. Often, it seems, the trade cycle, falling productivity and growing concentration of production combined to encourage insecurity and instability within the system of industrial relations.

This instability has always been reinforced by the special character of the mining workplace. It has often been observed that the discomfort, danger and unpredictability of the underground environment is likely to result in tension and discontent.

The mining industry differs from other industries, and particularly from manufacturing, in a number of ways . . . which have been summed up by Baldwin as 'the dynamic character of the working environment, its unpredictability and its lack of standardization' . . .
  Naturally these conditions have their effect upon those who work in them, and they create their own problems. The solidarity and indepen-

dence of the miners, for example, must in part be due to feelings engendered by working in a world of their own faced with an ever-present sense of danger. From the point of view of management these conditions mean, firstly, that plans must be flexible to take account of changes which may occur from day to day or week to week, and secondly, that, under the existing payment system, considerable time and energy must be expended in adjusting piece rates and allowances to take account of varying conditions.[7]

Certainly the nineteenth-century wages system was so complex that it tended to generate misunderstanding and disagreement. All miners' wages were based upon a regionally negotiated basis or standard rate and, after 1888, a percentage addition. Surface workers were paid by time, but in order to impose discipline in the hostile and unpredictable underground environment, nearly all haulage hands and faceworkers were paid according to the amount of work which they completed. So, in 1888, Northumberland and Durham haulage workers were 'usually paid from 11d to 15d per score of six tons, put an average distance of eighty yards with 1d extra per score for every additional 20 yards'. The calculation of hewers' earnings was 'accomplished by means of a colliery price-list and by weighing the coal which each man hews, and "measuring-up" any other kind of work'.

The principal item is the 'cutting price', or standard rate per ton paid for 'getting' coal from the face in a properly opened stall or place. The 'cutting price' may be anything from 1s. 1d up to 3s. per ton, and is subject to the addition of a percentage. If the latter is 60 per cent and the 'cutting price' of a particular seam is 1s. 8d, and if the man sends up 2½ tons of coal in one day, he earns 6s. 8d. Thus:

		s.	d.
1s. 8d × 2½	=	4	2
Add $\frac{60 \times 4s. 2d}{100}$	=	2	6
		6	8

But pieceworkers also received locally negotiated allowances for working in abnormal conditions. These were negotiated not only when a pit was opened or a new seam started, but whenever the state of the working altered in any way. 'The place that is normal one week is abnormal next week,' explained a Somerset hewer. 'Faults, and other interruptions, cause the place to be abnormal, and the best skilled miner is at a disadvantage to produce his usual output.'[8]

Even more destructive of smooth industrial relations was the nineteenth-century shibboleth that wages should follow prices. It was almost an article of faith with colliery owners (and some trade union leaders) that wage rates should be determined directly and exclusively by the selling price of coal. As the South Yorkshire employers asserted in 1879; 'The abstract question in all commercial affairs is what rate of wages will the selling price of the marketable article produced enable the employer to pay.' With selling prices fluctuating sharply, and wages accounting for as much as two-thirds of total production costs, it is not surprising that the coal owners should prove intransigent in negotiations. During the downswing of the trade cycle, when prices were falling, they tried to impose cuts; during the upswing, when prices were rising, they did their best to delay the increases demanded by the men.[9]

Viewed against this background of falling productivity, growing concentration of production, economic fluctuation, regional variation, a complex wages system and the employers' adherence to the simple tenet that wages must follow prices, it is possible to understand the course of industrial relations in the coal industry between 1875 and 1914. The unprecedented mining boom at the beginning of the 1870s had seen prices and wages rise and the county unions increase their membership to as much as 40 per cent of the workforce. In prosperous districts such as Scotland, Yorkshire and the North East, moderate union leaders were able to win recognition and secure collective agreements from the employers. By 1873 South Wales, Northumberland and Durham and South and West Yorkshire had all established *ad hoc* joint committees of employers and employed to deal with disputes at individual collieries. But, as so often, the end of the boom proved disastrous for the unions. In South Wales, the Black Country, South and West Yorkshire and the West of Scotland the men were roundly defeated when they tried to resist the wage cuts demanded by their employers as prices began to fall in 1874. Local union membership slumped and even the relatively broadly based Amalgamated Association of Miners was dissolved and its few remaining members advised to join the Northumberland and Durham-dominated Miners' National Association, now renamed the Miners' National Union. So, despite half a century and more of struggle, and despite a few years of relative prosperity, 1875 saw the employers confident and powerful, trade unionism patchy and weak, and no form of collective bargaining surviving outside Northumberland and Durham.[10]

It was trade union weakness which goes far towards explaining the course of industrial relations in coalmining, as in the iron trade, during the decade and a half after 1875. Union leaders like Thomas Burt of Northumberland, Alexander McDonald of Scotland and William Pickard of Lancashire tried to control the conflicts inherent in the industry, avoid direct confrontation with the employers, and work instead to safeguard the very existence of their organizations. Such a programme was unheroic, perhaps, but not ignoble; indeed it was a realistic policy designed to cope with the difficulties confronted by the unions between 1875 and 1888.

The unions' first priority was to stabilize, and then increase, their membership. But this was no easy matter particularly during the late 1870s when selling prices, and thus employment and wages, were all falling away sharply. (During the prosperous early years of the decade some Midlands men were said to have been earning ten shillings a shift whereas at its end many Nottinghamshire miners were earning no more than twelve shillings a week.) By 1879 even the employers' journal, the *Colliery Guardian*, had to admit 'that for a man having a family to provide for, the problem of how to exist on this limited income, without falling into debt, is difficult of solution'. In these circumstances it was easy for employers to impede union activity. A South Wales man remembers that there were

> so many ways to rid themselves of an awkward man. It is a long distance in to some of the workings, and stones or slags are often piled on the side of the roadway. Just a few stones pushed into a tram of coal in the darkness means a case of filling 'dirty' coal when the tram comes to daylight. Dirty coal means lost orders. How can a committee defend that case? How can the man prove he did not fill it? Or a collier may be kept so short of rails that he has to throw his coal four or five yards farther than the man in the next place. He may be kept short of trams or timber, or put in a place where the coal is very stiff or there is a lot of water. The man does not – he cannot – fill so much coal as those in other places, therefore he is lazy, is not trying; and with his job goes his house very often. The tied-cottage system of the farms has its ugly sister – the house owned by the colliery company.

Certainly in Scotland and the North East, where colliery houses were common, the threat of eviction was a powerful weapon. In 1879, for instance, Messrs Heley of Craghead near Chester-le-Street decided to employ no more union men and evicted from their homes every one of their workmen who belonged to the Durham Miners' Association. It was against this sort of hostility that many unionists had to contend.[11]

A further barrier to union efforts to expand their membership and influence the course of industrial relations was the fragmentation of the mining workforce. This may come as something of a surprise in view of the widely held belief that it was the very homogeneity of colliery communities which helped to produce their legendary union loyalty and industrial solidarity.[12] Such a view is altogether too simple. For one thing, there was a constant movement of men in and out of the industry; thus the expansion of the South Wales coalfield at the end of the century encouraged an influx of workers from England. But depression drove men to look elsewhere for work: it was said during the late 1870s for example that 'in consequence of the stoppage of pits' at Rhymney in South Wales, the miners were 'turning their attention to other branches of industry'. There was, too, a clear division of interest between the piecework hewer working at the coalface and the day-wage trapper opening and shutting the ventilation doors; a wide gap between the young man at the height of his earning power and the old man seeing out his days on the surface. Then again miners and their families did not always live in the closed communities of popular imagination. When they did, it might generate as much hostility as solidarity. One South Wales man recalls that in his village 'poverty was general and snobbery exactly as we find it today . . . The woman who lived in the main road would not admit even a nodding acquaintance with an equally respectable person living in a side street'. As in any industry, such heterogeneity made if difficult for a single organization to represent the entire labourforce, a difficulty exacerbated by the refusal of several unions to admit non-hewers to membership, let alone to allow them to stand for office.[13]

Confronted by the fluctuations of the trade cycle, the hostility of the employers and the fragmentation of the workforce, it is not surprising that the county unions found it so difficult to expand their membership. Slowly, however, from the beginning of the 1880s, the number of unionists did begin to grow. This was due in part to the increased attention paid by the unions to the two-thirds of the labourforce who did not work at the coalface. But far more important in encouraging membership was the economic revival of the early 1880s. Nonetheless, it is important not to exaggerate the extent of union support at any time between 1875 and 1888. Even in the mid-1880s no more than about a fifth of the country's miners were unionized.

In their efforts to strengthen their weak industrial position, union leaders turned increasingly to political and social action. Slowly, miners and other workmen began to play a part in local government and slowly, too, they began to aspire towards parliamentary representation. Indeed, the first workmen ever elected to parliament were the two miners' leaders, Thomas Burt and Alexander McDonald, who took their seats as Liberals in 1874. The extension and reorganization of the franchise in 1884–5 altered the balance of power in several coalfield constituencies with the result that six of the eleven Lib-Lab candidates successful in the 1885 election were miners. Thus Ben Pickard, the secretary of the Yorkshire Miners' Association, was elected at Normanton, a constituency in which over 60 per cent of the electorate were now miners. Such parliamentary activity was particularly important in this period of union weakness for it allowed miners' leaders a larger and more prestigious platform for their cautious and moderate industrial policies.[14]

Most unions also provided friendly benefits as a means both of remedying the deficiencies of existing sources of relief and of furthering their industrial policies. Thus it was agreed at an 1874 demonstration of the North Staffordshire Miners' Association that men 'should become members of the Widows and Orphans' Fund as, by so doing, it would be the means of strengthening the constitution . . . and further, it would secure its permanency'. Yet the primacy of the labour function was never left in any doubt. In 1877, for example, the secretary of the South Yorkshire Miners declared that he did not wish their 'Association to lose sight of the principle for which it was established, viz., the protection of labour, and dwindle into nothing more than a benevolent institution' and in the following year it was decided to deal with all business concerning the labour fund before considering anything relating to the widow and orphan scheme.[15]

Both political activity and the provision of friendly benefits did something to safeguard the unions' industrial interests. However the chief way in which miners' leaders, like those from several other industries, responded to their weak bargaining position during the 1870s and 1880s was by advocating the peaceful settlement of disputes. This, they hoped, might be achieved by either arbitration or conciliation agreements or by selling price sliding-scales, three methods which all seemed to offer solid advantages to a weak trade union movement. Efforts were directed at first towards the establishment of boards of arbitration whereby a third party was empowered to bring the two sides to an agreement. As Dr Porter has shown, 'The formation of the boards appears to have taken place when the unions had sufficient strength to convince the employers that . . . arbitration . . . [was] necessary, but insufficient power to make an openly militant policy more attractive for themselves'.[16]

Not surprisingly, union leaders like Alexander McDonald tended to make rather inflated claims for the benefits of arbitration: 'when we proposed the adoption of the principle of arbitration,' he maintained in 1875, 'we were then laughed to scorn by the employing interests. But no movement has ever spread so rapidly or taken a deeper root than that which we then set on foot.' Arbitration was no panacea however. Most miners were not covered by the thirty-nine awards made in the industry between 1873 and 1914, and those who were soon grew disillusioned with the way in which they operated. Because arbitrators embraced the conventional view of contemporary political economy that selling prices, rather than profits or regional comparisons, should determine the level of wages, they naturally awarded wage reductions at times of falling prices. Thus none of the twenty-one awards made between 1873 and 1896 (and only two of the eighteen made between 1897 and 1914) resulted in an advance for the men. So it was that arbitration awards became indelibly associated with wage reductions in the minds of the rank and file. 'Arbitration,' thundered the agitator Neddy Rymer, 'is but another means of concession to capital, for it allows them to use their organized knowledge in commercial matters against our ignorance.'

The significance of these arbitration awards was twofold. In the first place, they gave the unions a breathing space in which to gather their forces and secure some limited degree of recognition. In the second place, and this is somewhat paradoxical in view of the awards' growing unpopularity, they opened the way for the conclusion of selling price sliding-scales. The two sides selected a base year for both selling prices and wage rates and thereafter changes in the latter were determined by 'a given percentage change for each change in selling price'. The first sliding-scale in the coal industry was negotiated in South Staffordshire in 1874, and by the end of the decade the system had been adopted throughout Wales, in Northumberland and Durham, and over a good part of the central English coalfields. The major agreements covered South Staffordshire (1874–88), South Wales (1875–1903), Cannock Chase (1877–93), Durham (1877–89), Northumberland (1879–87), Cumberland (1879–88) and Lanarkshire (1887–9). By 1880 the whole of the Welsh labour-force, and well over half of all English miners, had their wage rates determined by selling price sliding-scales.[17]

It is not difficult to understand how the men's leaders, faced by a seemingly constant round of disputes, reductions and disaffection, should turn from one peaceful method of settling disputes to another. Unions in Yorkshire, South Wales and Northumberland lacked the strength to oppose the introduction of sliding-scales, but the leaders of the Durham Miners' Association, well aware of their county's reliance on the fluctuating export trade, believed positively that sliding-scales were 'the most equitable way of fixing and settling wages'. Like the employers, they hoped that the formalization of the already close relationship between wages and prices would accustom the men to fluctuating wages and provide a self-acting mechanism that would dispense with the need for constant and disruptive wage negotiations.

By their very nature, sliding-scales enabled employers to enjoy wage reductions when prices fell and workmen to secure increases when they rose. But during the 1880s both sides of the industry became disenchanted with this method of settling wage rates. The owners disliked the men's growing interest in their commercial policies, particularly when this took the form of recommending output restriction in order to maintain prices. For their part, the men and their representatives began to realize that the wage reductions forced upon them in response to falling prices did nothing to prevent short-time working and unemployment, yet did much to affect the viability of trade unionism. Even scales which contained provision for a minimum wage rate could not guarantee minimum earnings, for these depended of course upon conditions in the pit, the number of shifts worked, and the level of locally negotiated abnormal place allowances. But for both sides of the industry the most glaring weakness of the sliding-scales was that they did not produce the harmony which they had been designed to foster. There were major strikes in South Wales in 1875, and again in 1893; and not only did the scale negotiated in Durham fail to prevent conflict, it was actually one of the principal causes of a six-weeks' strike by 70,000 men in 1879. There were also a great number of local disputes concerning abnormal place allowances. Although these parochial and often short-lived disputes received little attention at the time and have not attracted much more interest since, they played a significant role in many coalfields in turning employers and employees alike away from the sliding-scale.

Sliding-scales have received a mixed press. The Webbs castigated their supporters for securing recognition from the employers only by accepting the principle that wage rates must fluctuate with the selling price: 'this victory brought results which largely neutralized its advantages . . . the men gained their point at the cost of adopting the intellectual position of their opponents.' Dr. Porter argues that: 'The criticism of conciliation and arbitration must lie in the proposition that a more militant policy would have secured even greater gains had the unions not been restricted by the boards and agreements and had they been able to take full advantage of periods of prosperity.' But as Clegg, Fox and Thompson point out,

> had Burt, Crawford, and Kane [of the ironworkers] not accepted the wage-price link during the seventies there would have been no unions of any strength in either industry a decade later. A recognition of the need for wage reductions was a condition of union survival at that time; and their sliding-scale agreements show a realization that automatic adjustments through the formal machinery of the boards were to be preferred to the frontal clashes which had destroyed so many unions in the two industries.[18]

Whatever their merits or defects, the abandonment of sliding-scales marked a significant stage in the evolution of coalmining's industrial relations. For just as the failure of arbitration in the late 1870s led to the introduction of sliding-scales, so a decade later did the demise of the sliding-scales pave the way for the emergence of a regional – even quasi-national – system of collective bargaining. Dissatisfaction with sliding-scales led directly to the establishment of the Miners' Federation of Great Britain in 1889. The initiative came from Yorkshire and Lancashire where Ben Pickard and Thomas Ashton had been collaborating informally since the beginning of the decade. It was clear that the Northumberland and Durham-dominated Miners' National Union could not be turned into an industrially militant organization and so, with the revival in trade, Pickard and Ashton began to co-ordinate wage claims from the central English coalfields. In the autumn of 1888 Yorkshire invited representatives of 'all miners now free from sliding scales' to discuss 'the best means of securing a 10 per cent advance . . . and of trying to find common ground for action'. The Federation was formally established in the following year. The county unions of Yorkshire, Lancashire, Nottinghamshire, Derbyshire, Warwickshire, Leicestershire, Staffordshire, Worcestershire, Cannock Chase, Shropshire, the Forest of Dean, Bristol, Radstock, Stirlingshire, Monmouthshire and North Wales retained their administrative and financial independence, but agreed to centralize their industrial and parliamentary policies.[19]

Outside the Federation remained Scotland and the exporting coalfields of South Wales and the North East, whose leaders continued to believe that the sliding-scale, or some form of arbitration or conciliation, offered the best way of dealing with their districts' peculiar sensitivity to changing market conditions. This did not necessarily weaken the new organization in the short term for it meant that its support was more homogeneous than would have been the case had the exporting districts been affiliated. Other developments, too, favoured the success of the Federation. The mining population as a whole was becoming more stable and more highly paid, and thus less difficult to organize. But most important of all was the revival of trade which took place during the first two years of the Federation's existence: between 1889 and 1891 the selling price of coal rose by about 60 per cent.[20]

The membership of the Miners' Federation grew rapidly. Increasing efforts were directed towards unionizing oncost and surface workers and overtures were made to those districts which remained outside the Federation. Scotland joined in 1894, although it was not until 1899 that South Wales could be persuaded, and not until 1907–08 that Durham and Northumberland were induced to join permanently. Between 1889 and 1914 the Miners' Federation of Great Britain consolidated its position as the largest bargaining unit not only in the coalfields, but in the country as a whole. In 1893 the 200,000 members of the Federation represented nearly a third of the mining workforce (and about a seventh of all trade unionists). At the end of the century the Federation numbered among its members nearly half of all miners (and a sixth of all unionists), while by 1908 the 600,000 members of the Federation represented 60 per cent of miners (and a remarkable one-quarter of all trade unionists).[21]

The Miners' Federation had two principal aims: a minimum wage, and an eight hour-day for all underground workers. Every means possible was used to strengthen the union's bargaining position. Like the cottonworkers and like other mining unions before them, the constituent unions of the Federation organized friendly benefits and took moderate political action. The mining vote continued to be concentrated in a relatively small number of constituencies: in 1910 there were eighty-six constituencies in which miners comprised a tenth or more of the voters, and eight in which they made up over half the electorate. Not surprisingly, the leadership could see little reason to collaborate with other, politically weaker unions. Nonetheless the Federation did not find it easy to return its own candidates favourable to the enactment of a statutory eight-hour day. It was difficult to dislodge the Northumberland and Durham Lib-Lab MPs, Thomas Burt, John Wilson and Charles Fenwick, with the result that throughout most of the 1890s the only Federation leader with a seat in the Commons was Ben Pickard. Not until the early years of the twentieth century was the Federation able to return a substantial number of its candidates: eleven in 1906, and fifteen in 1910. The long failure to oust the North Eastern MPs (or at least to convert them from Lib-Labism to independent Labour representation) was of crucial importance to the Federation's protracted struggle for an eight-hour day. Since hewers in the North East already worked less than eight hours a day, both the Durham Miners' Association and the Northumberland Miners' Mutual Confident Association were opposed to this plank of the Federation's policy. John Wilson, for example, attacked successive Bills, usually in close collaboration with the leader of the Durham coalowners, Sir James Joicey. It was not until 1908, after forty years' agitation, that underground workers finally won their statutory eight-hour day.[22]

The Federation's political moderation did not detract from its industrial militancy however. Opposition to the hated sliding-scales was turned almost into an organizing principle. Unity was enshrined in the famous Rule 20:

> whenever any County, Federation or District is attacked on the Wage question or any action taken by a general Conference, all members connected with the Society shall tender a notice to terminate their contracts – if approved of by a Conference called to consider the advisability of such joint action being taken.

During 1889 the Federation won two 10 per cent increases on the standard rates, and in February of the following year a special conference called for a further increase of 10 per cent. The delegates pledged 'to act jointly and unitedly' and agreed 'that if the advance be not conceded all round, no district, county, or federation be allowed to accept the advance of wages asked for'. It was in response to this challenge that the employers took united action. For many years colliery owners in Yorkshire, Scotland and South Wales, like employers in other industries, had joined together to present a united front when dealing with their workmen. Now Alfred Barnes, a Derbyshire coalowner and Liberal Unionist MP, pointed out that individual employers, or even county associations, 'must be powerless' against the might of the newly formed Miners' Federation. So it was that the establishment of the Federation led directly to the formation of a corresponding employers' association to cover the inland coalfields.[23]

The organization of both sides of the industry in the central coalfields led to two developments of the greatest importance: the growth of collective bargaining, and the proliferation of large, setpiece battles. The spread of collective bargaining, for all its deficiencies, was perhaps the outstanding change to take place in the industrial relations of the coal industry between 1889 and 1914. The dispute which led to the formation of the federated employers' association itself set the pattern: it was settled when the employers called for a conference with the Federation, an acceptance of the principle of the joint negotiation of wages over the whole of the federated area. By the early years of the twentieth century collective bargaining was established in every coalfield, and by 1910, when only a fifth of the labourforce generally was covered by collective bargaining, the agreements negotiated by the Federation applied to half of all British coalminers. So although true national collective bargaining was slow to emerge in coalmining, the formation of the Miners' Federation and of a parallel federated employers' organization clearly marked the beginning of nationwide collective bargaining, albeit on a regional basis.[24]

The second major development to flow from the growing organization of employers and employed was the proliferation of large, official, set-piece battles. Outside the Federation there were disputes in Scotland in 1894 (when 70,000 men came out), in South Wales in 1898 (when a five-months' lock-out resulted in the loss of nearly 12 million working days), and in Durham in 1892 (when 75,000 men lost over 4 million working days at a cost of £1,215,000).[25] Best known, however, are the two giant battles fought by the Miners' Federation: the 1893 lock-out and the 1912 Minimum Wage Strike. The 1893 lock-out was by far the largest industrial dispute which the country had ever seen; it lasted from July until November, involved

300,000 men, and resulted in the loss of 21 million working days. Its origins were deep seated. The selling price of coal had fallen by 35 per cent since the beginning of the decade and wages had fallen accordingly. Then, in the summer of 1893, the federated coalowners demanded a further reduction of '25 per cent off present rate of wages'. The Federation refused to acccept any reduction, and the men were locked out. It was not a national stoppage however; Scotland and South Wales were still outside the Federation; Northumberland had already voted against a strike, and Durham opted for arbitration. Moreover, in September the Federation decided to allow men to return to work for any employer who agreed to pay the rates which had been in force before the dispute. Within a month nearly 40 per cent of the men in the federated area were back at work and paying levies in support of those who were still locked out.

As winter approached, the dispute began to pose a serious threat to other industries and even, it seemed, to public order. The Prime Minister, Gladstone, wrote to Thomas Ashton:

> The Government have not, up to the present, considered that they could advantageously intervene in a dispute, the settlement of which would far more usefully be brought about by the action of those concerned, than by the good offices of others. But having regard to the national importance of a speedy termination of the dispute, and the fact that the conference which took place on the 3rd and 4th November did not result in a settlement, Her Majesty's Government have felt it their duty to make an effort to bring about a resumption of negotiations between the employers and the employees under conditions which they hope may lead to a satisfactory result.

The two sides met together under the chairmanship of the Foreign Secretary, Lord Rosebery, and agreed, first, that work should be resumed under pre-stoppage conditions; and secondly, that a conciliation board under an independent chairman should be established to determine wages in the federated area after February 1894.[26]

There has been considerable controversy as to whether this settlement represented a victory or a defeat for the Miners' Federation. Those who see the settlement as a victory point out that the government intervened on the side of the miners; that the men returned to work on pre-stoppage terms; and that the conciliation board did a good deal both to eliminate violent fluctuations in wage rates and to maintain those rates at least 30 per cent above the 'standard' 1888 level. The chief critics of the settlement, Dr. J.H. Porter and the late Dr. J.E. Williams, have viewed its consequences rather differently. They contend that the conciliation board acted as a restraining influence upon wages and that it reasserted the principle, so dear to the employers, that wages had to follow prices. Indeed, according to Williams, it was this failure to establish a minimum wage which made necessary the Minimum Wage Strike of 1912. But whether the settlement of the 1893 lock-out is regarded as a victory or defeat for the miners, it is generally agreed that it marked a decisive turning point in British industrial relations:

> the intervention by the State set a precedent for future industrial conflicts
> . . . And though Baldwin attempted in the twenties to take the State out of
> industrial relations it became exceedingly doubtful after 1893 whether
> the distribution of income could be left to negotiation between private
> parties. 1893 was the year in which the state became a party to industrial
> matters and voluntary collective bargaining started to decline.[27]

The Government intervened again in the 1912 Minimum Wage Strike. In this dispute the employers were seeking to attack, and the unions to defend, not the centrally negotiated percentage addition to the 'standard' wage rate which had been at the centre of the 1893 lock-out, but the additional 'abnormal' place allowances which were negotiated locally. Disputes about payments for working in 'abnormal' places were endemic in every coalfield, but particularly in South Wales where faulting and roof 'squeeze' constantly disrupted working conditions. Unable to pass on their increased costs (from workmen's compensation legislation, 1897 and 1905; the coal export tax, 1901–06; and the Eight Hours Act, 1908) to overseas customers who could look to other suppliers, the South Wales employers tried instead to reduce their expenditure on 'abnormal' place payments. This campaign was facilitated by a legal decision of 1907 which ruled that these allowances were *ex gratia*, and were therefore not recoverable at law. One dispute over these payments in 1910 led to a strike at the Ely colliery which belonged to the giant Cambrian Combine. By the end of the year 12,800 Rhondda men were on strike and they remained out until the following August, well after the Miners' Federation had withdrawn its support. The issue of 'abnormal' places, and thus of minimum earnings, rumbled on. As always, the diversity of the coalfields had its effect upon industrial attitudes. Employers in high costs areas, such as Scotland and South Wales, were implacably opposed to any idea of a minimum wage, whereas their colleagues in the federated district were less hostile because they believed that their wages were already higher than the expected minimum.

Early in 1912 the Miners' Federation took a ballot vote which resulted in a two-thirds majority in favour of strike action in order to secure minimum rates. The Prime Minister, Asquith, failed to get his compromise proposals accepted and a national strike began at the end of February. Within a week over a million men were idle and every colliery in Great Britain was at a standstill. As in 1893, the strike threatened to disrupt the whole economy and, as in 1893, the government intervened in unprecedented fashion, this time by accepting the principle of the statutory determination of wages in a private industry. The new Act, which became law at the end of March, provided that a minimum wage for each district, rather than for the country as a whole, should be settled by a joint district board under an independent chairman. The proposal was put to the men who voted by 244,000 votes to 201,000 in favour of continuing the strike. But because the majority was less than two-thirds, it was decided that the strike should come to an end. It is perhaps not surprising that the return to work was somewhat bitter.

The 1912 Minimum Wage Strike may stand as a symbol of the gains achieved by the Miners' Federation by the eve of the First World War. It demonstrated the Federation's ability to mount a national strike – and to get a reluctant labourforce back to work. The strike stands too as the culmination of increasing state intervention and supervision of industry. With the strike the Federation won statutory support for its view that wages should not be determined simply by the selling price of coal; wages, the state now decreed, were to be the first charge upon the revenues of the industry.[28]

There is no doubt that the growing organization of employers and employed encouraged large, set-piece battles, involving hundreds of thousands of men, millions of working days lost, and settlement by some form of government intervention. But the growing organization of employers and employed concealed, rather than removed, the centrifugal tendencies that were so fundamental a feature of coalmining's industrial relations. Indeed, it also led industrial relations in the opposite direction: towards local initiative, local action and local disputes.

The very success of the Miners' Federation and other unions led to difficulties. As unions grew larger, so their permanent officials tended to become isolated from the rank-and-file member. A South Wales miner wondered 'why our leaders always hold the conferences at pleasant places like Blackpool and Margate? I have heard men ask one another that question many times. Why not hold them in the Rhondda Valley, or at Landore or Llansamlefar or on the Tyneside?' The answer seemed obvious: 'Every year our leaders spend away from the very heart of the industry makes them feel more contented with the conditions of those they represent.' With the rank and file increasingly alienated from its leadership, with mining settlements sometimes physically and often socially isolated, and with conditions varying so much from district to district and from pit to pit, the local union branch came to assume a leading role. For most miners it had probably always been the local officials, rather than the nationally known general secretary, who represented the growing power and influence of the union. It was the branch secretary who collected subscriptions, paid out benefits, negotiated the price list and bargained for extra payment when working conditions deteriorated or when a member was required to undertake any job not shown on the price list. The power of the local officials was augmented still further in the 1890s when it became their duty to ensure that any awards made at district level were applied correctly to each individual price list. The local leadership benefited too from the growing grassroots dissatisfaction with both conciliation and collective bargaining. As Clegg, Fox and Thompson point out,

> For the union leaders, as joint authors of the new procedures, collective bargaining had come to stay. Despite its shortcomings, they saw in it the guarantee of union stability, one source of their own power, and the best means available for winning benefits for their members. The rank and file, anxious to protect their privileges and customs from encroachment by the employers, and responsive to the growing agitation for a 'living' minimum wage, did not see collective bargaining in the same light. It might have done much for their leaders, but what was it doing for them. By 1910 a rift between leaders and local militants was beginning to widen in a number of unions.[29]

In coalmining, as in other industries, this widening rift manifested itself in a number of ways. Disaffected union members pursued their own policies: in the Durham Miners' Association they tried to get their own leaders elected to the executive and campaigned for a minimum wage and for affiliation to the Miners' Federation; in the South Wales Miners' Federation they gave tangible expression to their discontent by the publication in 1912 of *The Miners' Next Step*.

The rift between leaders and local militants can also be seen in the growing number of local, unofficial strikes. Although it is never easy to assess the incidence of such informal, often short-lived, and frequently poorly reported disputes, there does seem reason to suppose that their number increased substantially towards the end of the period, especially in Durham and South Wales. It has been found that in Durham, for example, a high proportion of unofficial strikes were caused by putters who believed (correctly) that the Durham Miners' Association was not doing enough for the non-hewers.[30]

The fact that the growing concentration of employers and employed into hostile camps led, not only to large, set-piece confrontations, but also to local, unofficial disputes seems merely to confirm the coal industry's reputation for appalling industrial relations. Official statistics show that between 1898 and 1909, for example, coal-mining accounted for a quarter of all stoppages, a half of all workers involved in disputes, and a half of all the working days lost in the whole of British industry. Some caution is necessary however. Historians of industrial relations in the coal industry sometimes tend to see developments largely, if not exclusively, in terms of strikes and lock-outs. Certainly, there were few miners who never went on strike, and it would be absurd to deny that in certain districts at certain times a great deal of time was lost. Yet in a year like 1897 some 867,000 working days were lost as the result of industrial disputes. It appears a huge number; but it works out to well under $1\frac{1}{2}$ shifts for every person employed in the industry. Even if this figure is increased by 10 per cent to allow for the possible omission of unofficial disputes, it still means that the average miner lost fewer than two turns during the course of the entire year. When the same calculation is made for subsequent years, it transpires that between 1898 and 1901 the average miner lost twenty-three working days a year; eight days a year between 1902 and 1905, and no more than six days between 1906 and 1909.[31]

Industrial relations in the British coal industry underwent a substantial transformation between 1875 and 1914. Politically, the miners moved from dependance upon the Liberals to support for an independent Labour Party, while safety and welfare, hours and wages all became the direct concern of Parliament. There was also the emergence and growth of the Miners' Federation of Great Britain and the recognition and the collective bargaining procedures which it was able to secure from the employers. It was a transformation which in 1875 employers could scarcely have imagined; a transformation for which union leaders could scarcely have hoped.

References

1   I am grateful to Dr. W. R. Garside for his criticisms of an earlier version of this chapter.

2   J. Benson, R. G. Neville & C. H. Thompson, *A Bibliography of the British Coal Industry: Secondary Literature, Parliamentary and Departmental Papers, and a Guide to Sources*, (1981). For briefer guides, see J. E. Williams, 'Labour in the Coalfields: A Critical Bibliography,' *Bulletin of the Society for the Study of Labour History*, 4, (1962), and R. G. Neville & J. Benson, 'Labour in the coalfields (II): A Select Critical Bibliography,' *ibid.*, 31, (1975).

3   Recent general studies include J. Benson, *British Coalminers in the Nineteenth Century: A Social History*, (1980); N. K. Buxton, *The Economic Development of the British Coal Industry: From Industrial Revolution to the Present Day*, (1978); and A. R. Griffin, *The British Coalmining Industry: Retrospect and Prospect*, (1977).

4   A. J. Taylor, 'Labour Productivity and Technological Innovation in the British Coal Industry, 1850–1914,' *Economic History Review*, 14, (1961).

5   Benson, *op.cit.*, pp. 19–22; T. J. Raybould, *The Economic Emergence of the Black Country: A Study of the Dudley Estate*, (1973).

6   R. Walters, 'Labour Productivity in the South Wales Steam-Coal Industry, 1870–1914,' *Economic History Review*, 28, 1975; Benson, *op.cit.*, pp. 17–19.

7   W. H. Scott, E. Mumford, I. C. McGivering & J. M. Kirby, *Coal and Conflict: A Study of Industrial Relations at Collieries*, '1963), pp. 22–3.

8   The best guide to wages is still J.W.F. Rowe, *Wages in the Coal Industry*, (1923).

9   J. H. Porter, 'Wage Bargaining under Conciliation Agreements, 1860–1914,' *Economic History Review*, 23, (1970).

10   R. Challinor, *The Lancashire and Cheshire Miners*, (1972), pp. 112–33; J. E. Williams, *The Derbyshire Miners: A Study in Industrial and Social History*, (1962), pp. 126–70.

11   See for example, J. H. Morris & L. J. Williams, 'The Discharge Note in the South Wales Coal Industry, 1841–1898,' *Economic History Review*, 10, (1957); Benson, *op.cit.*, pp. 191–5.

12   G. V. Rimlinger, 'International Differences in the Strike Propensity of Coal Miners: Experience in Four Countries,' *Industrial and Labour Relations Review*, 12, (1959); M. I. A. Bulmer, 'Sociological Models of the Mining Community,' *Sociological Review*, 23, (1975).

13   Benson, *op.cit.*, *passim*; University College of Swansea: Edmund Stonelake, 'autobiography', ch. 2, p. 4.

14   R. Gregory, *The Miners and British Politics 1906–1914*, (1968); J.

Saville, 'Notes on Ideology and the Miners before World War I,' *Bulletin of the Society for the Study of Labour History*, 23, (1971).

15   J. Benson, 'English Coal-Miners' Trade-Union Accident Funds, 1850–1900,' *Economic History Review*, 28, (1975).

16   The best guide to arbitration is Porter, *op.cit.*

17   *Ibid*. But see also J. E. C. Munro, 'Sliding-Scales in the Coal and Iron Industries from 1885 to 1889,' *Transactions of the Manchester Statistical Society*, (1890); J. H. Porter, 'Wage Determination by Selling Price Sliding-Scales 1870–1914,' *Manchester School of Economic and Social Studies*, (1971); M. Duggett, 'A Comparative Study of the Operation of the Sliding-Scales in the Coal-Mining Industry in Durham and South Wales, 1875–1900,' (1977). The text of the 1875 South Wales sliding-scale is reproduced in R.P. Arnot, *The Miners: A History of the Miners' Federation of Great Britain 1889–1910*, (1949).

18   H. A. Clegg, A. Fox & A. F. Thompson, *A History of British Trade Unions since 1889*, I, (1964), p. 23. Also S. & B. Webb, *The History of Trade Unionism*, (1894), pp. 338–9; Porter, 'Wage Bargaining,' p. 475.

19   Arnot, *op.cit.*, pp. 92–119.

20   Benson, *op.cit.*, especially ch. 7.

21   J. H. Pencavel, 'The Distributional and Efficiency Effects of Trade Unions in Britain,' *British Journal of Industrial Relations*, 15, (1977).

22   For political developments see Gregory, *op.cit.*, Saville, *op.cit.* and F. Bealey & H. Pelling, *Labour and Politics 1900–1906: A History of the Labour Representation Committee*, (1958). For the eight-hour day, see B. McCormick & J. E. Williams, 'The Miners and the Eight-Hour Day, 1863–1913,' *Economic History Review*, 12, (1959).

23   The owners' side of the industry remains seriously neglected. But see, for example, L.J. Williams, 'The Coalowners of South Wales, 1873–80: Problems of Unity,' *Welsh History Review*, 8, (1976), and A. R. and C. P. Griffin, 'The Role of Coal Owners' Associations in the East Midlands in the Nineteenth Century,' *Renaissance and Modern Studies*, 17, (1973).

24   Clegg, Fox & Thompson, *op.cit.*, pp. 471–6.

25   R. Page Arnot, *A History of the Scottish Miners from the earliest times*, (1955), pp. 66–88; R. Page Arnot, *South Wales Miners: Glowyr de Cymru: A History of the South Wales Miners' Federation (1898–1914)*, (1967), pp. 42–66; W. R. Garside, 'Wage Determination and the Miners' Lock-out of 1892,' *Essays in Tyneside Labour History*, (ed.) N. McCord, (1977).

26   There were now conciliation boards of one sort or another in the federated district as well as in Durham, Northumberland, Scotland and South Wales. For the course of the 1893 lock-out see Arnot, *The Miners*, pp. 219–252, and Williams, *Derbyshire Miners*, pp. 314–43.

27   B. J. McCormick, *Industrial Relations in the Coal Industry*, (1979). Full references to the controversy are given in Neville & Benson, *op.cit.*

28   Arnot, *South Wales*, 274–89; Williams, *Derbyshire Miners*, pp. 393–441.

29   Clegg, Fox & Thompson, *op.cit.*, pp. 472–3; P. Spaven, 'Main Gates of

Protest: Contrasts in Rank-and-File Activity among the South Yorkshire Miners, 1858–1894,' *Independent Collier: The Coal Miner as Archetypal Proletarian Reconsidered*, (ed.) R. Harrison, (1978); D. Douglass, 'The Durham Pitman,' *Miners, Quarrymen and Saltworkers*, (ed.) R. Samuel, (1977).

30   Duggett, *op.cit.*; H. Francis & D. Smith, *The Fed: A History of the South Wales Miners in the Twentieth Century*, (1980), ch. 1.

31   For international comparisons see Rimlinger, *op.cit.*

10
Lancashire Cotton Textiles

Joseph L. White

The history of industrial relations in the Lancashire cotton textile industry between 1875 and 1914 is above all one of paradox and contradiction. On the face of it a workforce whose members were deeply divided by sex, age and occupational specialty would seem to be unpromising trade union material. Yet the cotton workers were, by 1914, the third best organized industry in all of Britain, behind only the (entirely male) coalminers and shipbuilding workers. Moreover, cotton trade unionism displayed an almost kaleidoscopic mixture of the Old and New Unionism, collaboration and struggle, subalternity and independence. Whether or not it exemplified a mature system of industrial relations, as Patrick Joyce has recently suggested,[1] long-term freedom from industrial conflict was not part of that maturity.

Economy and Technology

The broad economic history of the industry during our period may be described briefly and schematically: Cotton did *not* embark upon – let alone complete – the transition from competitive to monopoly capitalism. But this is not to say that the industry simply ossified and stagnated. Change did occur, in the forms of a reduced rate of growth and profitability, and a number of significant managerial adaptations and reactions to an increasingly competitive and inhospitable world market.

With respect to cotton's level of output and share of the world market, one detects a 'scissors movement'. The output of yarn and cloth more than doubled between 1870 and 1913 (measured in consumption of raw cotton, from 1,075 billion 1b. to 2,178 billion 1b.), with 1913 marking the highest point ever achieved.[2] At the same time, however, Lancashire's proportion of the world's output was declining. In 1875, the industry possessed 56 per cent of the world's spinning spindles; by 1893 the figure had fallen to less than 50 per cent and continued to decline. Cloth exports showed a similar trend, constituting 81.9 per cent of the world's exports in 1882–4, compared with 69.9 per cent in 1909–13.[3] To be sure, a shift away from textile production, either relatively or absolutely, was not a bad thing in itself from the standpoint of the overall development of the British economy, but as late as 1913 cotton exports still accounted for one-quarter of the economy's export trade.

As had been the case since the industry's earliest days, growth between 1875 and 1914 was anything but continuous and uninterrupted. The years 1875–96 witnessed a fall in prices, punctuated by three cyclical depressions in 1877–9, 1884–5 and 1891–3. The gross volume of production, which peaked in 1872, was not surpassed until 1904.[4] The years from 1895 to 1907 proved to be reasonably recession-proof, only to give way to a short but very deep recession in 1908–10, during which years spinning mill profits plunged from an average of £13,211 per mill in 1907 to an average loss per mill of £3680 in 1910. The ensuing recovery, from the Autumn of 1910 to May–June 1914, was mainly a production boom and not one of profits: the average profit per mill reaching £5584 in 1912 and £5366 in 1913.[5]

The impact of these market forces upon the industry's structure and technology were minimal, considering their force. Rather than resulting in vertical integration and the concentration of capital into fewer hands, the period saw the completion of the separation process by which spinning and weaving became two virtually separate industries. By 1914 Lancashire had about 2000 firms, of which the number of giants had long since ceased to expand. Although the triumph of limited liability in the coarse spinning trade, centred on Oldham, created larger mills (averaging over 100,000 spindles by 1900), in weaving capital requirements for entering the industry remained low and as a result firms tended to be small – 350 looms being a representative figure. Not the least import implication is that weaving now possessed a chronic tendency toward over-capacity and over-production.[6]

What technological change there was also tended to move along already established lines. As spinning mills grew in size, so did the length of the mules inside them. But although some firms were beginning to shift to the more technologically elegant and productive method of ring spinning, the number of mule spindles actually increased in the first years of the twentieth century by a couple of million, at a time when the rest of the world was phasing out their mules.[7] In weaving, the number of fully automatic Northrup looms amounted to only 5409 out of more than 800,000 in the industry in 1911. The argument that union opposition inhibited the adoption of new technology has recently been advanced by L.G. Sandberg, but the safest verdict appears to be: not proven.[8]

How then did Lancashire manage to survive as well as it did? One can single out three managerial strategies. The first was a reorientation of the industry's product mix in the direction of both higher quality yarn and cloth aimed at the domestic and western European market, and coarse cloth for Third World markets, sometimes so heavily sized that it literally had to be dug out of the holds of ships![9] According to D.A. Farnie, 'a wide and extending range of products dissolved the industry's superficial unity into a congeries of dissimilar and unconnected complexes of firms, producing different goods for different markets'.[10] In addition to making the industry's wares more attractive to prospective buyers, the trend toward a more variegated product mix also appears to have reduced intra-industry competition, and thus enable smaller and less efficient firms to survive, though the two were not necessarily the same. Indeed, the number of formal bankruptcies averaged only 31.6 per year between 1873 and 1896, and by the early 1900's decreased further.[11]

The second and third managerial strategies bore directly upon labour. The period saw a significant increase in the size and speed of machinery and was accompanied by a persistent movement towards the use of cheaper, shorter-staple cotton as a raw material.[12] From the standpoint of enhancing productivity these two parallel developments were problematic in the extreme, particularly the use of inadequate raw materials which, far from representing best managerial practice, was essentially a throwback and an evasion of managerial functions. The same can be said for the practice – particularly during periods of slack trade – of not providing weavers with a full workload.[13] At its worst 'playing for work' might result in a four-loom weaver having only one loom to tend. In light of management's ham-fisted approaches to productivity, it is perhaps remarkable that significant gains were actually recorded. The best estimates available are that in spinning output per worker rose from 5520 1b. per worker in 1880–2 to 8737 1b. per worker in 1913. In weaving, the amount of cloth produced per worker appears actually to have fallen – from 4039 1b. per worker in 1880–2 to 3868 lb. per worker in 1913. However, it is to be noted that the value of cloth produced increased from £222.25 per worker in 1891–3 to £280.76 in 1913, which figures represent not only the general rise in prices, but the industry's tendency toward the production of finer cloth of higher value.[14]

But whatever its ultimate effect upon productivity, the dual irritants of speeded-up machines and inadequate materials were an unambiguous disaster from the standpoint of inducing peaceful industrial relations. Historians of labour are still debating the direction of long-term trends of working conditions in Western capitalism. As far as the 'Indian Summer' of the Lancashire cotton industry is concerned, there is little doubt that they saw a significant deterioration.

Workers and the Labour Process

Work and its discontents figured prominently in the industrial conflict that the cotton workers engaged in between 1875 and 1914. To understand their propensity and ability to respond to them, a grasp of the composition of the workforce, and of the division of labour within the industry, is essential.

Economic historians have made much of the cotton industry's more archaic features, and so have we. But to the (extreme) extent that the division of labour within the industry was developed and to the extent that a wedge was deeply driven between what Harry Braverman has called the conception and execution of work,[15] the industry was utterly precocious and fully deserves the fascination (and, on occasion, horror) displayed by observers and critics over the centuries. For cotton was indeed the world's first continuous flow, mass production industry staffed by workers on whom the French term, *operatif specialisé*, sheds a much clearer light than the nearest English equivalents, 'unskilled', or 'semi-skilled'.

This is to say at the outset that the work people, whose numbers grew from 450,000 in 1870 to some 577,000 in 1907, were not a common labour pool of undifferentiated 'hands'. Workers were slotted by age and sex into jobs whose specifications and manning levels were rigidly determined by the machinery, managerial preferences, and, in one very important instance, by the workers themselves. A survey of the major occupational specialties in the industry will make this clear. In spinning mills, breaking open the bales, mixing and carding the cotton were jobs performed entirely by men. The slubbing, intermediate and roving machines, which attenuated the carded cotton into thin strands called rovings, were staffed exclusively by women who were usually (but not invariably) in their teens and early twenties. The actual spinning of the rovings into yarn, of which more than 80 per cent was done by mule, was performed by a team headed up by an adult male spinner (or minder, as he was significantly called) and one or more youthful (again male) assistants, called piecers. This division of labour in the mule room was unique to Lancashire and was the handiwork of the Spinners' union, which in most districts was powerful enough to enforce it.

On the weaving side of the industry, occupational groups were just as sectionalized, but ordered quite differently. Winding yarn into packaged lengths suitable for warping was, again, exclusively women's work. Weaving also possessed cotton's few truly skilled craftsmen – warpers, tapesizers, and loom maintenance men called tacklers. But the largest occupational grouping of all, powerloom weavers, who numbered about 200,000 in 1914, included both men and women.

The fact that so large a proportion of the jobs consisted of more or less routine machine minding and tending was bound to leave its mark on the workers themselves and on the pattern of industrial relations. First, the cotton workers, especially women, shared in common with 'unskilled' workers in other countries and industries the trait of going out on strike in protest over the dismissal of overlookers known to be friendly and helpful (which characteristics all too often had something to do with their dismissal in the first place). Second, many of the workers staffed machinery over whose speed they had no control and could not therefore emulate the skilled craftsmen's work ethic of the daily 'stint', and of a 'manly' refusal to work in the presence of the boss or his deputies. Third, the spinners were keenly aware that the self-acting mule required less strength and skill than its predecessor, the (only semi-automatic) hand mule, which did not disappear altogether from the fine spinning Bolton district until the 1880s. Their struggle for control of the spinning team was a tacit admission that in the absence of union the employers could all to easily and profitably adopt the joiner-minder system, in which two men and one lad minded two pairs of mules and resulted in more work and lower earnings for the men. Worse yet, employers might hire women spinners, as some had in fact done in the Wigan district which, both geographically and economically, was on the margin of the industry.

And yet the more closely one considers the question of the cotton workers' putative lack of skill, the more doubts arise. Another habit of unskilled workers the world over was high turnover rates, particularly in non-unionized periods and industries. If the Lancashire employers had any difficulties keeping their unskilled workers between 1875 and 1914 they have left no record of their troubles. This of course is negative evidence. On the positive side, the spinners, despite their frequently noted obsession with high output, may have fashioned for themselves the functional equivalent of the daily stint to a far greater extent than has been recognized. As will be seen below, the most intractable problem in industrial relations between spinners and managers was 'bad spinning', that is, an unacceptably high (to the spinners) number of broken ends of yarn per draw of the mule carriage. The sticking point in the elusive search for objective criteria of what constituted bad spinning was the employers' querulous complaint that 'there are many indirect ways in which minders can affect the spinning in such a way as to bring about a breakage of any number of ends desired'.[16] In other words the problem (from the employers' perspective) was that the spinners had not lost all control of the labour process. What is more, the spinners appear to have universally adopted the custom of making personal adjustments and minor alterations on their 'own' pair of mules with a view to maximizing production and making it difficult if not impossible for anybody else to operate them![17] Here, then, is an instance of workers' reinserting the skill factor after the employers had done their historic best to remove it.

The spinners were not alone. Both men and women weavers took pride in the mastery of their jobs.[18] That is to suggest, if the work had been totally diskilled, there would have been nothing to master. In addition, they prided themselves on their ability to mind their looms and do other things as well, like the socialist weavers of Nelson who boasted that they could finish reading the morning papers before the breakfast break at 8 o'clock. If the overlooker complained, he would be curtly reminded that payment was by result and that he was therefore to mind his own business.[19] Even jobs that to the uninitiated outsider appeared to be utterly monotonous and without redeeming merits could be turned to advantage by knowledgeable and canny workers, like minding the winding frames, which ran so quietly that workers could engage in conversations above the hum.[20] In sum, then, it would be a serious error to see the cotton workers as either cowed and deferent 'hands', or as an early version of the 'embourgeoisified' worker.

If the division of labour and the skill content of the occupational specialties had their effect upon workers' consciousness, so did the massive presence of women and children in the industry. The related phenomena of pooled family earnings and of the family hierarchy in the mill have continued to attract the attention of historians. Again, as with the problem of skill, there is more to the question than meets the eye. On the one hand, it is unquestionably true that some families managed to achieve very high earnings – upwards of £7 a week was theoretically possible, if seldom realized – and that right down to 1914 a majority of workers supported the retention of the half-time system, which allowed twelve-year-old youngsters to work in the mills half the day and attend school the rest of the day. But it is altogether likely that the size of pooled family pay packets was declining by 1914 because of smaller sized families and because of the decline of child labour: down from 14 per cent of the workforce in 1875 to under 5 per cent in 1911.[21] Analysis, however, is made difficult by the lack of mill personnel and wage records for our period. One piece of evidence we do possess, however, shows that however frequently the sons of spinners may have followed in their fathers' occupational footsteps, the majority of youngsters working in Bolton and West Lancashire mills in 1898 were *not* the children of cotton workers.[22] Also, it is noteworthy that by 1914 the leaders of the cotton unions had come round to a stance on child labour either of direct opposition or of unconcern because as they saw it the half-time system was 'dying on its feet'. This was in sharp contrast to the position they adopted before the Royal Commission on Labour of 1892, when all of them defended child labour and opposed the statutory eight-hour day in the face of Tom Mann's pointed questioning.[23]

The depth of sectionalism made it all but inevitable that trade unionism should assume the form of loose sectional federations as opposed to one centralized industrial union that included all grades of millworkers. The weavers were first off the mark, forming the 'First Amalgamation' in 1858. The weavers' defeat in the Great Strike of 1878 and the only limited success of the First Amalgamation in bringing together all of the local weavers' societies appear to have been the chief impulses that resulted in the establishment of the Second Amalgamation in 1884. By 1888, the union claimed 40,000 members, roughly one-quarter of the weaving labourforce, and this figure rose to 109,000 in 1900. By 1914 membership had reached 179,000, close to 85 per cent of all weavers in the trade and possibly as many as 95 per cent of the male weavers.

The full measure of the Weavers' Amalgamation's success cannot be gauged just from their own membership figures. Their success in organizing the bulk of the trade's operatives – weavers made up three-quarters of the average weaving shed's workforce – appears to have directly stimulated the unionization of the industry's other crafts and specialties which by 1914 was also essentially completed. What is more, a majority of the weavers were women, making them the most highly unionized and best paid manual women workers in the entire country. By the end of our period the union had its sights set on transforming weaving into a 'high-wage' industry.[24]

If the weavers exemplified the emergence of modern industrial unionism among semi-skilled operatives, the Spinners Amalgamation represented an equally successful attempt to maintain a semblance of craft status and privilege for mule spinners for whom, as has been argued, control of the job by means of skill had been largely undercut by the adoption of the self-acting mule. The union's response was to insist that each pair of mules be staffed by one adult spinner and his piecer assistants. This was *not* an apprentice system. Rather than limiting the supply of fully-trained workers, the piecer system guaranteed a permanent surplus fully initiated into the arts and mysteries of operating a pair of mules. Despite (or, more precisely) because of their numbers, the union's policy was to keep the piecers in a condition of permanent industrial subordination by means of their equally successful insistence that the spinners be paid by results, whilst piecers were paid a flat weekly wage, thus ensuring wage differentials between spinners and big piecers of more than 2:1 and wages for spinners what were the highest in the spinning industry.

From the late 1870s onwards, the Spinners' degree of organization was more than 90 per cent. However, their policy toward the unionization of the piecers was equivocal to the point of fraudulence. Since the condition of their favoured position was the continued subalternity of the piecers, opening their union to the piecers on the basis of full membership was out of the question. What the Spinners did – in an apparently sporadic and half-hearted way – was to set up 'Piecers' Associations' with low dues which could well have been deducted by the spinners from the piecers' pay packets, as it was the custom in many mills for the spinners to pay the piecers directly. (This holdover from the days of true sub-contracting was another 'archaic' feature of the cotton industry.) In addition, the Spinners often provided strike pay for piecers with a view to avoiding their acting as scabs.

The upshot was that the piecers, who numbered over 40,000 by the end of our period, remained the most exploited and ill-used section of work people in the entire industry. Wastage was high. Often a piecer would have to wait until his late twenties before he landed his pair of mules – hence the spinners' fear of piecers acting as strike-breakers as a shortcut to promotion. From the spinners' side of the fence, the system also meant difficulties for ageing spinners as well as a severe restriction upon their lateral mobility within the industry. Accordingly, in order to maintain high wages, the spinners had to sacrifice just about everything else. I have suggested elsewhere that the spinners are best regarded as contrived labour aristocrats and that their often-noted conservatism might well have had more to do with this contrived set of working arrangements that with any other single factor.[25]

Because of the Spinners' organizational introvertedness, the task of organizing spinning millworkers outside the mule rooms fell to the Cardroom Workers Amalgamation. An unambiguous creature of the 'Great Depression', it was founded in 1886, and of all the cotton unions most resembled a general union in terms of its membership composition and strategies. At the union's core were strippers and grinders – whose job was to superintend and maintain the long banks of carding engines that straightened the cotton fibres. Although the objectives of the strippers and grinders were identical to those of the spinners – namely, the attainment of high wages and job security for themselves as semi-skilled adult male workers – the CWA realized from the beginning that its strength depended upon numbers and not skill, with the result that it organized the women workers who operated the tenting and ring-spinning frames. By 1914 it was looking for members as far away as the lace mills of Derbyshire. Having survived the difficult years of 1891–3, the CWA grew to 20,000 members in 1900 and 55,000 in 1910. Although more than 80 per cent of its members were women, and although the leaders delivered sizeable material gains to its female members, nevertheless women remained very much second-class union citizens, as strippers and grinders monopolized the union's permanent officials and lay officers from the outset.[26]

The conservatism and bureaucratic tendencies of the cotton unions' leaders have been well known ever since the appearance of the Webbs' *Industrial Democracy*. An important reason for their reputation as trade union mandarins was the complexity of the wage lists that lay at the heart of the unions' trade policies and which were absolutely essential if a degree of order was to be brought to the industry's payment of its wage bill. The officials were certain that ordinary workers – and particularly women – were quite incapable of making the mathematical calculations required to protect themselves against 'nibbling' by the bosses. (Whether they were in fact correct is a separate matter, but it is the perception that counts.) As early as the 1850s the Weavers instituted a written mathematics examination for their prospective paid officials,[27] and there is little doubt that for this and other reasons the distance between officials and shopfloor was very wide – and eminently 'modern'.

This distance between leaders and ranks could cut both ways. Sometimes the leadership was 'ahead of' the members: as already noted, most of them had, by 1914, no brief to make out for the half-time system whilst a majority of the workers still supported it. Although many cotton workers were Tories, James Mawdesley, general secretary of the Spinners until 1902, appears to have been the only Tory cotton union leader aside from an oppositionist weavers' movement in north-east Lancashire which by 1914 had been driven back to one branch in Blackburn thanks to a series of wildcat strikes in 1913 led by ILP weavers in Nelson. On the other hand, socialist officials appear to have been equally rare, and the union leaders participated in the fight for women's suffrage only for a couple of years around 1904. Indeed the President of the Bolton Spinners was one of four delegates to the 1913 TUC annual conference who voted against a resolution favouring votes for women.[28]

But the penchant of the cotton men for labour statesmanship and industrial peace had its limits. Concurrent with their being 'mere calculators', they were unabashedly economistic in their overall trade policy for an industry whose tendential rate of profit appeared to come right out of the pages of classical political economy. In addition, they were unswerving supporters of the strike weapon and opponents of compulsory arbitration, or, indeed, any outside interference in the industrial affairs of the trade, convinced as they were that only they and the employers fully understood its intricacies. But because the union leadership were thus committed, they had to offer the employers something by way of a trade-off, and that something was industrial peace and control of their membership. However, they could deliver industrial peace only intermittently, as over time, the heaving pressures upon working conditions did not abate and the workers showed that they had a collective will of their own. The result was industrial conflict, to which we must now turn.

Strikes

Industrial relations between 1875 and 1914 can be divided into three periods. The first was one of defence against wage cuts and the quest for recognition, 1875–1893–4. The second, which lasted until around 1906, was a period of consolidation and relative industrial peace, to be followed by a final wave of conflict which peaked in 1913 and only began to subside with the signs of an impending recession in the months just before the outbreak of war in August 1914.

Before 1888 our information is limited to about a half dozen long strikes.[29] Their pattern is clear: all were fought over the employers' demand for reductions in wage rates and all were successful from the employers' standpoint. The weavers' Great Strike of 1878, for example, which was the largest strike (involving 100,000 workers) that the cotton industry had experienced up to that time resulted not just in an 'official' reduction of 10 per cent, but in further cuts imposed by individual employers as well. According to one estimate, some weavers were earning more than 35 per cent less at the end of the year than before the dispute began; and this is to say nothing of the sixty-eight strikers who were convicted and sentenced to as many as fifteen years' imprisonment for – among other offences – burning down the house of one of the Blackburn employers. On the spinning side of the industry, wages fell some 20 per cent between 1877 and 1879. Not until 1886 were the workers strong enough to turn back demands for further reductions, as the Oldham Spinners were able to do, partly because of their ability to convince the employers that cutting wages would not cure their economic headache as long as margins remained low and markets remained glutted.[30]

With the return of good trade in the late 1880s and early 1890s, the unions' defensiveness gave way to an offensive strike wave of major proportions. In this respect the cotton workers were clearly part of the 'New Unionism'. In the five years from 1888 to 1892 no fewer than 643 strikes took place involving all sections and districts, but centred mainly in the coarse spinning towns of south-east Lancashire and the plain cloth weaving districts around Blackburn. The old adage that 'every strike is a wages strike' receives a certain amount of confirmation from the fact that 478 of the strikes were fought directly over wages and having to work with bad materials, which had the invariable dual effect of making work more burdensome and reducing pay packets. But to compress the strikes of these years into the narrow categories of wages or, what amounts to the same, recognition of the union wage list, is to distort their meaning. What stands out is the broadness of the range of demands – from the right of workers to take Easter Monday as an (unpaid) holiday, strikes against the practice of fining weavers for cloth judged by management to contain imperfections, excessive steam in weaving sheds (itself a direct consequence of the trend toward the use of bad yarn and heavy sizing), equal pay for women weavers doing the same work as men, to spinners' striking against excessive mule speeds. The strikes of 1888–92 represented not so much the emergence of a 'mature system of industrial relations', as a different maturing process on the part of workers that if union recognition and acceptable working conditions were to be achieved, the strike weapon would need to be resorted to early and often.[31]

As the number of strikes mounted, the decisive confrontation of their offensive phase occurred in the coarse spinning town of Stalybridge. From early 1891 the spinners and piecers at the Stalybridge Mill Company had been complaining about the high number of yarn breakages and, consequently, reduced earnings, due to the poor quality of the material. When management promises to improve matters brought no relief they went on strike on 25 September 1891.

The Stalybridge strike was particularly alarming to the employers because the spinners were demanding *retroactive* monetary compensation for bad spinning, and because employers in Ashton-under-Lyme and north-east Cheshire feared that spinners working in their mills would also raise the bad spinning issue in order to gain a general wage advance. To forestall this happening, the employers, who had hastily re-formed and expanded their organization under the stimulus of the strike, imposed a lock-out on 60 per cent of the south-east Lancashire/north-east Cheshire spinning trade on 15 April 1892. It took three weeks to arrange a compromise settlement which, while upholding the principle of compensation for bad spinning, nevertheless fell far short of satisfying the Stalybridge strikers who had been demanding that agreed-upon criteria for establishing the fact of bad spinning be laid down *before* they returned to work. Because the Spinners' officials had agreed to settlement terms that compelled the strikers to return to work first, they felt they had been sold out.

In the outcome of the Stalybridge strike and lock-out we have a clear-cut instance of the Spinners' officials' desire for industrial peace being at sharp variance with the members' desire to improve conditions in the mule room by any means necessary. Mass meetings of spinners in Stalybridge and several other districts criticized and heckled union officials, and workers were reported to be showing a new interest in the arguments of local socialist agitators for the legislated eight-hour day. Whilst their union leaders were giving testimony in London against the eight-hour day, a mass meeting of workers in Oldham voted for the statutory control of the hours of work in August 1892.[32]

But the rank and files opportunity for continued insurgency was short-lived for business conditions took a sharp turn downward in 1892. The employers, having tasted the fruits of success brought about by their organization and solidarity, moved to impose a second lock-out, this time for a 5 per cent reduction in wages. Beginning on 7 November 1892, the lock-out eventually stopped 16 million spindles and idled some 45–50,000 workers. For the first time, the coarse spinning millowners succeeded in enlisting the support of their fine spinning brethren in the Bolton district, whom they persuaded to run on short-time. Although the lock-out was peaceable – the employers wished to clear stocks as well as win the 5 per cent reduction and therefore did not try to bring in scabs – passions were running high. J.B. Tattersall, the secretary of the employers' federation, spoke darkly of the socialist menace and of 'men of small intelligence and large pockets' who constituted 'a public nuisance which requires to be suppressed'. Mawdsley of the spinners portrayed the employers as men whose 'best friends never accuse . . . of having brains, but nevertheless having got some money, and being put on the directorate of three of four mills . . . they at once begin to consider how they can justify their entrance into middle-class rank by jumping on the men whose labour has placed them where they are'.[33]

It is in this context that the Brooklands Agreement of 23–24 March 1893 is to be understood. Singled out for praise by the Webbs as a model of industrial statesmanship, it provided for a wage reduction of 2.9 per cent – i.e., only slightly more than half the employers' original demand. Just as importantly, the Brooklands Agreement set up a trade-wide system of grievance machinery and placed a limit upon wage movements of plus or minus 5 per cent in any one year. Both sides were thus able to claim victory; and indeed a giant step toward the 'routinization of conflict' had been taken.[34]

In the following years it looked as though the Brooklands Agreement and its spirit had transformed industrial relations. For the next ten years the trend in the number of strikes and working days lost was steadily downward, until by 1903 there were only twenty-three disputes resulting in 37,829 lost working days compared with 104 strikes and 481,676 lost working days in 1894. Even the boom of 1905–07 did not produce a major strike wave: ninety-four strikes in 1907 caused the loss of only 449,616 working days, again fewer than in 1894.

One cannot state with confidence the exact causes of the relative placidity of industrial relations during these years. From one angle, they can be seen as a period of union consolidation following the upsurge and struggles of 1888–93. Another consideration is the mildness of economic fluctuations: really good years were rare, and recessions were shallow. Finally, it is permissible to speculate that the eleven years of Unionist rule that included the Boer War exerted a diffuse but real dampening effect on cotton workers' militancy. But in any case, industrial peace came to an abrupt end in 1908 when the employers, who had also maintained their organization over the years, demanded a 5 per cent wage reduction, citing the end of the boom and the onset of depression as the reason. Ballots taken by the Spinners' and Cardroom Workers' Unions show the depth of rank-and-file opposition to the proposed reduction. The spinners voted 15,916–1301 against acceptance, and the cardroom workers' vote was equally lopsided: 34,714–2818. Despite a final suggestion from the unions that the mills shut down for a month to clear glutted markets, the lock-out commenced on 19 September. The Spinners' officials had by this time reconciled themselves to giving into the demand for the reduction and were able to persuade their members narrowly to go along. An 80 per cent affirmative vote was required to authorize a strike and fell short by just 6 per cent; that is, 74 per cent of the working spinners ignored the counsels of the leadership. Nonetheless, the lock-out lasted until 9 November and cost some $4\frac{3}{4}$ million working days, owing to the stubbornness of the Cardroom Workers' Amalgamation, which was now powerful enough to buck the wishes to the Spinners. (Cf. 1891–3, when the CWA was reduced to having to solicit other unions for financial support.) Their militancy was a possible factor in the employers' decision to defer the 5 per cent cut until March 1909.[35]

So alarmed was the Liberal Government by the confrontation and lock-out that it initiated a conference between the unions and the employers' federation to consider an automatic wage-regulating scheme, or sliding-scale for the industry. The conference failed to reach agreement on the key question of whether current wages were at or 5 per cent above the 'standard', and as a result the whole idea was unceremoniously dropped. But failure aside, the talks marked the first instance (though as will be seen shortly, not the last) of governmental intervention into trade-wide collective bargaining in the cotton industry.[36]

The failure of agreement on the sliding-scale scheme, coupled with the continued and deepening recession throughout 1909, led to a demand by the employers for a second cut of 5 per cent to take effect in March 1910. The officials of the Spinners and Cardroom workers were now in a tight bind indeed. The Spinners' leadership had only narrowly received a mandate to agree to the first cut, and the CWA leadership and rank and file remained as opposed as ever. The outcome – after months of secret negotiations – was yet another compromise. In return for the employers' rescinding their demand, the unions agreed to freeze wage rates for a period of five years. In form the compromise was reminiscent of the Brooklands Agreement. But whereas the Brooklands Agreement had signalled the establishment of industry-wide collective bargaining, the agreement to suspend the wages question for five years in effect put collective bargaining into cold storage. Here indeed was an instance of what Keith Burgess has called 'collective bargaining in the interests of the employers'.[37] For the CWA, the five-year freeze also meant a moratorium in its quest to eliminate (or at least substantially reduce) the differential between the wages of strippers and grinders and of mule spinners. This explains their marked reluctance to ratify the agreement. Although both spinners and cardroom workers voiced opposition to the freeze, it was neither widespread nor organized, and came to nothing.

The recession-plagued and nearly strike-free years of 1909 and early 1910, along with the five-year wage freeze in the spinning trade, proved to be a deceptive overture to the final years before August 1914. For in late 1910 a new wave of insurgency arose. Once again as in 1888–92 workers in all sectors of the industry struck – officially and unofficially – over a very broad range of issues. The CWA, by now set in its independent ways, triggered a one week lock-out of the spinning trade. In order to protect the on-the-job autonomy of the strippers and grinders, the union had instructed one of its members to ignore management's instructions on how to clean the operative parts of carding engines, for which act of insubordination he was sacked. Talks to resolve the dispute snagged on the union's claim that the firm had refused to employ the grievance procedures laid down in the Brooklands Agreement and on the firm's counter-assertion that their right to dismiss workers for insubordination was absolute. The dispute remained deadlocked until October 1910 when the employers – eager to break the impasse and restart the mill now that the recession had ended – declared a general lock-out. It took the intervention of George Askwith, the Board of Trade Labour Department's chief trouble-shooter, to bring in a settlement. This Askwith was able to do by locating an imperfection in the Brooklands Agreement: it had been drafted in such a way that unless one side or the other came forward as the 'plaintiff' in a dispute, the grievance machinery could not be started up. Because Askwith was able to confine the conflict to its procedural aspects, a compromise was rapidly agreed to, and the discharged union man was rehired by a neighbouring mill. Militancy had paid.

Just over a year later, Askwith found himself back in Lancashire, this time to mediate a general lock-out in weaving, the first since 1878. The initiative for starting the conflict lay squarely with the Weavers' Union, which, in 1911, had lodged a demand for an industry-wide closed shop. This was the first time in the history of the cotton trade that the weavers, or any other section, had sought by means of agreement with the employers the goal of making union membership a condition of employment. Notwithstanding the fact that the closed shop had no 'upfront' price tag attached to it, the employers were adamant in their refusal to entertain the demand, and at Christmas 1911 closed their mills.

The leaders of the Weavers' Unions were caught by surprise over the employers' tactic and appear to have made no contingency plans whatsoever. In addition, Askwith showed little sympathy with their cause, and neither did liberal opinion-makers in Lancashire, led by the *Manchester Guardian*. But precisely because the closed-shop campaign proved to have the enthusiastic backing of working weavers, the leadership could not immediately back down from the confrontation they themselves had created. As a result the lock-out dragged on for four weeks before the Weavers' officials finally – and from their viewpoint, with the greatest sense of relief – surrendered.[38]

Although it was the two trade-wide lock-outs that rivetted the attention of the nation and most subsequent historians, they were not totally representative of the 1910–14 unrest. In scale and content they marked a continuation of the workers' propensity to weave a small, dense pattern of strikes fought over local and immediate issues. At the same time, however, comparative analysis of 1910–14 and 1888–92 reveals some crucial differences, and allows us to see just how far the cotton workers had come in the course of a generation.

Contrary to Joyce's assertion[39] that strikes in late Victorian Lancashire had become routinized and ritualized to the point of strikers being assured of getting their jobs back, the figures speak otherwise. In no fewer than fifty-nine of the 643 strikes between 1888 and 92 (9.2 per cent) do we find the terse entry in the columns of the *Annual Report on Strikes and Lock-outs*; 'hands replaced'. By 1910–14 the figure comes down to eight out of 244 (3.3 per cent). The point is that it took employers a very long time to take the occurrence of strikes in their stride; indeed they never fully did so in our period. Other indicators point in the same direction of strikes becoming more effective. In 25 per cent of the strikes over compensation for bad materials in the earlier period, no compensation was paid at all: that is, the strikes failed totally. By 1910–14 in only two out of thirty-seven weaving strikes over bad material did the strikers go back empty-handed. (Spinners, as has been shown above, won the battle for compensated bad spinning as early as 1892.)

Ever since its inception the Weavers' Union had sought to eliminate the practice of employers' imposing fines on weavers producing cloth judged to be spoiled or otherwise substandard. (That the standard practice of firms was to go ahead and sell the 'imperfect' cloth on the open market rankled all the more.) Between 1888–92 twenty-nine strikes were fought over the question of fines, and a flurry of nine more were fought in 1894. By 1910–14 only one strike over fining occurred. Similarly, overlookers struck fifteen times between 1888 and 1892, almost all of them over dismissals or 'poundage' rates, as it was the practice for overlookers also to be paid by results. Only two strikes between 1910 and 1914 involved overlookers, who were now highly organized and earned a flat weekly wage irrespective of the output of the workers under them.

Finally, one notes a significant change in the number and cause of piecers' strikes. Along with the spinners, piecers had to cope with the problem of bad spinning, and joined their senior colleagues in bad spinning disputes during both periods. But, as we have seen, their greatest industrial discontent was that of equitable promotion. The figures for 1888–92 indicate that only five out of twenty-six of their strikes were over promotion. By 1910–14 the figure had leapt to thirty-two of forty-six (69.6 per cent), indicating a growing sense of impatience, urgency – and power. As in the earlier period, piecers in 1913 took the step of organizing their own trade union, independent of the Spinners. Its survival, however, was cut short by the coming of the war.

How should these findings be interpreted? First, it is clear that militant strike action on the part of the unions and their workers succeeded in curbing or eliminating some practices seen by the workers as being abusive and unfair. Second, the workers had broadened and improved the art of fighting and winning 'perishable disputes',[40] that is, those grievances which if not acted upon at once cannot be acted upon at all. Alongside of these tendencies we find in the years before the war the re-emergence of industrial struggles taking on a political dimension (which, to take one final glance back to 1888–92 appears to have happened only once, in the aftermath of the Stalybridge strike). In 1912 the socialist weavers of Burnley succeeded in replacing the Lib-Lab officials of the Burnley Weavers' Association. A few miles away in Nelson, which boasted an 800 member ILP branch, the second largest in the country, ILP members appear to have commanded a majority on the union committee, and in 1913 led the wildcat strikes against Tory dual unionists. A final instance of politics intersecting with industrial concerns occurred in the spinning centre of Middleton, where the branch executive and president of the spinners became converts to industrial unionism and hostile critics of the Amalgamation leaders' handling of the bad spinning strikes of 1913. So threatening did they appear that the Amalgamation officials placed the Middleton branch in receivership – an unprecedented move by any cotton union leadership during the entire period 1875–1914.[41] To summarize, by 1914 some cotton workers were pushing to its limits the sectional, moderate unionism of earlier years, and, if the war had not intervened, might well have continued to do so.

The years 1875–1914, then marked the coming-of-age of the cotton workers as modern industrial workers and trade unionists. At the level of trade-wide policy-making, they had perfected what David Montgomery has graphically called 'cash and carry' trade union-ism,[42] whilst the rank and file has perfected to quite as high a degree shopfloor unionism – with or without the aid of their own officials – to ensure that wages and working conditions attained humanized standards. All in all, it was a considerable achievement.

References

1 Patrick Joyce, *Work, Society and Politics: The Culture of the Factory in Later Victorian England*, (1980), p. 64 ff.
2 R. Robson, *The Cotton Industry in Britain* (1957), pp. 331–5.
3 D. A. Farnie, *The English Cotton Industry and the World Market, 1815–1895*, (1979), p. 185.
4 *Ibid.*, p. 171.
5 L. G. Sandberg, *Lancashire in Decline*, (1974), p. 105.
6 Farnie, *op.cit.*, p. 191 and *passim*.
7 Sandberg, *op.cit.*, p. 26.
8 *Ibid.*, pp. 221–3. For a searching critique of Sandberg's argument see A. Fowler, 'Trade Unions and Technical Change: The Automatic Loom Strike, 1908,' *North-West Labour History Society Bulletin*, 6, 1979–80, pp. 52–3.
9 Interview with Mr. Harry Kershaw, former general secretary of the Amalgamated Weavers' Association.
10 Farnie, *op.cit.*, p. 191.
11 E. J. Hobsbawm, *Industry and Empire*, (1968), p. 184.
12 Farnie, *op.cit.*, pp. 196–7; K. Burgess, *The Origins of British Industrial Relations*, (1975), pp. 234–5; J. L. White, *The Limits of Trade Union Militancy*, (1978), pp. 15–24. Farnie's assertion that the 'use of inferior cotton . . . necessitated . . . an increase in the spindle speeds necessary for the conversion of such cotton into yarn' (p. 196) is diametrically

opposed to the opinions and behaviour of those spinners and piecers who struck against inferior materials – that is, cheap cotton of too short a staple-length for the counts being spun. A *reduction* of spindle speeds and a lowering of the counts being spun constituted a satisfactory resolution of these strikes. See PP 1893/4, LXXXIII Pt. I, *Report on the Strikes and Lock-outs of 1891*, p. 174; and PP 1896, LXXX Pt. I, *Report on the Strikes and Lock-outs of 1895*, pp. 152–3. There are few instances in the history of work where strictly technical factors have determined machinery speeds, and it is unlikely that spinning was one of them.

13 David Montgomery, *Workers' Control in America*, (1979), p. 38.
14 White, *op.cit.*, p. 19.
15 Harry Braverman, *Labor and Monopoly Capital*, (1974), pp. 50–1, 75–83 & 113–14.
16 White, *op.cit.*, p. 19.
17 Harold Catling, *The Spinning Mule*, (1970), p. 149.
18 Farnie, *op.cit.*, p. 300; Robert Roberts, *The Classic Slum* (1971), p. 20.
19 Interview with Mr. Harry Kershaw.
20 J. Norris & J. Liddington, *One Hand Tied Behind Us*, (1979), pp. 91–3.
21 Burgess, *op.cit.*, pp. 238–9; White, *op.cit.*, pp. 27–30.
22 White, *op.cit.*, pp. 56–8.
23 PP 1892 XXIV, Royal Commission on Labour, *Minutes of Evidence* [Group C, Vol. I], pp. 13–14, 24–7 & 43–5.
24 White, *op.cit.*, p. 77; H.A. Turner, *Trade Union Growth Structure and Policy*, (1962), pp. 108–68. Turner's book is the definitive study to date of the history of the cotton unions.
25 White, *op.cit.*, pp. 24–7.
26 *Ibid.*, pp. 76–7.
27 S. & B. Webb, *Industrial Democracy*, (1897), pp. 196–9.
28 Trades Union Congress, *Annual Report*, (1913), p. 330; Norris & Liddington, *op.cit.*, pp. 158–166.
29 PP, 1889, 70, *Report on the Strikes and Lock-outs of 1888*.
30 Burgess, *op.cit.*, p. 267.
31 Figures calculated from data in the *Reports on Strikes and Lock-outs*, 1888–92 inclusive.
32 Burgess, *op.cit.*, p. 283.
33 *Ibid.*, p. 283; H. A. Clegg, A. Fox & A. F. Thompson, *A History of British Trade Unionism Since 1889*, (1964), p. 116.
34 S. & E. Webb, *op.cit.*, pp. 202–03; Burgess, *op.cit.*, pp. 284–7; Clegg, Fox & Thompson, *op.cit.*, p. 117.
35 PP 1989, 69, Pt. II. *Report on the Strikes and Lock-outs of 1908*, pp. 55–60.
36 White, *op.cit.*, pp. 80–4.
37 Burgess, *op.cit.*, pp. 288 & 290.
38 White, *op.cit.*, ch. 8.
39 Joyce, *op.cit.*, p. 67.
40 Richard Hyman, *Strikes*, (1972), pp. 23–4, 39 & 114.

41 White, *op.cit.*, pp. 173–6.
42 David Montgomery, *Beyond Equality: Labor and the Radical Republicans, 1862–1872*, p. 295.

11
Transport

Philip Bagwell

In the forty years between 1871 and 1911 employment in the transport sector of the British economy rose by 240 per cent. This represented a much faster rate of growth than that of employment as a whole which, increased by only 55 per cent in the same time span. Within the transport industry employment on the railways and trams grew at a faster rate than it did in docks and harbours while there was a reduction in the numbers employed on the canals – the consequence of railway competition – as well as in the cab service, where employment opportunities declined with the growth of metropolitan and underground railways, and the spread of cheap bus and tramway services. In 1871 road transport employed more than twice as many people as did the railways; in 1911 there were as many railway jobs – around 625,000 of them – as there were jobs in road passenger and freight transport. Meanwhile employment at sea, on the canals and in the docks had grown to 292,000 in 1911 compared with 191,000 in 1871, an increase principally due to the expansion of British foreign and commonwealth (as distinct from coastal) trade.[1] These shifts in the structure of employment affected the bargaining strength of labour and capital and the pattern of industrial relations in the different sectors of the transport industry.

On the British railway network of 1875 collective bargaining was absent because trade unionism was almost non-existent. After abortive attempts had been made to establish unions on a craft basis in 1848–9 and 1865–7 an enduring union, the Amalgamated Society of Railway Servants (ASRS) was established in the boom conditions of the winter of 1871–2. In the first flush of enthusiasm, 17,000 men joined the new organization. But deficiencies in union management, inter-regional rivalries and the economic depression of the late 1870s brought about a decline in membership to an all-time low of less than 6000 in 1882. At no time before 1914 was a majority of the railway workforce unionized. In 1880 fewer than one in twenty railwaymen held a union card. In that year a new union, the Associated Society of Locomotive Engineers and Firemen (ASLEF), was established on a craft basis. Ten years later another craft union, the United Points-men's and Signalmen's society (UPSS) sought the allegiance of the men in those grades while the General Railway Workers' Union (GRWU) aimed at enrolling the poorer-paid unskilled grades and the men employed in the railway workshops. It was not until 1897, a year of intensive union activity, that the Railway Clerks' Association (RCA) was formed to recruit those employed in the clerical and supervisory grades. Despite the subsequent wooing of railway employees by no less than five trade unions, a majority continued to remain unorganized until the upsurge in industrial strife in the years 1911–13.

It was this failure of staff to organize which enabled the chairmen and general managers of the great railway companies to cling with impunity to their policy of non-recognition of the unions.

In 1907 Mr. Cosmo Bonsor, Chairman of the South-Eastern Railway Company, expressed the 'power to manage' viewpoint, often associated with employers in the engineering industry, but also characteristic of the majority of his contemporaries in railway management: 'The company had refused, and would continue to refuse, to permit a third party to come to their Board Room to discuss with them as to how they were to carry on their business'.[2] The railway companies used a variety of arguments to justify their refusal to negotiate with the unions. In common with the shipowners, railway general managers maintained that trade unionism was incompatible with the strict military-style discipline it was necessary to enforce if the safety of the travelling public and the staff was to be assured. Sir George Findlay, general manager of Britain's 'senior' railway, the London and North-Western, declared in 1892: 'If the railway company were to deal with the Amalgamated Society on questions affecting matters of discipline and good order, I say no discipline and good order would be maintained.'[3]

Those who charged the railway companies with authoritarianism in their dealings with labour were assured that the directors were always ready to hear complaints on an individual basis. The Railway Companies' Association, an organization established in 1867, asserted in 1907 that 'there was no substantial grievance among the men that could not be remedied by personal negotiation'.[4] Management also maintained that members of staff put a high value on railway employment, as evidenced by sons following their fathers in the service. Mr. Birt, general manager of the Great Eastern Railway, asserted that it was 'considered a great privilege to get a son into the service', and that he knew of many instances of his company employing members of three generations of the same family.[5] His chairman agreed. But for the activities of members of the ASRS, he claimed, they would be 'a fairly happy and contented family' on the Great Eastern.[6]

There were many reasons why the majority of railwaymen apparently preferred to accept the strong paternalism, mixed with rigid discipline, of company managements rather than to back the trade unions in an effort to establish collective bargaining. Since the volume of business on the railways fluctuated less severely than it did in other industries, such as building construction and the merchant marine, a job on the railway was more dependable and regular than were jobs elsewhere. Furthermore, the railway network and the volume of traffic were both expanding and the chances of promotion were good for sober and loyal servants of the companies. Cautions, suspensions, fines, and, in extreme cases, sackings, were ever-present reminders of the all-seeing eye of management; but for the dedicated man a job on the railways was a job for life. At a time when the loss of one's employment could mean resort to the dreaded workhouse, employment security was highly prized. This must have been true of accident-prone Peter Lythgoe of Chester Locomotive Works who started work as a cleaner, earning 12s a week in 1864, and rose to become a main line driver at the top rate of 7s 6d a day in 1869. He was kept on in the service until 1914 when he reached the age of sixty-nine, having been fined ten times, cautioned fourteen times, suspended thirteen times and reprimanded twice in his fifty years at the depot. His case was untypical only in respect of the *number* of punishments he received.[7]

A further attraction of the railway service was the existence of company-based friendly societies providing sickness and retirement benefits. The first of these, the Great Western Railway Provident Society, was founded as early as 1838. Dr. Kingsford discovered that there were sixty similar organizations in 1870. Sir George Findlay believed that his company's policy of contributing to the various benevolent funds for different grades of staff had been well worth while since 'it prevented the servants of the North Western to any considerable extent joining the Trades Union Association, that is the Amalgamated Society'.[8]

Encouraged by the divisive tactics of the companies, many railwaymen were more concerned with conditions of employment in their particular grade and with the prospects for promotion within the grade hierarchy – e.g. from engine cleaner to fireman to driver – than they were about joining forces with men in other grades to advance the welfare of the whole. A long campaign of education by the leaders of the ASRS and the GRWU was needed before rank-and-file railwaymen recognized the advantages of working together to wring concessions from the companies.

Although the ASRS enrolled only a small proportion of the railway workforce, its strength varied from region to region, and from grade to grade. In the late 1880s it was strongest in the territory of the North Eastern Railway and in South Wales, both regions in which there was an established tradition of trade unionism among the miners and the engineers – and it was more successful in recruiting footplatemen and guards than it was platelayers, porters and shunters. It is not surprising, therefore, that before the union's officers launched the first national All Grades Campaign of 1896–7, the greatest initiative in formulating demands for improved working conditions came from the best organized regions. In July 1888 branches in the North East drew up the Darlington Programme for reduced working hours and higher pay for the principal grades of railwaymen. The union's AGM that October simplified the claims, stressing only the guaranteed week's work, and a ten-hour day, with payment for overtime on a daily basis.[9]

Two months later on the NER a campaign organized by the Tyneside and national Labour Union and backed by the ASRS for a reduction in the working day, persuaded the directors to agree to arbitration. The award of Robert Spence Watson, announced early in January 1890, granted a reduction in working hours to some, though not all, of the company's goods workers. When they were faced with further demands for reduced hours nearly a year later, the Board, on 18 December 1890, resolved 'to meet any committee of the men either alone or associated with any advisers whom they select to accompany them'. Although the union officers attending a conference with the board two days later were reminded that they were only there as 'advisers', their presence may be seen as a significant milestone in the development of collective bargaining on the railways. An important reason why it had happened was that the NERs directors were 'drawn from the region's leading trade' and were 'men who were well used to dealing with organized labour'.[10]

In August 1890, the directors of the Taff Vale, Rhymney and Barry Docks railways, confronted with similar demands for a reduction in the working day, at first refused to allow Mr. Harford, general secretary of the ASRS, to accompany a deputation of the men. It required an eight-day strike, which disrupted the industry of South Wales, to persuade Mr. Inskip, chairman of the TVR, and spokesman for the companies, to negotiate a settlement with Mr Harford.[11]

In Scotland, the boards of the three principal railway companies, the North British, Caledonian and Glasgow and South Western, refused both direct negotiations and resort to arbitration on the question of excessive overtime working. A bitterly fought strike, which began on 21 December 1890 and was backed by the Scottish ASRS (founded in March 1872), ended in complete defeat on 29 January 1891 and the merger of the union with its stronger English neighbour in the following year.

A number of grade conferences of members of the ASRS were held in Birmingham in the summer of 1896, culminating in an aggregate conference on 11–12 October to draw up the first national All Grades Programme with comprehensive demands for shorter hours and improvements in pay. On 24 October 1897 the general managers of all the principal railway companies in the UK received copies of the document with a request from Richard Bell, the union's general secretary, to negotiate. Hitherto each company had felt perfectly competent to manage its own labour problems. Now, with narrowing profit margins, the result of the application of expensive safety measures under the Railway Regulation Act of 1889 and a government-imposed freeze on freight charges from 1894, the chairmen and general managers felt the need to stand together. Two hundred of them met at Euston on 4 November 1897 to plan a concerted *riposte* to the union. A fortnight later an informal sub-committee of general managers of six of the largest companies drew up a four point plan to beat the ASRS in the event of its calling a strike. None of the companies, with the one important exception of the North Eastern, would agree to negotiate. Faced with the determined opposition of the overwhelming majority of companies, the ASRS did not press its programme to the point of a strike. However, it could claim one success. The board of the NER not only discussed the union's demands with its officers but also agreed to submit the entire All Grades Programme to arbitration, and to allow Richard Bell to be the spokesman for the staff. The award of the arbitrator, Lord James of Hereford, presented in August 1897, shortened hours and improved overtime rates and Sunday payments.[12]

The ten-day strike on the Taff Vale Railway at the end of August 1900 stiffened the resolve of the hard-line directors in the Railway Companies' Association. They approved the company's hiring of blacklegs through William Collison's National Free Labour Association and contributed £5000 to its legal expenses. The Law Lords' decision in favour of the TVR in the Taff Vale Judgment of 1901 and the severe financial liabilities incurred by the ASRS took the sting out of union activity until the passing of the Trade Disputes Act in 1906 nullified the Lord's decision.

On 18 January 1907 all railway general managers received a copy of the ASRS's new All Grades Programme, including demands for an eight-hour day for traffic grades, a ten-hour maximum for other railwaymen, and a 2 shillings a week rise in pay. Although Richard Bell's three separate appeals for negotiations were fruitless, the times were more propitious for the unions than they had been ten years earlier. The rise in food prices helped to generate militancy and to boost ASRS membership from 57,462 in 1905 to 97,561 in 1907. In October 1907, a members' ballot vote of 76,925 to 8773 in favour of strike action hardened the resolve of the union's executive which met to fix the date for a national stoppage.

At this point Lloyd George, President of the Board of Trade, intervened. He invited the union's officers to a meeting with representatives of the companies in Whitehall on 6 November. Both parties accepted. Early on the day of the meeting the directors met separately at Euston and resolved unanimously 'not to yield in the slightest degree' in their resolve to deal direct with their men 'without intervention by the unions'[13]. As a sign of that resolve they refused to meet in the same room with the union leaders and Lloyd George was obliged to flit between the two parties as the discussions advanced. That the negotiations did not breakdown was due to Lloyd George's persuasiveness and charm and to the union's abandonment of its claim for recognition by the companies in return for its acceptance of the company's offer to submit to arbitration all questions concerning pay and hours of work which could not be settled in the Sectional and Central Conciliation Boards which were established under the agreement.[14] The die-hard directors objected to yielding to arbitrators the right to decide important questions about the conditions of service of railwaymen but were consoled by the decision to exclude from membership of the boards all full-time officers of the union. In their public statements they stressed that the conciliation scheme with a *substitute* for union recognition, not a stage in its progress. The moderates on the management side, notably Sam Fay, general manager of the Great Central Railway, were relieved that a national railway strike had been averted, were less hostile to the unions, and were therefore prepared to accept the settlement with equanimity, especially since they believed it was to be of a minimum duration of seven years.[15]

By August 1911 rank-and-file railwaymen, caught up in the wave of industrial unrest of that hot summer, were disillusioned with the working of the conciliation scheme. In 1908 'trade went down with a bang' and the somewhat niggardly settlements reached in the conciliation boards or awarded by arbitrators reflected the depressed state of the companies' revenues.[16] The railwaymen's average weekly wage in 1910 at 25s 9d was a penny less than it had been in 1905.

The railway strike of 1911 began unofficially on 5 August when men employed by the Lancashire and Yorkshire Railway came out with a demand for a 2 shillings a week increase in their wages. Its spread was rapid. In an endeavour to keep it under control the executives of all the railway unions, except the Railway Clerks' Association, met in Liverpool on 15 August and decided to offer the companies twenty-four hours in which to open negotiations, failing which a national railway strike would be called. In the belief that 'the government had undertaken to put at the service of the railway companies every soldier in the country', the directors stood firm, confident that the strike would be ineffective. The events of 15–20 August, when much of the industrial life of the North and of South Wales was paralysed, revealed the extent of their miscalculation.

With the threat of war over the Moroccan crisis overshadowing the scene, Lloyd George succeeded in bringing together in one room, for the first time, the representatives of the companies and the leaders of the railway unions. The companies agreed to reinstate the strikers without penalties and both sides agreed to resume negotiations in the conciliation boards and to participate in the work of a Royal Commission on the working of the 1907 Conciliation Scheme.[17] After the union's rejection of the Report of the Royal Commission, the threat of a further strike and the passing of a Commons' resolution urging the resumption of negotiations, there was a renewal of discussions between the two sides on 7 December. Four days later a revised conciliation scheme was agreed. It was noteworthy in that for the first time, the companies conceded the right of full-time trade union officials to represent the men on the conciliation boards.

Meanwhile, the union leaders who had co-operated to prosecute the strike of 1911 considered the question of a more permanent fusion of forces. The outcome of their labours was the merging of the ASRS, GRWU and UPSS to establish the National Union of Railwaymen (NUR) on 29 March 1913. Albert Fox, general secretary of ASLEF, ceased to attend the discussions after his scheme for a federation, rather than a merger, was rejected. Nevertheless the enthusiasm for the 'New Model' of 1913 was immense. The *combined* membership of the three merging unions in 1913 had been 141,000. In 1914 the NUR membership was 273,362 – 44.3 per cent of the workforce. With ASLEF's 32,900 and the RCA's 29,394 the percentage unionized was now 56. This transformation broadly coincided in time with railway management's acceptance of the need to negotiate regularly with union leaders.

Many of the obstacles to union recruitment experienced by the pioneers of the ASRS in the last quarter of the nineteenth century were also experienced by leaders of the merchant seamen: but the seamen's problems were of greater magnitude. The establishment of an enduring trade union as well as of collective bargaining came later in the merchant marine than it did on the railways. The National Amalgamated Sailors' and Firemen's Union (NASFU) was not founded until 1887, and nationwide collective bargaining to determine the pay and working conditions of seamen was only achieved in 1917.

It was not for want of trying that seamen were without a union, Stephen Jones found evidence of no less than seventeen strikes of sailors based on the north-east coast between 1768 and 1854.[18] J. Havelock Wilson, who led the NASFU from its inception, had been a member of the Seamen's Union of Sunderland, founded in 1878.[19] On the Mersey, a Liverpool Seamen's and Firemen's Bowl Union organized a strike of more than 10,000 sailors in 1879.[20] In Hull both the Marine Firemen's Mutual Association and the Amalgamated Society of the Seafaring Men were functioning in 1881.[21] But all these organizations were local and ephemeral.

The principal impediment to the unionization of sailors was their widespread dispersal. In 1903, Havelock Wilson considered they were 'the most difficult body of men to organize'. 'They were,' he said, 'difficult to get at and away a good deal.'[22] Furthermore, there was no single labour market. Rates of wages and conditions of service varied from region to region. On ocean-going vessels monthly payments were the rule: but rates were higher for able-seamen serving in steamships than they were for those employed in sailing vessels. The man employed on the collier sailing brigs of the North East, who was paid by the round-trip to London and back, found little in common with his contemporary employed at a weekly rate of pay on the ships of the City of Dublin Steam Packet Company's regular packet services to Ireland.

Although desertion from one's ship was treated as a criminal offence until 1880, there was a constant seepage of men at American ports where higher wages were on offer. Shipowners often replaced vacancies thus caused by recruiting lower paid sailors on the European continent. Thus trade unions were losing members across the Atlantic and trying to recruit in their place men unfamiliar with the English language. The number of foreign sailors employed in British ships rose from 16,673 in 1886 to 42,856 in 1910.[23] The employment of foreigners was not an insuperable obstacle to unionization and Wilson found that where they had served any length of time in British ships they stood 'better together' than did many British sailors.[24] But the rapid turnover of staff which the increased employment of foreigners indicated increased the cost and difficulties of union recruitment.

Shipowners and ships' masters were inclined to take the same view of trade unionism as an impediment to discipline and safety as did the general managers of the railway companies. In 1892, when G.E. Laws, a shipowner and general manager of the Shipping Federation, was asked whether 'to allow unions to interfere would be danger-ous', replied: 'Most dangerous in every way, because you lose that authority over men which is necessary at sea, especially in times of danger when everything has to be done promptly and effectively.'[25]

The combined evils of the advance note and the crimping system demoralized the labour force and constituted one of the greatest obstacles to unionization. The advance note was given to the sailor on leaving ship and was a promise to pay the sum it specified to its bearer some days after the ship had again put to sea. Ostensibly, it was designed to help the sailor 'tide over' the period until his back wages were paid. (Until 1880 it was not obligatory for the shipowner to pay wages until six days after the ship docked. Thereafter the maximum delay was two days.) The crimps boarded the newly arrived ship, plied the sailors with drink, offered cash (at a heavy discount) for the advance note, and provided shore accommodation. Subsequently their primary concern was to return sailors to their ships – if necessary in a drunken state – so that the advance notes could be redeemed on shore after the ship's departure.[26]

From February 1878 the Board of Trade employed a small ship *The Midge* in the pool of London to convey its officers to incoming ships where, after negotiations with the ships' masters, they cleared the accounts of the crews, brought them ashore and provided them with rail passes to their home ports. The 'Midge' system was extended to other ports in 1880 and played a major part in undermining the influence of the crimps.[27]

Only in times of booming trade, as in 1870–2 and 1881–90, did shipowners find some difficulty in recruiting sailors to man their ships. The normal situation was of a glut of labour. In 1911 the Board of Trade estimated that there were over 28,000 seamen out of work,[28] and this was not a year of trade depression such as 1908. Given this situation in the labour market the seamen's trade unions had an uphill task to prevent shipowners beating down the level of wages.

One reason why the strongest tradition of sailors' trade unionism was to be found in the North East was that the men employed on the collier brigs of Tyneside-and-Wear made, on average, nine round trips to London and back in a year. Thus they were more frequently in their home ports than were men employed in the ocean-going vessels and were consequently easier to organize. Nineteenth-century seamen's trade unionism often originated in Shields or Sunderland and would spread southwards, London experiencing 'the last echo of the thunder rolling down the coast'.[29] This pattern was, in part, repeated with the NASFU after its foundation in Sunderland in 1887. That it survived longer than its predecessors was partly due to the fact that it was established a few months before the boom of 1889–90 when seamen's labour was in short supply, and shipowners felt obliged to concede some of the union's demands. The union endeavoured to secure the goodwill of the employers by stressing the reliability and good character of its members. In the third quarter of 1888, fourteen members of the Sunderland branch were expelled for various offences, the principal one being 'neglecting to join their ships after they had signed their articles'.[30]

The growth of the NASFU through the years 1888–90 was spectacular. In September 1888 it had only three branches and no more than 2000 members. By mid-May 1889 there were 65,000 members in forty-three branches and by midsummer that year Wilson claimed a membership of over 70,000. By the end of July 1889 the £1 a month increase claimed by the union in the strike which spread round the coast in the preceding weeks had been conceded by most shipowners in twenty of the country's principal ports.[31] In Liverpool in the winter of 1888–9 seamen were on strike for a total of fourteen weeks and won numerous concessions; but the Cunard Company led a determined campaign of resistance to the union's demands, particularly to the claim that the shipowner should employ only union men.[32]

The catastrophic fall in NASFU membership from 75,000 in 1890 to 6000 in 1894 was partly the result of a decline in trade and the return to the normal position of a glut in seamen's labour. But of greater importance was the counter-offensive launched by the Shipping Federation from 1890. The new organization – originally called the Shipowners' Federation – was spurred to action by the demands of the ships' masters organized by the Mercantile Marine Service Association (Liverpool, 1857), the British Shipmasters' and Officers' Protection Society (North East, 1873), the London Shipmasters' Society (1876), and the Scottish Shipmasters' Association (1887). The ships' officers saw the concessions made to the sailors by the shipowners in 1889–90 as threatening their authority, status and income differentials. At a meeting with the committee of the Shipowners' Federation in London on 16 September 1890, Mr Bolan, the shipmasters' spokesman, warned that 'if the trade unionists' coercion continued the officers would have to join the union against their will'. He urged that the Federation should 'take the officers under their wing . . . attend to their grievances and . . . protect them from intimidation'.[33] Those representations had the desired effect. They strengthened the determination of the shipowners to break the stranglehold of trade unionism. Mr G.E. Laws, the first general manager of the Federation, conceded in July 1891 that his organization was formed because of 'the coercion of the union' and of

Wilson's attempt to ensure 'that every master and officer who sailed' belonged to a trade union.'[34]

The Shipping Federation used three tactical devices to break the power of the union. First, employment was limited to holders of a Federation ticket, obtainable at the offices of any of its shipping company members. The holder of the ticket undertook not to object to working alongside non-unionists whose names were entered in the companies registers of free labour. Secondly, men were required to sign their articles on board ship, under the master's eye, rather than on land where they might come under the influence of the union pickets. Thirdly they employed depot ships in strike-bound ports as bases for accommodating blackleg labour.[35]

Although not all shipping companies belonged to the Federation, the outsiders, such as The Cunard and White Star companies, were often strong enough on their own to defy the union. With the other shipping companies the Federation's policy was very effectively applied. From October 1890 in London the British India Line ships were manned with free labour and this company's example was quickly followed by the Shaw Saville Line and the New Zealand Shipping Company. The NASFU persuaded the other water-side unions that the introduction of free labour was a threat to them all. In the Wades Arms Manifesto of December 1890 the United Labour Council of port workers called for a blacking of the free labour companies. The response was initially widespread but the strike ended in crushing defeat in the following March.[36] In Hull the showdown between the Federation and the unions was delayed because of an initial pro-union stance by the largest shipping firm in the port, Messrs C.H. Wilson. On 20 March 1893, however, the Federation opened a Free Labour Exchange on the water-front and put pressure on Wilsons to comply with its policy. The firm yielded, and reversed its earlier policies. With its most powerful support gone, the water-side trade union movement in the city suffered immeasurably.[37]

In 1894 the NASFU's bankruptcy was not simply due to the counter-offensive of the Federation. The union was administratively top-heavy, and was heavily involved in expensive legal cases. After its reconstruction as the National Sailors' and Firemen's Union (NSFU) it moved to less expensive headquarters in Camberwell (it had been in the Strand) and reduced its staff.[38] Its loss of membership was matched by that of other water-front organizations and the influence of sailors' and dockers' unions was minimal until well into the twentieth century.

In June 1911 seamen at Southampton started an unofficial strike for higher pay. The NSFU was low in funds, but it took a gamble and called a nationwide strike, anticipating that the seamen would respond, hoping to gain concessions. The gamble paid off. Within a fortnight 65,000 sailors were on strike and the Shipping Federation which for twenty years had coped successfully with local disputes suddenly found a situation quite beyond its control. Not only was it necessary for the shipping companies to make concessions on wages – a standard increase of ten shillings a month was generally granted – but at Cardiff, London and Liverpool joint union management negotiating arrangements were adopted. Negotiating machinery was one thing: the achievement of the principal objectives of the union-standardized port rates and union recognition-quite another. After the heady gains of the summer of 1911 there were setbacks, and it was not until the emergency of the First World War that either of the objectives were attained.

The leaders of the dockers had at least one problem in common with those of the seamen: the glut of labour. Except in the early 1870s and in 1889–90, there was always competition for the unskilled jobs. In London, in 1892, 7000 of a workforce of 22,000 were idle.[39] This situation did not greatly disturb the dock employers whose bargaining position was strengthened by it. In fact they 'deliberately spread the work out' in a conscious effort to maintain a large pool of labour.[40]

Although most dock labour was casually employed, an 'infinite variety' of job specialisms created sectional interests, inhibiting a common approach to the employer. Shipboard workers – principally the stevedores – were a distinct class from those who worked ashore. Among the dock workers, coal porters, corn porters, cotton porters, deal porters, and many others, all had specialized experience which rendered them geographically and occupationally immobile. In Liverpool and Glasgow Catholic and Protestant antagonisms were a stumbling-block both to mobility and to union co-operation.[41]

In 1890 the tonnage of UK steam ships for the first time exceeded that of sailing vessels. The change was associated with an increase in the size of ships and the concentration of capital ownership into the hands of large companies. In London, Bristol and elsewhere, activity shifted from inner dockland to downstream wharves or outports, loosening the control of craft unions of the stevedores and lightermen over conditions of employment. The larger shipping companies were in a stronger position to defy trade unionism than were the more numerous, competing, owners of sailing vessels.

Throughout the period 1875–1914 shipowners aimed at a quick turn-round of ships through the use of 'a pliable labour force, worked for long hours and at high speed'.[42] The success of the gasworkers in gaining improved conditions of employment from the gas companies obliged the employers to modernize equipment, thereby increasing both labour productivity and its rewards: the failure of the water-front unions to establish significant improvements in the rewards of labour reduced the shipowners' incentives for dockside modernization and kept the productivity of the workforce and its rewards at a low level, despite the intensification of labour.[43]

Apart from the lightermen, watermen and stevedores who were continuously organized from the early 1870s on a craft basis with restricted entry and relatively high entrance fees, the organization of water-side labour was characterized by sudden bursts of expansion, as in 1870–3, 1889–90 and 1911–12, interspersed by long periods of stagnation or retreat.

A major exception to this general pattern was the strike of 30,000 Merseyside dockers and sailors in February 1879, in the depths of the trade recession, to resist the wage cuts unilaterally imposed by the Liverpool Steam Ship Owners' Association and other employers. Although unions were formed in both north and south ends of the port, the strike was defeated through the importation of 'free' labour from Bristol and Glasgow. When agitation was renewed in the following Spring, both sides agreed to arbitration and accepted the Earl of Derby's award restoring the pre-1879 rates of 4s 6d per day for dockers with 8d an hour for night work. These basic rates remained unchanged until 1915.[44]

The great leap forward in organization of waterside workers in 1889 affected all ports. The demands of Ben Tillett's Tea Operatives' and General Labourers' Union, founded in London in 1887 and later entitled the Dock, Wharf Riverside and General Labourers' Union (better known as the Dockers' Union), were for the abolition of sub-contracting, a guaranteed four hours' employment (such as already operated in Liverpool) and the dockers' 'tanner' – a minimum wage of 6d an hour, with 8d an hour overtime. Decisive factors in the success of the five-week-long strike included a steady flow of financial support coming from Australian dockers, starting at a critical stage in the struggle, the backing of skilled waterside workers including the stevedores, and the mediation of Cardinal Manning and others leading to the Mansion House Agreement of 14 September 1889[45]. This success of the dockers encouraged the growth of trade unionism in a wide range of occupations throughout the country.

The Liverpool South End dockers, through the National Union of Dockers (founded in 1889) were more successful in sustaining collective bargaining than were their North End and London contemporaries because they were able to maintain the practice of labour recruitment outside the dock gates where union cards could be checked. They were also dealing with small-scale sailing ship owners who found the 'union rate' some protection against unbridled competition. On the other hand the shipping companies which dominated Liverpool's North End and became increasingly important in London were determined to control their own labour supply by recruiting inside the dock gates where 'free' labour was possible.

The failure to enforce the closed shop on the Thames was fatal to the Dockers' Union, which by 1906 was nearly extinct. When large-scale agitation was renewed in London in 1911 it was led by the National Transport Workers Federation to which seventeen unions affiliated earlier that year. It gave the shipowners until 1 July to concede union recognition, port rates, and an hourly rate of 8d, with one shilling for overtime. Lord Devonport, Chairman of the Port of London Authority, brought together 'the first fully representative gathering' of water-side labour and capital. An increase to 7d a hour in the basic rate was conceded: but the chairman firmly refused any other improvements and a general strike of water-front labour was called on 3 August. After arbitration through the Board of Trade, there were more concessions, but the NTWF lost out on the key question of control of the labour supply. In Liverpool, on the other hand, the strike led to full union recognition. A joint committee of shipowners and union representatives established the Dock Scheme. This was so much valued by the men that, in 1912, when the London dockers appealed for support in their struggle to achieve control of the labour supply, the Liverpool men sat tight, fearful of losing their hard won gains.

After 1875 there was very little competition in the long-distance freight charges of British railway companies: by contrast, distribution from the railheads was intensely competitive and of great frequency. The number of carmen and rulleymen proliforated, though their employers often claimed inability to pay them more than 2½d an hour – half the basic rate of London dockers in 1888 – because of the uneconomic nature of the traffic. With the simultaneous rapid expansion of road distribution from factories and docks the number of carmen, carters and waggoners rose from under 150,000 in 1881 to 314,000 in 1901 and 351,000 in 1911.[46] Very few of these men were organized. (In 1901 no more than 12,000 of them can have been unionized.[47])

The growth of trade unionism was impeded, in the case of the larger employers, through the existence of 'stable societies', akin to company unions, paying friendly society benefits.[48] The division of carters into separate categories employed by the railway companies, railway contractors, the large carrying firms, municipal corporations and co-operative societies, created an infinite variety of conditions of service, a formidable obstacle to the trade union organizer. In the Clydeside area and London, at least, employers blacklisted union activists.[49] In some regions there were too many unions. In Manchester there were five which 'took in horsemen indiscriminately'.[50]

Nevertheless, improvements in working conditions were achieved by the unions. In Scotland the switch from collecting union dues in the stables to collecting them in the men's homes helped to put a stop to blacklisting and victimization. The fact that municipal corporations employed many carters either directly, or indirectly through contractors, was seized upon by Hugh Lyons, general secretary of the Scottish Carters' association, to gain union recognition from Glasgow Corporation in 1904 and thereafter to put pressure on other corporations to follow suit.[51] A widespread strike of Glasgow carters in 1910–11 prompted the employers to form the Glasgow Carting Contractors and Horse Owners' Association. The dispute was settled in February 1912 by an arbitration award fixing the minimum wage for contractors men at 25 shillings a week. Hours were to be limited to 62½ per week. Two years later the Clydeside workers struck again and, with the employers' association in disarray, secured a further rise to make the minimum wage 27 shillings.[52]

Meanwhile in London the strike of the carmen, backed by the NTWF, resulted in an agreement with the London Master Carmen and Cartage Contractors, limiting the working week to one of six days and no more than seventy-two hours, with a maximum daily turn of duty of fourteen hours. This 'for the first time in history made it possible for a man to see his children – once a week at least'.[53] But London and Glasgow, with a few other urban areas, represented only isolated pockets of successful organization by the carters. A more general growth of collective bargaining in this large sector of transport was not achieved until after the First World War.

The rapid urbanization which was characteristic of British population growth in the forty years from 1875 was accompanied by an unprecedented expansion in public passenger transport services. The tramway network grew from 321 miles in 1879 to over 2500 miles in 1914. In the nineteenth century, horsedrawn trams predominated, but by 1906 electrified mileage was 2069 compared with a mere ninety-six miles over which trams were horsedrawn.

W.J.C. Wain, a leading representative of the tramway companies, conceded in 1892 that 'there was no difficulty at all in finding tramway labour'. This enabled him to take a firm line with the unions. 'I absolutely refuse to recognize the interference of outsiders,' he said. The Tramways Institute, of which he was chairman, represented thirty-five companies.[54] The recognition of trade unions was delayed through the sacking of the activists and the sponsoring of company-based friendly societies.[55] Under the rules of the London Tramway Company (1885 edition) an employee could be sacked without the company giving a reason, and wages could be 'varied at any time by giving twenty-four hours' notice'. Conductors were encouraged to report the misdemeanours of their drivers.[56]

Under the Tramways Act, 1870, local authorities had the right to purchase tramway undertakings, generally after twenty-one years, and invariably under remarkably favourable terms. Under the Act the authorities were not permitted to operate the tramways themselves, but under radical political pressure they often included clauses in the leases to the companies which safeguarded the welfare of labour. Some corporations acquired parliamentary powers to run their tramway services themselves, as did Huddersfield in 1883. In 1897 the LCC leased important tramway mileage north of the Thames to the North Metropolitan Tramway Company. In the following year five horsemen with good service records were dismissed within forty-eight hours of attending a union meeting, and the council brought the case to the arbitration of Lord James of Hereford who found the company in breach of the leasing agreement which contained clauses protecting employees from dismissal on account of union activity.[57] This experience helped to convince the council of the merits of outright municipalization: between January 1899 and July 1904 it brought out the tramway companies.[58] In Glasgow, the Trades Council in 1889 brought to the attention of the corporation 'the shocking condition of the tramway servants' who worked a 16–17 hour day for a wage of 20 shillings a week. The agitation was effective, and the corporation decided to acquire the city's tramways when the company's lease expired in 1894.[59]

The progress of trade unionism was eased under municipal ownership. In London, the Amalgamated Omnibus and Tram Workers' Union, which had been established just before a strike in 1891, was absorbed a decade later by the provincially-based Amalgamated Society of Tramway and Vehicle Workers, a union which secured recognition from the LCC in 1905. Collective agreements were well established in Manchester and Salford by 1901. By 1909 London had a Tramways Conciliation Board modelled on that of the railways.[60] Five years later, working conditions of tramwaymen, with hours reduced to $8\frac{3}{4}$ per day and a maximum of seven days' holiday after four years' service, were superior to those of water-side labour and the cabmen.

Through the competition of the faster and cheaper trams the popularity of horsedrawn buses declined in the first decade of the twentieth century. The numbers employed in buses in the UK actually fell from 12,310 in 1901 to 11,836 in 1911.[61] At least 7000 of the total were employed in London. The glut of labour which was present on the water-front and in the tramway depots was also to be found in bus operation. 'When we want six conductors' said the London General Omnibus Company's general manager in 1877, 'we probably have sixty or eighty candidates.'[62] The policy of his company was to oppose union recognition and to dismiss those who were known to be union activists.[63] The result was that turns of duty of up to seventeen hours a day were common, and Sunday working was a widespread practice. The horses were better cared for than the men. A bus driver told Henry Mayhew in 1861: 'Every horse in our stables has one day's rest in four, but it's no rest for the driver.' This was still true a quarter of a century later.

When a major strike of London busmen took place in June 1891 the London Trades' Council raised almost £1000 in support of the strikers, and paid £10 a month to Fred Hammill to organize the Amalgamated Omnibus and Tram Workers' Union.[64] The Union's general secretary claimed that the principal object of the strike was to achieve a twelve-hour day: but the secretary of the LGOC considered that his company's introduction of the ticket system (to match the practice of other companies) was the main cause of the disputes. It was a long tradition in London to allow conductors 'earnings on the side', the legacy of coach guards being allowed to keep the 'short stage' fares. The LGOC on introducing the ticket system increased wages by one shilling a week and after the strike the daily wage of conductors was raised from 4s to 4s 6d, while hours were reduced by three per week.

Influenced by the policy of union recognition adopted by the Tramways Committee of the LCC, the bus companies changed their policies just before the First World War. Albert H. Stanley, who was managing director of the LGOC from 1912, in 1913 recognized the right of the union to negotiate with the company on wages and working conditions. By this time the working day had been reduced to 9–9½ hours.[65]

The organization of the cab drivers was hampered by the existence of a labour surplus as was that of the tramwaymen and the busmen. In London and some other British cities the 'cabbie' hired his hansom, his four-wheeled cab, or his motor taxi by the day, as did his contemporaries in Paris and St. Petersburg, and endeavoured to earn a living by taking in fares more than he paid in rental. Since it was generally the case that there were more men looking for work than there were cabs available, the proprietors were able to keep up the daily rental to a level which squeezed the potential earnings of the cabbie to an almost unbearable extent. The rental was fixed higher from about April until after the date of the Eton and Harrow match at Lords, and was at its lowest in the winter months.

Before the mid-1880s the London Cabbies found their most lucrative stumping ground in the City where men of affluence made short trips to meet other businessmen. The increased use of the telephone reduced earnings from this source, at the same time as the extension of hours of operation of buses, and then trams, undermined the cabbies' late night pickings.[66]

The effect of these developments was to compel the cabbies to work a longer day in order to gain a livlihood. Whereas in the early 1880s a twelve-hour stint was sufficient, a decade later an average of fifteen hours daily was being worked. Understandably, the principal objective of unions such as the Amalgamated Society of Metropolitan Cab Drivers (1874–88), the Edinburgh and Leith Cab Drivers' Association (1885–) and the London Cab Drivers' Union (1894–) was to negotiate with the proprietors for a reduction in the rental of cabs; for when this objective was achieved the driver could anticipate both shorter hours and better take-home earnings.

However, the owners, for the most part organized in London through the United Cab Proprietors' Protection Association, sometimes blacklisted union men and generally refused to recognize their organization since, it was claimed, no more than 4000 cabbies out of 15–16,000 had union cards.[67] In April 1891, the proprietors brought on a strike of the drivers by raising cab rentals during exceptionally cold weather when fares were scarce, and by refusing to answer letters from the union's officers and rejecting arbitration. A few of the larger proprietors, however, broke away from their Association and offered their cabs at the lower rate of 16 shillings a day.[68] Three years later there was a general strike of cab drivers in the capital, lasting from 15 May–11 June. The cabbies complained that the fares they charged to the public were subject to official regulation while the price they paid for the daily use of the cab was determined by market forces. This dispute was referred to the Home Secretary and after investigations a new scale of charges ranging from 10–16 shillings per day was agreed.[69] This was a much better deal for the drivers.

Clearly an outstanding influence on industrial relations in this huge sector of the economy was the unskilled or semi-skilled nature of much of the work. An important influence inhibiting the success of trade unionism, and hence the growth of collective bargaining, was the abundance of labour and the absence of control over its deployment into the transport services. Only in the case of railways, where jobs were secure and not greatly subject to seasonal fluctuation, was the turnover of labour slow, providing better opportunities for union organization. Even in this sector, however, collective bargaining came late in the day since job security was accompanied by authoritarian company rule and draconian discipline.

References

1   Department of Employment, *British Labour Statistics: Historical Abstract 1886–1968*, (1971), table 102, p. 195. D. L. Munby, *Inland Transport Statistics Great Britain 1900–1970*, (1978), tables A 8 1, p. 47 and B 4 2, p. 277.
2   *The Times*, 31 July 1907.
3   Royal Commission on Labour, Minutes of Evidence, Group B PP 1893–4, 33, Q.25, 949.
4   Railway Companies Association, *Conditions of Railway Service and the National Programme*, reprinted from the *Railway News* 19 October 1907.
5   Select Committee on Railway Servants' Hours of Labour PP 1890–1, 16, Qs. 9449–56.
6   Royal Commission on the Railway Conciliation and Arbitration Scheme of 1907, Minutes of Evidence, PP 1912–13, 65, Q.10,011.
7   PRO, British Transport Archives, LNW, 15/175 Staff Register, Chester Locomotive Depot.
8   P. W. Kingsford, *Victorian Railwaymen*, (1970), Appendix 1, pp. 194–7. Royal Commission on Labour, Minutes of Evidence, Group B PP 1893–4, 33, Q.25,953.
9   P. S. Gupta, 'Railway Trade Unionism in Britain, c 1880–1900' *The Economic History Review*, 29, 1, (1966), p. 129.
10 R. J. Irving, *The North Eastern Railway Company 1870–1914*, (1976) p. 59.
11 P. S. Bagwell, *The Railwaymen*, (1963), pp. 137–9.
12 *Ibid.*, pp. 181–3.
13 C. Wrigley, *David Lloyd George and the British Labour Movement*, (1976), pp. 55–6.
14 G. Alderman, 'The Railway Companies and the Growth of 'Trade Unionism in the late Nineteenth and early Twentieth Centuries,' *The Historical Journal*, 14, (1971), p. 140.
15 Sir Guy Granet, general manager of the Midland Railway told The Royal Commission on the Railway Conciliation Scheme, 1907, that: 'A solemn bargain was made . . . that for seven years from 1907 the question of recognition should not be pressed upon the railway companies,' PP 1912–13, 45, Q. 12,912.
16 The observation was Sam Fay's. Royal Commission on the Railway Conciliation Scheme, 1907, Minutes of Evidence, PP 1912013, 45, Q. 11,813.
17 C. Wrigley, *op.cit.*, pp. 64–5.
18 S. Jones, 'Community and Organisation, Early Seamen's Trade Unionism on the North-East Coast 1768–1854,' *Maritime History*, 3, 1, (1973), p. 35.
19 J. H. Wilson, *My Stormy Voyage Through Life*, (1925), pp. 94–5.
20 E. L. Taplin, *Liverpool Dockers and Seamen 1870–1890*, (1974), p. 26.
21 R. Brown, *Waterfront Organization in Hull 1870–1900*, (1972), p. 26.

22 Select Committee of the Board of Trade on the Merchant Marine, Minutes of Evidence, PP 1903, 92, Q. 6065. In reminiscent mood, more than half a century afterwards, Emmanuel Shinwell (later Lord Shinwell), confirmed the truth of Wilson's observation: 'In a flush of zeal a seaman would join the union, pay his dues, and proceed to sea on a long voyage. On his return he would indulge in the traditional spending spree, for his amusement and also to meet the debts which his family had accumulated in his absence. By the time Wilson had caught up with him and demanded past and current contributions he had no money left.' *Conflict Without Malice*, (1955).

23 F. J. Lindop, *A History of Seamen's Trade Unionism to 1929*, (unpublished M. Phil. Thesis, University of London, 1972) p. 22.

24 Select Committee of the Board of Trade on the Merchant Marine, Minutes of Evidence, PP 1903, 62, Qs. 5306, 5401.

25 Royal Commission on Labour, Group B Minutes of Evidence PP 1892, 35, Q. 5019.

26 T. Brassey, *The Advance Note: What it is and Why it ought to be Abolished*, (1875).

27 *Merchant Ships: British Seamen, Report to the Royal Commission on the Loss of Life at Sea*, PP 1886, 59, pp. 205–6.

28 28 Royal Commission on Labour, Group B Minutes of Evidence PP 1892, 35, Q. 5019.

29 Jones, *Maritime History*, p. 42.

30 *Seafaring*, 28 October 1888.

31 *Seafaring*, 1, 8, 15 June and 27 July 1889.

32 Taplin, *op.cit.*, pp. 65–72.

33 *Seafaring*, 20 September 1890.

34 Royal Commission on Labour, Group B Minutes of Evidence PP 1892, 35, Q. 5018.

35 L. H. Powell, *The Shipping Federation*, (1950).

36 J. Lovell, *Stevedores and Dockers*, (1969), pp. 138–40.

37 R. Brown, *op.cit.*, pp. 66–87.

38 J. Sexton, *Sir James Sexton, Agitator*, (1936).

39 Lovell, *op.cit.*, p. 34.

40 *Ibid.*, p. 33.

41 Taplin, *op.cit.*, p. 10.

42 Lovell, *op.cit.*, p. 29.

43 E. J. Hobsbawm, *Labouring Men*, (1968 edn.), chs. 9 & 11.

44 Taplin, *op.cit.*

45 The best account of the strike and settlement is contained in H. Llewellyn Smith & V. Nash, *The Story of the Dockers' Strike*, (1889).

46 H. A. Clegg, A. Fox & A. F. Thompson, *A History of British Trade Unions since 1889*, (1964), p. 88. D. L. Munby, *Inland Transport, Statistics Great Britain 1900–1970*, Table B 41, p. 275.

47 A. Tuckett, *The Scottish Carter*, (1968), p. 101.

48 *Ibid.*, pp. 44–5.

49 Royal Commission on Labour, Group B Minutes of Evidence, PP 1893–4, XXXIII, evidence of R. Lemmon and W. Cuthbertson,

National Scottish Horsemen's Union Qs. 23,082–5 and E. Ballard, Organizing Secretary, London Carmen's Trade Union, Q. 17,746–8.

50 *Ibid.*, Evidence of John Kelly of the Manchester, Salford and District Lorrymen's and Carters' Union, Qs. 18548–9.

51 Tuckett, *op.cit.*, pp. 85–7.

52 *Ibid.*, pp. 116–22.

53 B. Tillett, *History of the London Transport Workers' Strike 1911*, (1912), pp. 62–3.

54 Royal Commission on Labour, Group B Minutes of Evidence, PP 1893–4, 33, Qs. 23123–45.

55 *Ibid.*, Evidence of Thomas Sutherst, Qs 15646–7.

56 Greater London Council, Archive Department, TWYS/GEN/4/3.

57 GLC, TWYS/GEN/1/15.

58 T. C. Barker & M. Robbins, *A History of London Transport*, Vol. 2, (1974), p. 313.

59 Tuckett, *op.cit.*, pp. 34–6, Royal Commission on Labour, Group B Minutes of Evidence. PP 1893–4, 33, evidence of Walter Paton Qs. 19,023–38.

60 GLC TWYS/GEN/1/18.

61 Munby, *Inland Transport Statistics*, Table B 4 1 p. 275.

62 Barker & Robbins, *op.cit.*, p. 280.

63 Royal Commission on Labour, Group B Minutes of Evidence, PP 1893–4, 33, evidence of R. T. Kingham, secretary, LGOC, Q. 18,186, Atkinson, treasurer, Amalgamated Omnibus and Tram Workers' Union, Q. 16,457, and H. Bowdrick, the Union's general secretary, Q. 16,208.

64 London Trades Council, Minutes 16 July 1891.

65 Barker & Robbins, *op.cit.*, p. 314.

66 Committee of Enquiry of the Home Secretary on the Cab Service of the Metropolis, Minutes of Evidence, PP 1895, 35, evidence of F. White, president of the London Cab Drivers' Trade Union, Qs. 4616–4757.

67 Royal Commission on Labour, Group B Minutes of Evidence, PP 1893–4, 33, evidence of A. Mills, secretary of the United Cab Proprietors' Association, Qs 18627–38, and W. R. Levick, member of the London Cab Drivers' Trade Union, Q. 1, 857.

68 *Ibid.*, Evidence of R. Jenkins, London Cab Drivers' Trade Union, Qs. 17822–3.

69 Barker and Robbins, *op.cit.*, p. 276.

12
The Iron Trade

Jeffrey Porter

'We do not wish to intimidate or coerce our employers.'

John Kane, 1863

The manufactured iron trade was a key sector in the conciliation movement which developed in Britain in the last four decades of the nineteenth century. In the 1860s the principal propagandist for the concepts of conciliation and arbitration was A. J. Mundella, the Nottingham hosier and Liberal MP. Mundella instigated the Nottingham hosiery board, assisted in the formation of the Nottingham lace board and was to influence David Dale, a leading member of the Iron Manufacturers' Association and a director of Consett Iron Company. Mundella himself was to arbitrate in the iron trade and he was on friendly terms with several other arbitrators such as Rupert Kettle, G. Shaw Lefevre and David Dale.[1]

The conciliation movement spread to several major industries such as coal mining, cotton textiles, building, engineering and the boot and shoe industry. The iron trade, however, attracted public attention as one of the earliest schemes and superficially one of the most successful. The operation of the conciliation boards in this industry was clearly distinct from the others in that delegates to the boards in the manufactured iron trade were generally elected on a works basis and not necessarily controlled by the trade unions. For an explanation of this curious position there has to be an examination of the experience of the iron trade and its workers before the creation of the boards and the nature of the economic and technological hazards which affected the industry.

The iron trade was adversely affected by both secular and cyclical movements. In the long term the industry was suffering from competition from steel products particularly following the spread of the Gilchrist and Thomas process after 1879. The technological developments linked with steel production adversely affected the demand for manufactured iron, that is for sheets, rails, plates, angles and bars. Furthermore the northern centre of production suffered particularly from its traditional concentration upon the production of iron rails for which the demand, declined greatly during the 'Great Depression' and never recovered. During the course of these changes there occurred a switch in the relative importance of the production of the English regions of the North East and of Staffordshire with which we are principally concerned. In 1882 the north-eastern area had ranked above Staffordshire in terms of output, but by 1894 the southern output was twice that of the north, and by 1914 was three times as important.[2] The division of the English industry into two main districts also meant that there was rivalry and competition between them as manufacturers sought to undercut each other and this was to bedevil union activity throughout the nineteenth century.

This latter point is particularly important when the extreme volatility of demand for manufactured iron products is taken into account. One example will illustrate this. In 1890 the output of firms affiliated to the northern iron trade board was 283,711 tons; by 1893 this output had been reduced to 128,000 tons. Nor can this drop be explained by firms resigning their membership of the board. In 1890, eight firms owning twelve works were affiliated, whilst in 1893 nine firms owning eleven works made the returns.

In such economic conditions union membership and activity was likely to be difficult to maintain. However, these were not the only problems, for there were divisions between the workers in the different processes and between forehands and underhands. Forehands were a species of subcontractor. It was the custom to pay forehands tonnage rates each fortnight. Customarily iron trade wage rates were one shilling for each pound of selling price with the addition of an 'extra'. The forehand would pay the subordinate underhands daily or weekly. The customs of the trade did not appear to permit the forehand to squeeze the underhands, by tradition underhands' wages generally moved in proportion to the fluctuations imposed upon, or negotiated with, the forehands by the employers or their association. Underhands by their nature were young and inexperienced and so inevitably the key figures in the trade were the skilled forehands and conflict with the employers was led by them. The only effect the underhands could have on a dispute was the possibility of some of them being deemed by the employer to be suitable for promotion to forehand and so to be used as replacements for the striking forehands.[3]

The labourforce was further splintered by antagonisms between the forehands in the different processes. The most numerous and lowest paid of the forehands were the puddlers. The puddling process was the most uniform and traditional. This combination of homogeneity, technological backwardness and low pay meant that this group was usually the most militant. After being refined by the puddler the iron was hammered into the form required in the mills and forges by the shingler. Then it was converted into sheets, plates, rods or bars, etc. by the roller, millman and furnaceman. This last group employed teams of between ten and twenty underhands and was the real aristocracy of the iron trade's labourforce. Their consciousness of this superior position was a constant irritation to the puddlers and was to influence the number of unions formed in the industry and the unity, or lack of it, within individual unions.

Conflict in such conditions was hardly surprising and in the 1860s the iron trade was marked by strikes, lock-outs and attempts to form effective trade union organizations. The experience of this decade was to influence union leaders in the industry for the rest of the century.

The formation of trade unions in both English districts of the iron trade was mainly the result of strikes. In August 1862 a strike at Gateshead led to the formation of the National Association of Puddlers, Shinglers, Rollers and Millmen. The following year the puddlers of South Staffordshire struck for a 10 per cent rise in wages, although it took them five months to achieve the advance. The consequence of the Staffordshire dispute was the formation of union branches which became in 1866 the Associated Iron Workers of Great Britain. During the dispute the southern men had sought the assistance of the northern union and agreed to adopt its rules but right from the start there was disagreement over where control of any national union ought to be. In addition, the southern millmen disliked the possibility of being overruled by the more numerous puddlers and as a result a breakaway Millmen's Union was established in Staffordshire, though not in the north.[4]

The response of the employers to the formation of this new group of unions was prompt, the next year saw the establishment of a national employers' organization and the likelihood of a trial of strength increased. Leeds proved to be the next cockpit of the iron trade. In 1864 men at seven works in Leeds were locked out for refusing to sign the 'document' and agree to leave the northern union. This lock-out lasted for twenty-seven weeks, and whilst initially the three unions provided support for the 10,000 men in the end the Leeds workers went down to defeat. The ironmasters took full advantage of this and dismissed those who continued to attend union meetings. The Leeds branches never recovered from the blow, and iron trade unionism in the area died out. The dispute also displayed the disunity of the two unions based on Gateshead and Brierly Hill. Attempts were made by the two executives to promote unity, but the suspicions in the south of northern domination led the Staffordshire men to withdraw support from the Leeds dispute. This may have been because the fight seemed hopeless, but the dispute cost the National Association £17,000 and reinforced the mutual suspicion and distrust.

Events during the following year had a depressing familiarity. The North Staffordshire men determined to strike against a wage reduction and gained support from the north. The national Association of Ironmasters met in Birmingham and decided on a national lock-out. The employers were much better organized for conducting a national dispute than the union, and when twenty delegates from the two iron unions met at Brierly Hill John Kane from the north persuaded them not to call a national strike. The employers showed no inclination to respond to this peace initiative and in any case the North Staffordshire men refused to return to work and stayed out for five months. Since it was clear that the two unions' leaders had no real influence in North Staffordshire the employers rescinded their call for a national lock-out as it would now have been purposeless.

Current attempts at co-operation between north and south collapsed in 1866. The northern men opposed their employers' demands for a reduction and for five months some 12,000 men in the area were laid off. In October the southern iron workers formally established their own union, the Associated Ironworkers, and cut off financial aid to the northern men whom they believed were trying to dominate them. The consequence of defeat and schism for the membership of the two unions was disastrous. The Associated area claimed a membership of 6000 in 1865, 2000 in April 1867 and a mere 900–1000 in November 1867. The National Association claimed 5000 paid-up members in July, and only 500 by the end of the year.

Wage reductions followed in the south in 1867 and further reductions in 1868. By that time there were only 350 union members in the north and 750 in the south. In such a situation the clear choice facing the unions was extinction or amalgamation. Support from the north during an eight-week strike paved the way for the creation of the National Amalgamated Society of Ironworkers, a gradiose title for a struggling union with less than 500 members and little in the way of funds.[5]

To have survived as a union leader in that cockpit of a decade was in itself a sign of toughness but it was inevitable that such an experience would influence the union leaders' expectations of success through militant strike action. It is apposite, therefore, to consider the leading personalities in the Ironworkers' Union.

The outstanding figure in the formation of the Ironworkers' Union was John Kane who was born in 1819 and who had been trying to form a union for twenty years before his eventual success in 1862. When the National Association was formed in that year, on the crest of an iron trade boom generated by the American Civil War, John Kane was elected president and chief executive. After thirty years' employment with the same firm, he was dismissed for his part in the Leeds dispute and subsequently elected to be full-time president of the Union. Consequently his experience led him to believe that disputes were 'very prejudicial to all classes and, like war, leave the track of misery behind them'.[6] John Kane died suddenly in 1876 and was succeeded as general secretary and as operatives' secretary of the northern conciliation board by Edward Trow (born in 1833).

Exceptionally amongst the union leaders Trow had held union office in both English districts. In his mid-thirties, Trow had been a branch secretary of the Brierly Hill union. In 1867 he moved to a job in Darlington and joined the National Association. Five years later he was elected president and assistant secretary of the new Amalgamated Malleable Ironworkers' Union (formed in 1868) and vice-president of the northern board. In 1874 Trow took over the paid position of assistant secretary and treasurer. The presidency then passed to William Aucott. When the union was reorganized yet again in 1887 as the Associated Iron & Steel Workers of Great Britain, Trow was elected general secretary. He died in 1899.[7] Aucott had joined the Staffordshire Union at its creation, then, after its failure, passed over to Kane's Union, and with James Capper had been influcntial in the affairs of the southern hoard. As well as having held the presidency of the Amalgamated Malleable Ironworkers, Aucott was elected president of the Associated Iron and Steel Workers on its formation. In 1889 the secretaryship of the Midland Board fell to Aucott on the indisposition of James Capper, and Aucott held this post until his death in 1915 and combined it with the union's presidency till 1912.[8]

This brings us to the last of the 'Big Four'. James Capper, born in 1829, was one of the staunchest supporters of independence for Staffordshire from the north and so was in opposition to Edward Trow's ideas. Capper was the operatives' secretary of the Staffordshire board from 1876 and actually left the Amalgamated Malleable Ironworkers and seems to have rejoined the Associated Iron and Steel Workers in 1887 merely to preserve his position on the Board. However, in 1888 a stroke incapacitated him from further Board work.[9]

These four brief biographical sketches show how the four most influential men in the union had all experienced the vicissitudes in the fortunes of the iron trade unions and could be expected to be antipathetic to strikes which in the past had left the union weakened and divided in the face of the more strongly organized employers. Moreover, those who were secretaries of the wages boards were paid by the Board and in some respects could afford to ignore criticisms from union members who were only a part of the total membership of the boards.

It is clear from the account so far that when the employers and their Association were in the dominant position they had no time for suggestions of conciliation or arbitration. When Kane had made such suggestions in 1866 he had been ignored. The following year, however, Dale had proposed a resolution in favour of schemes like Mundella's board in Nottingham at a meeting in London of the Associated Chambers of Commerce, but he received little support from his fellow ironmasters when he circularized them in 1868. In that latter year the Union had moved its head office from Gateshead to Darlington, and this put Kane into closer contact with Dale.[10] Kane had advocated the formation of such boards in evidence to the Royal Commission on Trade Unions and was already an enthusiastic supporter of the concept and practice of conciliation and arbitration.[11]

Perhaps Dale anticipated, as Mundella certainly did, that the next revival of trade might give the unions their opportunity for revenge. For when trade began to revive in 1869 the employers' leader W. Whitwell thought 'any increase in the demand for iron would be the signal for peremptory demands on the part of the workmen, tending to a renewal of the confusion of the previous years'.[12] Kane and Trow were both impressed by the Nottingham board and Kane pushed the idea through the newly established *Ironworkers Journal* which he edited. Consequently the employers' opportunistic support for conciliation found a ready audience in the union leaders.

Although the northern employers had by now decided in favour of a conciliation board they had no intention of granting recognition to the union. At the first meeting of the representatives from the two sides they objected to John Kane's presence on the grounds that he was not a 'practical ironworker'. The accepted solution was to make Kane and Daniel Jones, the employers' secretary, joint secretaries of the Board. Dale was elected president. Representation was on a works basis so that all workmen took part in elections and the existence of the union was not recognized.[13] Five weeks after the establishment of the Board a meeting of workers' delegates decided that the five operative representatives on the Board's Standing Committee should act as the Union's General Council. This continued to be the practice. So in consequence the union leaders could be elected by a majority of non-unionists.[14] A similar Board with a more informal structure was adopted in Staffordshire after a successful strike in 1872. In this case twelve representatives from each side formed the Board. The employers leader, E.J. Barker, thought it would diminish the likelihood of strikes when bargaining power was increasing.[15]

The employers in the north in 1869 were unwilling to grant an increase in wage rates and the Middlesborough workers were so incensed that the Board members were finding 'the utmost difficulty in keeping them quiet and convincing them of the advantages of arbitration'. As a result Rupert Kettle, a County Court judge and frequent advocate of conciliation was chosen as arbitrator by the Board. Kettle accepted the previous custom of basing wage fluctuations on price changes. 'Price,' he said, 'forms the only legitimate fund out of which wages can be paid and the enquiry should be strictly confined to this.' He awarded 5 per cent, and the Board agreed to look at his suggestions for the adoption of a selling price sliding-scale which would automatically vary wage rates in response to changes in the selling price of manufactured iron.[16]

In any comparison of prices and wages the choice of base year is obviously crucial. Much argument on these lines took place in 1870 in an arbitration before Thomas Hughes, author and Christian socialist. Although a well-known public figure, Thomas Hughes proved an unwise choice as he confessed himself unable to understand the evidence and instead persuaded the employers to offer a 10 per cent increase for a year. Then prices temporarily turned and a 5 per cent reduction followed in 1871 as the delegates agreed that prices had fallen. In that year Hughes also took two further arbitrations and incurred unpopularity in both. The first, a reduction of 5 per cent, reduced the men to 'a dreadful state of excitement' and the second, a 5 per cent increase for nine months kept 'the men bound hand and foot . . . without monetary compensation'. According to union leaders, the employers had previously admitted that a long agreement was in itself worth 5 per cent regardless of a change in prices. Hughes attacked his critics for behaving 'like spoiled children'. There were excited demands for strike action, and Hughes' language could hardly be described as diplomatic.[17]

Again Hughes had suggested a sliding-scale and by 8 January 1872 a committee chaired by Dale had worked out a scheme. Wage rates were to be changed each quarter, and Board meetings were to be reduced to two a year. However, the Dale Scale gave the men less than was granted in Staffordshire and in the face of mounting discontent the employers conceded the balance. The problem of parity with Staffordshire continued in 1873 but no agreement could be reached and Kettle was called on to make two further arbitrations in the north.

Meanwhile the Staffordshire Board was facing similar strains. E.J. Barker attacked union leaders as 'paid professional disturbers' and told them bluntly that the union was in no position to fight and should accept the same as Kettle awarded in the northern boards' two arbitrations. This was reluctantly accepted.[18] The continuing divergence in rates between the two areas led to a joint meeting at Derby to negotiate a joint scale, a scheme was arranged but the delegates proved unable to sell it to the members. However, after the employers had secured a reduction of 10 per cent in both regions the 'Derby Scale' finally came into operation in July 1874 and over 1874–5 reduced wage rates by a further 20 per cent. The northern employers secured a further reduction of 5 per cent. The price-wage bargaining tide had clearly turned again.[19] A ballot of the northern men agreed to a further arbitration which would determine wages for the first half of 1876 by 1908 votes to 958. A local ironmaster and A.J. Mundella were chosen. Mundella was given strict instructions not to compromise by Kane. But he did, and gave a reduction of $7\frac{1}{2}$ per cent, not on the basis of lower prices but with the idea of stimulating demand. As soon as the award was known men at Stockton, Middlesborough and Sunderland came out on strike. They were, however, thus in breach of the Board rules and the union leaders insisted they return to work.[20]

In the south the parallel reductions led to strikes at the end of 1875 and the men refused to return to work. Aucott and Capper were accused by the employers of losing control of the men. Capper complained 'The men are so disorganized and dissatisfied that we cannot give any pledge on their behalf'. As a result the Board was of no use to the employers and it was dissolved.[21] A new Board was then drawn up on the lines of the northern Board with representatives being elected from each works; Aucott was vice-chairman and Capper secretary; Joseph Chamberlain agreed to be umpire.

By 1877 the union was so weakened in the south that its membership was almost entirely confined to the north-east. In that area further arbitrations by Dale in 1877, 1878 and 1879 further reduced, or failed to increase, wages as did an award by the Liberal MP G. Shaw Lefevre in December 1878. Joseph Chamberlain awarded the Staffordshire men reductions in 1876 and 1878 even though he felt 'that the reduction would not be to the advantage of the trade and knowing the operatives to be receiving wages barely sufficient to provide for necessities'.[22] A slight recovery occurred in the southern area towards the end of 1879 and Chamberlain was able to award two increases and, in the temporarily more optimistic climate, recommend the negotiation of a new sliding-scale. This came into operation in July 1880 with an 'extra' of 6d awarded by Richard Chamberlain who had succeeded his brother as umpire. Prices, however, were now falling once more and therefore so did wages. This scale lasted until 1882 after which arbitration was again adopted.

The north shared a similar experience. In November 1879 the men had claimed an increase and a new scale came into operation at the end of April 1880 with a 1s. 6d 'extra' decided by Dale as arbitrator. This scale also awarded reductions and strikes followed. In 1882 there were signs of improvement and the employers granted a $7\frac{1}{2}$ per cent increase plus an arbitration by J.W. Pease, MP for Durham and an ironmaster. He based his award on past and expected prices, the latter being unverifiable guesses provided by the employers. Only three works accepted his award: twenty-one others were shut by strikes. This was the occasion for the cumulative discontent to be expressed. A ballot of 9807 subscribers to the Board found 4117 in favour of its continuing, while 3229 were against. The Board delegates decided to continue nevertheless and held a second ballot later in the year. This revealed no less dissatisfaction. Of 10,307 subscribers, 5418 were in favour and 1320 against, but 393 did not bother to vote and 148 spoilt their papers.[23] Discontent with the Board and with arbitration was really a reflection of the link between selling prices and wages. If prices were volatile around a downward trend, and if prices were accepted as the principal determinant of wage changes, then this could only be at the expense of the concept of a minimum standard of living.

In these circumstances it is surprising to find Pease arbitrating again, and again making his award on expected iron prices. He awarded a reduction from 25 November 1882 of 5 per cent. More strikes ensued. The following year a modified '1880 Dale' sliding-scale was introduced with wage changes every two months. Reductions in wages followed once more and it was terminated. In practice the termination meant nothing since it was followed by four arbitrations by Robert Spence Watson in 1884–5 and he based his decision mainly on changes in selling prices. After the collapse of the Chamberlain Scale in the south in 1882 Alderman Thomas Avery had arbitrated and presided over discussions for a new sliding-scale. This was repudiated by the men when wages were reduced. Some 15,000 workers struck, there was much violence and fourteen arrests, but the employers' unity defeated the strikers. However, Avery awarded further reductions. By January 1886 wages in the south were lower than at any time since 1871.[24] Union organization was so weak that it could not enforce any decisions and firms were actually leaving the Board to secure further local reductions.

Another low point in the union's existence had now been reached. As an attempt at recovery, the new Associated Iron and Steel Workers' Union was formed in 1887, and the Amalgamated Association wound up in 1891, and its remaining members transferred to the new union which had, in 1892, a membership of 10,000. This fell to 5000 in 1896, recovered to 8000 in 1900 and by 1916 when the union was merged into the British Iron, Steel & Kindred Trades Association membership was 9798.[25] These figures suggest that while membership still fluctuated with the state of trade, a more stable floor to membership had been achieved and it is perhaps in this later period that the iron trade gained – and perhaps deserved – its reputation for pacific industrial relations.

After the reformation of the union Spence Watson had arbitrated once more in the north and again suggested a sliding-scale. This was agreed from July 1889 for a period of two years. Twelve works were in favour, four against and two neutral.[26] With the recovery of prices the sliding-scale was repeatedly renewed and discontent abated.

The Staffordshire district took more time to settle. After Sir Thomas Martineau, Mayor of Birmingham, had become president, the Board was reorganized in 1888 as the Midland Iron and Steel Wages Board and the improved condition of the union was recognized by the employers when it was agreed that only 'compliance' members of the union could be elected to the Board. The removal of Capper shortly afterwards through ill-health facilitated change. Until a new scale was arranged, Sir Thomas Martineau made three awards on the basis of changes in selling prices, and by October 1889 a new scale was agreed.[27] The problem of comparability with the north continued to cause dissension and in 1890 the scale was suspended. Attempts to establish a joint sliding-scale for both districts came to nothing in 1892 when the northern men rejected the idea. By 1893 the divergence between northern and southern prices was such that the Midlands' representatives from each works wanted links with northern rates abolished and the Midlands Board reorganized to cover all works in the area. Sixty-two out of sixty-nine works in the Midlands area agreed to this.[28] A new sliding-scale was brought in but gave little comfort to the men, and Aucott conceded that men were leaving the union because they thought it useless.[29]

Not until 1899 did wages in the south rise significantly to reach a level not seen since 1879. Then stagnation hit prices again, and that sliding-scale ended in 1904. By 1906 a new sliding-scale had been agreed which in the event continued until the outbreak of war. Despite earlier protests from the men, the link with the north continued so that rates did not diverge from their customary difference.

The output of the Midlands manufactured iron trade was 229,968 tons in 1907 compared to the 67,312 tons in the north. Consequently the shifts in the location of the trade had left the northern area with the tradition of union strength and policy dominance, but had given the Midlands the greater productive capacity.[30]

The history of industrial relations in the manufactured iron trade does not bear out the optimistic propaganda put out by its supporters in the nineteenth century. It is hardly possible to agree with Professor Munro, writing in 1885, when he described the selling price sliding-scale as 'the greatest discovery in the distribution of wealth since Ricardo's enunciation of the law of rent'.[31] Indeed, the concentration on selling prices, initially dictated by the employers, destroyed any ability to secure a minimum standard of life. Yet, what alternative lay open to union leaders in the early years of the Boards, they had few members and fewer funds? The employers anticipated future strength by securing the organization of the Boards on a works basis. At the reorganization of the union in 1887 perhaps more active bargaining ought ot have been undertaken to take advantage of strength from a more secure membership. It was, however, unlikely that the union leaders who had experienced the 1860s and early 1870s would risk returning to that level of conflict.

In the circumstances the statement by John Kane which heads this chapter can only be regarded as ironic.

References

1   V. L. Allen, 'The Origins of Industrial Conciliation and Arbitration,' *International Review of Social History*, 9, (1964), pp. 253–4. J. H. Porter, 'Wage Bargaining under Conciliation Agreements 1860–1914,' *Economic History Review*, 23, (1970), pp. 460–75.

2   T. H. Burnham & G. O. Hoskins, *Iron and Steel in Britain 1870–1930*, (1943), p. 157; J.H. Porter, Industrial Conciliation and Arbitration 1860–1914, (Ph.D. Thesis, University of Leeds, 1968,) pp. 96–241.

3   N. P. Howard, 'The Strikes and lock-outs in the Iron Industry and the Formation of Ironworkers' unions 1862–69,' *International Review of Social History*, 18, (1973), pp. 396–427.

4   E. Taylor, 'James Capper,' *Dictionary of Labour Biography*, Vol. 2, (ed.) J. M. Bellamy & J. Saville, (1974), pp. 80–5.

5   Howard, *op.cit.*, pp. 396–427.

6   E. Taylor, 'John Kane,' *op.cit.*, Vol. 3, (1976), p. 119.

7   E. Taylor, 'Edward Trow,' *ibid.*, pp. 187–92.

8   E. Taylor, 'William Aucott,' *ibid.*, Vol. 2, pp. 22–25.

9 E. Taylor, 'James Capper,' *ibid.*, pp. 80–5.

10 Sir Edward Grey, *Sir David Dale*, 1911, pp. 36–8.

11 *Royal Commission to Enquire into the Organization and Rules of Trade Unions*, Fifth Report and Minutes, 1868, Q. 8329–79.

12 *Royal Commission on Labour*, Minutes Group A, Vol.2, c. 6795–iv, 1892, Q. 14798.

13 *Report on Rules of Voluntary Conciliation and Arbitration Boards*, cd. 5346, 1910, pp. 156–61.

14 Howard, *loc.cit.*, p. 425.

15 *Royal Commission on Labour*, Minutes Group A, Vol. 2, B. Hingley, Q.15486; *Ironworkers Journal*, 1 April 1873.

16 J. H. Porter, 'David Dale and Conciliation in the Northern Manufactured Iron Trade 1869–1914,' *Northern History*, 5, (1970), pp. 157–71.

17 *Ironworkers Journal*, 1 March–1 June 1870, 15 March–15 May 1871; C. E. Mack & W. H. G. Armytage, *Thomas Hughes*, (1952), p. 198.

18 *Capital and Labour*, 18 March 1874; J. H. Porter, 'Management, Competition and Industrial Relations, the Midlands Manufactured Iron Trade, 1873–1914,' *Business History*, 11, (1969), pp. 37–47.

19 L. L. F. R. Price, *Industrial Peace*, (1887), p. 64; J. E. C. Munro, 'Sliding-Scales in the Iron Industry,' *Transactions of the Manchester Statistical Society*, (1885–6), pp. 1–27.

20 *Ironworkers Journal*, 1 February 1876.

21 *Bee-Hive*, 18 September 1875.

22 *Ironworkers' Journal*, November 1878.

23 *Ironworkers' Journal*, July, November 1878.

24 J. E. C. Munro, 'Sliding-Scales in the Coal and Iron Industries from 1885–9,' *Transactions of the Manchester Statistical Society*, 1889–90, pp. 119–47; E. Taylor, *The Better Temper, a Commemorative History of the Midland Iron and Steel Wages Board 1876–1976*, (1976), pp. 13–15.

25 Taylor, 'Edward Trow,' pp. 187–92.

26 *Ironworkers' Journal*, May 1889.

27 *Ironworkers' Journal*, November 1889.

28 *Ironworkers' Journal*, July 1893.

29 *Ironworkers' Journal*, March 1896.

30 Porter, *Northern History*, pp. 157–71; *Business History*, pp. 37–47.

31 See also J. H. Porter, 'Wage Determination by Selling Price Sliding-Scales 1870–1914,' *Manchester School*, 39, (1971), pp. 13–21.

Index